Additional Praise for ESPN The Company

"If you love the business of sports, or the sport of business, you will love this book!"
—**Larry Probst,** Chairman, United States
Olympic Committee, and Chairman, Electronic Arts

"Tony Smith's captivatingly insightful story of how ESPN defied convention in its pioneering journey—having fun all along the way—is a must read for sports, entertainment and brand marketing aficionados."
—**Jon Katzenbach,** Founder, Katzenbach Partners,
Former Director, McKinsey and Company, bestselling author
of several books, including *Peak Performance* and
The Wisdom of Teams

"Most sports fans are "fan"atics. ESPN has become the public face of this devotion. But ESPN is more than a sports channel or a media company; it is a brand. This readable, engaging, and interesting book shares the story behind the brand. Like being in the huddle or locker room, we learn about how ESPN leaders made choices that turned sports fanaticism into business results. The principles in the ESPN story apply to a broad spectrum of companies and leaders. A wonderful business read of a sports journey."
—**Dave Ulrich,** Partner, The RBL Group, Professor,
Ross School of Business, University of Michigan,
Ranked the #1 Management Educator and
Guru by *Businessweek*

"Leading a business through a fast-growth cycle has its challenges and Dr. Smith has captured not only the interworkings unique to ESPN but also broadly applicable lessons for anyone either starting, running or growing a major enterprise."
—**Thomas Ryan, Jr.,** President & CEO, PODS Inc.

"Leadership is about visualizing an exciting future, and making it happen by combining the passion of true believers with the power of core values. Nothing brings this idea to life more than the ESPN story, and no one could have told it better than Anthony has in this very instructional and inspirational book."
—**Rajeev Peshawaria,** Chief Learning Officer,
Morgan Stanley

"Knowing first hand the excitement and the challenges of leading a company, particularly in this environment, I found Dr. Smith's account of ESPN to be both inspirational and instructional. The authentic leadership throughout their history combined with the intense passion of the employees were obviously key to ESPN's success, and are key to creating enduring brands forever. I am a big fan of learning from the best, and no one can argue with the fact that ESPN is the best at what it does, so enjoy the learning—I certainly did."

—Carl Liebert III, CEO, 24 Hour Fitness Worldwide

"Dr. Smith has been a valued advisor to ESPN for over 20 years. In fact, he became a Board member of the V Foundation based on the strong recommendations from ESPN. He has had a front row seat on watching ESPN grow, develop, and become the incredible company that it is today. His account of their evolution combined with his expertise in leadership and organizational science has culminated in this fascinating and compelling book.

ESPN has become enormously important to the world of sports and media, not to mention a great business story. I, along with my brother Bob, are honored to be associated with such a wonderful company, and I know my late brother Jimmy felt the same way. Both ESPN, the "actual" company and Dr. Smith are tremendous supporters of the V, and I am touched that he is giving a large percentage of the profits from this book to our foundation to support our mission to find a cure for cancer."

—Nick Valvano, CEO, The V Foundation for Cancer Research

"American companies have done a lot wrong in the past few years. It is great to learn from one that has done a lot right! The greatest sports story of the decade is not about a game or a player—it's all about a company—ESPN! Smith's book is filled with great lessons on leadership and team work from this American winner!"

—Marshall Goldsmith, *New York Times and Wall Street Journal* #1 bestselling author of *What Got You Here Won't Get You There* and *Succession: Are You Ready?*

THE COMPANY

ESPN
THE COMPANY

THE STORY AND LESSONS BEHIND THE MOST FANATICAL BRAND IN SPORTS

ANTHONY F. SMITH
WITH
KEITH HOLLIHAN

WILEY

John Wiley & Sons, Inc.

Published by John Wiley & Sons, Inc., Hoboken, New Jersey.
Published simultaneously in Canada.

ESPN ia a registred trademark of ESPN, Inc.

For general information on our other products and services or for technical support, please
contact our Customer Care Department within the United States at (800) 762-2974,
outside the United States at (317) 572-3993 or fax (317) 572-4002.

Wiley also publishes its books in a variety of electronic formats. Some content that appears
in print may not be available in electronic books. For more information about Wiley
products, visit our web site at www.wiley.com.

Library of Congress Cataloging-in-Publication Data:

Smith, Antony F.
    ESPN : the company : the story and lessions behind the most fanatical brand in
    sports/Antony F. Smith, with Keith Hollihan.
        p. cm.
    Includes bibliographical references and index.
    ISBN 978-0-470-54211-8 (cloth)
        1. Television broadcasting of sports—History. 2. ESPN (Television network)—
    History. I. Hollihan, Keith.   II. Title.
    GV742.3.S528   2009
    384.55'5—dc22
                                                                    2009023147

Printed in the United States of America

10 9 8 7 6 5 4 3 2 1

I dedicate this book to the wonderful people who introduced me to ESPN, trusted me over the last 20 years to be their partner, and allowed me to share in this incredible story with them—a story which, by the way, is far from over. Thank you, Michael Gorman, for providing me with the initial opportunity to work with you in the early days at ESPN. I still remember the day I drove with you from New York City to Bristol over 20 years ago, anxious but excited about this small cable company.

Thank you, Rick Barry and Jim Allegro, for trusting me enough to introduce me to your new CEO, Steve Bornstein, who had an enormous impact on my thinking and approach over the years, which in turn made me a better consultant.

Thank you, Steve, for letting me work with you and your talented and dedicated team over the years, including your successor, George Bodenheimer. All of you have been wonderful clients, and have become dear friends, cherished by me and my family.

Finally, thank you, George, for trusting and allowing me and LRI to continue to work with you and your gifted team of leaders, many of whom I met more than 20 years ago, including Sean Bratches, Ed Durso, Christine Driessen, Rosa Gatti, John Walsh, Steve Anderson, John Wildhack, Chuck Pagano, Ron Semiao, David Pahl, Len Deluca, Chris Laplaca, Norby Williamson, John Skipper, Russell Wolff, Jed Drake, Al Jaffe, and the many other wonderful ESPN employees who continue to build the legacy of the most fanatical brand in sports!

Contents

Acknowledgments

As you will read in this book, ESPN is a company that is about the fans and their sports, not about themselves. Therefore, having someone write about "them" is not part of their corporate DNA. However, as a student of organizations and leadership, I felt compelled to share this incredible *business and leadership* story of this company that most only know because they love what they do, not because they love who they are; just as sports are inspiring to the fans, ESPN's story is inspiring to anyone who is interested in starting, developing, growing, leading, and institutionalizing a phenomenal business enterprise; so thank you, ESPN!

I would also like to thank several people who gave up their precious time to be interviewed for this book: Steve Bornstein, Mark Shapiro, Rick Barry, Jim Allegro, Mark Quenzel, Roger Werner, Bill Creasy, Michael Gorman, Howard Katz, Geoff Mason, Lee Ann Daley, and Dick Glover. I would also like to thank Rosa Gatti, who gave up so much of her precious time to help support me with last minute details in the frantic last hours of the editorial process.

ACKNOWLEDGMENTS

Thank you B.G. Dilworth, my wonderful agent, Patti Judd, my talented PR consultant, and the great and talented team at Wiley. Debra Englander, Jocelyn Cordova, Adrianna Johnson, Todd Tedesco, and Kelly O'Connor, your heroic efforts to get this book out on ESPN's 30 year anniversary was truly inspiring.

I would be remiss if I didn't thank my family for all their support while I wrote this book. Writing is a labor of love, but it did take me away from spending precious moments with my true inspirations—my sweet daughter Estelle Rose Smith and my wonderful son, Dominic Thomas Smith.

Lastly, I would like to thank Steve Bornstein (President/CEO, 1990–2003) and Jim Allegro (CFO, 1990–1995), who introduced me to the V Foundation for Cancer Research; I proudly serve on their board, along with Steve, Jim, George Bodenheimer (President, 1998–present), and many other ESPN family members. ESPN supports the V Foundation in many significant ways, and I will continue to support The V Foundation by donating a significant percentage of the profits from this book. Knowing that we have all been touched in some way by cancer, I would invite you to look into, and perhaps support, The V Foundation for Cancer Research, where 100 percent of your dollars go toward finding a cure for cancer. As Jimmy Valvano stated in his inspiring speech at the ESPY awards, "Never give up. . . never ever give up!"

Thank you.

Anthony F. Smith

The V Foundation for Cancer Research was founded 15 years ago by ESPN and Jim Valvano. The V Foundation has earned a top four-star rating from Charity Navigator, America's largest charity evaluator. The V Foundation can be contacted at their headquarters:

The V Foundation for Cancer Research
106 Towerview Court
Cary, North Carolina, 27513
Phone; 1-800-454-6698
www.jimmyv.org

Introduction: The Biggest Business Story In Sports

The headline read, "25 Years Ago, The Biggest Story In Sports Didn't Even Make The Sports Page." Today, sports coverage is a 24–7 media phenomenon and ESPN is the brand and the sports outlet synonymous with nightly highlights, morning updates, athlete interviews, must-see games, and major sideshow events like the ESPYs and the NFL draft. When ESPN put its full-page twenty-fifth anniversary ad in the *New York Times* on September 7, 2004, it was calling attention to the impact the organization has had on changing the nature of the sports media game. As Chris "Boomer" Berman stated in the foreword to *ESPN 25* (a book of 25 years of sports highlights), "History now tells us that the television sports landscape was forever changed. Funny though; those of us who worked at ESPN back in the fall of 1979 and the beginning of the 1980s weren't so sure."

At first it's hard to remember how incredibly different the business of covering and broadcasting sports was before the arrival of ESPN in 1979. Remember when ABC's Wide World of Sports (... *The thrill of victory, and the agony of defeat. . . .!*) was the weekly outlet for sports fanatics? Remember when the best you could do for a recap of the night's games was watch the scores and highlights crammed into a few sparse minutes between news and weather on your local television channel? Thirty years ago, sports coverage was produced as though the topic was a sidebar unworthy of serious news time. That mindset shifted when Bill Rasmussen, an unemployed sports announcer, and a group of committed sports junkies in Bristol, Connecticut decided to lease unwanted satellite transponder space to broadcast Connecticut college sports and New England Whalers hockey games. Before the Entertainment and Sports Programming Network even launched, the dream of sports coverage broadened and went national. Fans who loved sports—the types who watched prime time games, late night games, pro games, college games, amateur events, and anything else that involved uniforms and competition—couldn't get enough.

Today, ESPN is the most powerful and prominent name in sports media. The Bristol campus—and who could have envisioned Bristol as the center of the sports world?—has 27 satellite dishes feeding more than 97 million subscribers as one of cable television's biggest networks. The channels, which have multiplied fourfold and gone international, putting them in more than 200 countries, include ESPN2, ESPNEWS, ESPNU, ESPN Deportes, and ESPN Classic. Piling on, *ESPN The Magazine*, ESPN the store, ESPN Radio, ESPN Zone Restaurants, ESPN.com, ESPN Books, ESPN Original Entertainment (Movies and Shows), the X Games, ESPY Awards, and many other brand extensions that feed the fans' insatiable hunger for sports stories, statistics, communities, and memorabilia.

But, ESPN is not just impressing its fans and customers, it's impressing the media analyst on Wall Street. Although parent company Disney reports on the revenues of their media group and cable groups, it does not report the economics of ESPN per se. The consensus view of Wall Street analysts, however, is that the combined revenues of the ESPN enterprise, conservatively speaking, totaled roughly $5 billion in 2007, with profits in the range of $2 billion. At a New York conference in 2007, UBS announced that they had determined ESPN's value to be $28 billion. They went on to say that ESPN accounted for 40 percent of Disney's $70.7 billion market capitalization, based on prevailing cash flow multiples in the industry.

While the appetite for sports and the suitability of cable television as an outlet strike most of us as self-evident now, the traditional networks completely missed the early opportunities ESPN scooped up. In part, that innovative vision explains the early success of the organization in staking its large claim on the sports wilderness, but it does not explain the sustained growth over three decades or the ability of ESPN to maintain market leadership in the face of new and heavily backed competitors. If jumping into the game early was the primary requisite for long-term success, then Starbucks would be only one of many globally recognized coffee shop chains, and ESPN would be just another jumble of letters providing sports entertainment. There were other ESPNs around the country, known by other initials. For example, there was Ted Turner and Time Warner's CEO, Gerald Levin's attempt at Cable Sports—CNN/SI, which closed down after six years of operation. So, how did the ESPN we know today succeed? Thirty years ago, ESPN may have been the biggest sports story not to make the front page, but the even bigger story, a story that remains untold, is how ESPN managed to sustain its growth, its strong and special culture, its innovation, and brand in a highly competitive and rapidly evolving marketplace. That's a business and leadership story, not a sports and media story, and I tell it in this book.

Through my 20 years of consulting at ESPN, not to mention interviewing many of the top executives for this book, I have come away even more impressed about what they have accomplished.

It was probably 12 years ago that I mentioned to Steve Bornstein, who was president at the time, that someone should write a book about ESPN. "Steve, what you guys are doing here, not to mention what you have done, is an inspirational and instructional lesson for all big and small companies alike." He quickly agreed, and said that I should be the one to write it: "You are the perfect outside 'insider,' Dr. Smith" (as he would always say with a grin). As you will read in the forthcoming pages, when Steve "mentions" something, you take it very seriously. Well, surprise, surprise, I started taking notes and documenting the many best practices of ESPN that day!

Based on my observations, experiences, and research, I have organized the book to first give you, the reader, an inside look and feel for the type of organizational psychology and culture that exists internally at ESPN, both from a leadership perspective as well as an employee's. I then focus on the external dynamics, describing their creative and innovative spirit and practices, which drove the programming, products, and services. I conclude with the lessons of how ESPN dealt with their many partners, and how they handled mistakes and missteps along the way. And finally, the old professor in me attempted to distill each of the core lessons throughout the book, which you will find at the end of each chapter. But, before I get started, I want to further explain my relationship with ESPN.

"Welcome to Bristol, Dr. Smith"

As you will discover in this book, I love working with ESPN, and like many of ESPN's "older" viewers, I am a sports fan, although I haven't worn a uniform since Little League in lovely Santee, California and I know as little about television as the average father who needs to Tivo Sponge Bob or Hannah Montana for his children. And although I have now spent several years consulting at sports and media companies, I do not consider myself a "sports or media expert" per se. My field of expertise is corporate leadership, and I am a consultant who considers himself a lifelong learner and teacher in the field of organizational behavior and psychology.

My relationship with ESPN began over 20 years ago when Roger Werner was president of the network. Initially, Werner was an outsider who came into the media industry through consulting. He was a McKinsey consultant and ABC executive who had impressed the leadership at Getty Oil (the original investors) with his entrepreneurial spirit and visionary and strategic acumen. After spending several years in various roles at ESPN and ABC, he was asked to take the helm at ESPN and make this start-up profitable. So, he took the plunge. Although Werner had followed a few men who had been president since Rasmussen (Chet Simmons, Stuart Evey, who actually held the title of CEO, and Bill Grimes), it was Roger and another ex-McKinsey consultant who introduced me to this incredible company.

Replacing the founder Rasmussen so early may have surprised many, but the management advisors at Getty understood that, although Rasmussen and his team loved sports and had learned enough about satellites and transponders, if ESPN was going to live up to its rapidly growing potential, a business leader with vision and robust operational capability would have to be in charge.

As these things go, Werner looked to his old colleagues at McKinsey for some help overhauling ESPN's functions. One of the members on that team was a young finance jock named Michael Gorman, who impressed Werner so much that he asked him to stay on as the new CFO. For Gorman, there was only one problem. While he could run numbers as well as anybody, he had no managerial experience whatsoever. Now he was being asked to lead a function with a staff of 60 through a difficult transition period.

I knew Gorman from my own days serving McKinsey. He asked me to come in and help him manage his team, get the right divisional structure in place, coach him on leadership issues, and essentially be a thought partner in navigating his team to success.

Across the leadership team, Gorman's experience and his development needs were not unusual. If you've ever enjoyed the privilege and the pain of working for a start-up that's on a heady skyward trajectory, you know what it means to learn on the run and grow into a role. At ESPN, people with terrific technical skills—whether in cost accounting or camera angles—were being asked to take on leadership roles all over the organization. One year, you might be managing a single remote team at a college basketball game; the next year, you could be the VP of production, managing 50 camera crews all over the nation. Of course, start-ups aren't alone in facing this challenge. In business, you typically get promoted for your technical ability and character. But it's rare that anyone has prepared you with the leadership skills needed to manage people—whether that's a group of 200 or a global organization of 50,000.

My knowledge of leadership and my experience with the challenges of management and organizational structure became highly valued within ESPN over the years to follow, and I was asked by a number of different Michael Gormans to help them grow into their new roles. Guys like Ron Semiao, who created the X-Games, would say to me, "Tony, I know how to produce a competition in which people fly 80 miles an hour on skateboards down Nob Hill in San Francisco, but now I've got to manage a wacky and creative staff of over 100. Can you help me?" Keeping up with the promotions in the programming and production area, as well as on the business side, Gorman and other executives basically became my full-time job.

After spending a little over a year working with several executives besides Gorman, Steve Bornstein, an executive whom I had only known by reputation, not personally, was named president of the company. Bornstein was a sports nut who had gone to the University of Wisconsin, where he'd covered sports as a cameraman. He then became a programmer at a sports affiliate in Milwaukee, and made his way to Bristol on an invitation from ESPN executive Bill Creasy, who was hired from CBS, and later became a dear friend and mentor of Steve's.

In the media world, programmers are the people who come up with the best menu of program offerings, in particular developing shows and scheduling shows that feed into one another strategically to keep you watching. There are those in the industry who consider Bornstein one of the best programmers ever, but when he was appointed head of ESPN, he had some rough edges. While Bornstein was clearly bright, creative, and hard-driving, he was also extremely tough, brash, and intimidating—qualities that could paralyze people and, in turn, not always bring out the best in others.

Jim Allegro, an ABC/Cap Cities guy who had been recruited to oversee the finance function as a kind of technical mentor, encouraged me to work with Bornstein so that he could fulfill his incredible potential as a CEO. The only problem was that brash, tough, and intimidating Steve Bornstein didn't know who I was, or understand why he should be working with me.

The three of us and another executive, Rick Barry, who I worked with on several HR initiatives and who became a great friend and supporter of mine, went out for dinner at a restaurant in Westport, Connecticut. The goal of the meeting was to convince Bornstein that I was a consultant worth listening to. Bornstein was as blunt and gruff as I had been led to expect, and the meeting had its uncomfortable moments. Allegro said I'd be a good guy to give Bornstein a little support in his new role. I remember a few of Bornstein's polite inquiries about my qualifications: "Who the hell are you?" "What qualifies you for such a role?" "If I do need an advisor, why in the hell should it be you?"

I told Bornstein that if he hired me as his consultant, I'd look him in the eye, be up-front and honest about every aspect of his leadership, study the organization vigorously, and tell him the tough things he didn't want to hear. If my memory serves me, I think Bornstein leaned back in his chair and yawned. I knew the meeting wasn't going well when I noticed that both Jim and Rick were sweating profusely, with pained looks on their faces.

That's when I noticed the watch Steve was wearing. I'm a watch nut and Bornstein was wearing a beautiful Patek Phillipe. With enthusiasm, I asked him where he had gotten it. Bornstein said it had been his father's. Like the commercial says, you don't own a Patek Phillippe, you look after it for a while and then pass it on to the next generation. We talked about my collection of watches for a few minutes and forgot about business and leadership development. Then, at the end of dinner, Bornstein shook my hand and asked me when we would begin working together. From the looks on Jim and Rick's faces, you would have thought they had just witnessed one of their kids graduating summa cum laude from an Ivy League college.

Fasten Your Seatbelt

"Where do we start?" Bornstein asked me when we met in his office a few days later. I told him that every great leader begins with the question, "Where do I want to take this organization?" Coming up with the answer means formulating the vision, mission, and values of the enterprise. But as I said to Bornstein, "If you're going to be the messenger and the one articulating where you're taking ESPN, and what others need to do to realize the vision, we need to make sure that your credibility is as strong as it can be; and given that leadership is a receiver-based phenomenon, we need to figure out what people think about you, and what you need to do differently to have as much impact as possible."

So, one of the first things I did with Bornstein was to develop the Mission and Values of ESPN. For other clients, such a project could take several months to complete—multiple meetings, whiteboarding, drafts, soliciting input from key executives, and so on. Although we went through these steps, Steve had a very clear sense of ESPN's mission and what people, particularly the leadership, needed to value and embrace to grow the organization at an unprecedented pace. This phase took a few weeks to complete; a pace of change and completion that one learns quickly working with Bornstein (for the record, he developed and launched the NFL Network in a matter of months). Once we finalized the Mission and Values statement, and incorporated input from the other executives, we developed a 360 feedback instrument (an assessment that surveys direct reports, colleagues, managers, etc.) to reinforce the values and assess and develop the company's top leaders. The first leader we used it on was Steve Bornstein.

I asked the top 15 executives at ESPN what they thought of their new leader. They had all worked with him before when Bornstein was head of programming. "What were you happy about? What's going to make him succeed in his new role? What can he leverage even more? What's going to trip him up? Where is he most vulnerable?"

The messages were incredibly consistent; "He's as bright as they come, and he's the right guy to take us to the next level," "he knows the business cold, and he needs to share his vision with all of us," but there were also tough criticisms. When I met with Bornstein, he told me to skip all the good stuff and just give him the things he needed to work on.

To his credit, Bornstein took the tough stuff as well as anyone I have ever seen. I gave it to him as straight as I said I would when we had dinner in Westport. I won't go into the personal details but the essence was clear: Bornstein was so critical and brilliant that he could strip people down in a New York minute, often in meetings when the entire executive team was present. He intimidated them so much that they were reluctant to challenge him, and if they had opposing ideas, they would rarely bring them to his attention. He needed to soften that impact while still maintaining the demanding qualities that made him a very effective and hard-driving leader.

We came up with some ways to work on that, and I promised to keep my ears and eyes open on his leadership interactions and let him know what I was picking up. Bornstein grinned and said, "Okay, let's make sure all the other top guys get their feedback, too." At this time, I feel it is appropriate to point out that Bornstein was a great student as well as a wickedly smart leader and teacher. Although I may have been considered Bornstein's organizational consultant and teacher, I learned a lot from the standards and example that Steve set. I witnessed the positive impact he had that resulted in the tremendous growth and development of the other senior leaders at ESPN.

As both a teacher and a student, I've devoted my career to trying to understand what leadership is all about, what great leaders do, how they create strong performance cultures, and how successful organizations are structured and run. I was able to share some of that knowledge with ESPN over the past 20 years, and hopefully played a minor role in their success. Along the way, my experiences with larger, more established organizations in mature industries were consistently valuable. I'd introduce leadership and management ideas I'd seen work at large financial institutions or professional service firms. Inevitably, Bornstein would complain, "Tony, we're not American Express. We're not McKinsey. We're not a big company." And I'd reply, "Yes, but I think you can learn from those organizations, and I also believe they can learn from you as well."

The *lessons* of ESPN are applicable to whatever type of business you are in, and yes, the *story* is probably a bit more entertaining than that of a bolt company—but even bolt companies can benefit by embracing the best practices of ESPN. For instance, the best organizations invest in their people. They train them. They believe that if you spend time and resources turning talented performers into leaders, you're going to get better organizational performance and engender higher levels of commitment and sweat. You want employees at all levels to believe in your company if you're going to succeed. I told Bornstein that a key predictor of that kind of loyalty was how staff felt about their immediate boss. Bringing leadership awareness to all levels of the organization, and coaching managers to become more effective leaders, was critical for long-term performance. I spent the next 18 years working with other talented executives to implement that kind of systematic leadership development at ESPN.

Along the way, I saw a wild start-up become an industry threat and finally the industry leader. I got involved with ESPN at a crux moment, when the company was scrambling with the transition to achieve the scale and capabilities of its future self. I saw how they managed that shift, and how they maintained it. I mentioned that I consider myself a lifelong learner as well as a teacher. What I've learned firsthand at ESPN about growing a great company I've written down in the chapters that follow.

For one thing, I learned that ESPN had one consistent priority when they hired someone, whether that person was the head of human resources or a production assistant. They wanted people who loved sports first and foremost. It didn't matter whether you were a Baker scholar from Harvard Business School like Michael Gorman.

The main concern ESPN had was whether you were a sports junkie, too. What's your favorite team? How much did it hurt when they lost the big game? What is the first section of the newspaper you read? How many stadiums have you visited? How many times do you watch SportsCenter in a day?

For sports fanatics, those answers come quick and clear, without hesitation, straight from the heart. Being a fan—being a *fanatic*—may set you apart from your families, your loved ones, even your spouse, but it puts you into select company with other fans. You know how the others think, you feel sports in the same way, you get it, and you want it all the time.

Those are the kinds of people who launched ESPN and those are the kinds of people who were brought on board and groomed over the last 30 years. Is it any wonder ESPN has a visceral connection with its customers? What's more, that same connection extends to many of the athletes they cover. Inside a lot of professional athletes and coaches is an obsessed fan, juiced up on the game and on competition and the drama of winning and losing. I can think of few other companies that do as good a job of creating an atmosphere of fun and excitement for its people and its customers—maybe Southwest in the airline industry, Starbucks in the consumer goods space, or Apple and Google in high tech. But it's hard to surpass ESPN.

I learned a lot from ESPN. I learned about people and expecting the most out of them, being aggressive about new ideas, grabbing a market, giving leaders room to run, and rewriting the rules of the game by making the most of the opportunities that are available. I became convinced that smarts combined with passion (skill and will) accounted for 99 percent of the variance when it comes to performance. I saw strategies and approaches that made me shake my head in amazement, sometimes at the audacity, sometimes at the sheer brilliance. Imagine watching Ford Motor Company invent the assembly lines and mass production of automobiles, grow like crazy, and then transform into Toyota, constantly innovating and leading the market. That's the kind of evolution and success ESPN has experienced in the media industry. I'm not claiming that ESPN's story is over, or that they're the perfect company without any failures on their record, or that there isn't treacherous terrain to come, but what they pulled off and how they did it is a story worth telling.

My friend and mentor Mac Stewart, who retired as a senior director at McKinsey and Company, says that consultants provide the bumblebee function in the business world. We go from company to company, picking up a little bit of knowledge here, spreading it elsewhere, bringing other best practices or management innovations back. In this book, I want to share the lessons I learned at ESPN about launching and growing a wildly successful enterprise. This is my raison d'être—to first learn and then teach others how they can create and grow phenomenal organizations by creating opportunities for people to grow and have impact, all while enhancing economic and human value. I hope you find the lessons here to be rich and applicable anywhere. They were a lot of fun to learn, and if you're a fan of business, competition, or sports, I bet they'll be a lot of fun to read, too.

Chapter 1

TURNING FANATICS INTO FANS

You arrive in Bristol, Connecticut, and you think ESPN. This is the epicenter of the known sports universe. The corporate headquarters are approached by highway, but when you near the gate you are greeted rather quietly by a small sign in simple letters reading "Welcome to ESPN." The sign looks as though it hasn't changed much since the organization was founded 30 years ago, utterly subdued compared to ESPN's often boisterous shows, hosts, and guests. Very subtly, this is an important part of ESPN's message to its people every day when they come to work: It's about the fans and the sports, not ESPN.

Inside the gate, there are a myriad of parking lots and sprawling buildings, and a forest of satellite dishes, like a field of giant white mushrooms tilted skyward. Twenty years ago, when I first drove to ESPN, there were only a half-dozen satellite dishes, a couple of finished office buildings, and rows of temporary trailers—everything in flux, everything growing. Now, instead of giving off a corporate vibe, like stalwarts such as IBM or GE, the grounds of ESPN have the big-time aura of an Ivy league campus, but the look of a state-of-the-art high tech company. The rank-and-file employees are dressed casually and look about as young and diverse as undergrad students anywhere, though they are always in a hurry. The managers are often dressed more formally, a bit like professors at a business school, and the older executives could pass for top administrators and deans. There is often an expression of pride and—dare I say it—happiness on the faces you see. I'm not claiming ESPN is a utopia, and I describe its ways of doing business with candor and curiosity in this book, but the giddy energy always strikes me. This is the place to be if you are engaged by sports and television. Just by being here, the young people have achieved something special. The older hands who have been around for many years are noticeably proud of what has been accomplished, the growth of the business reflected in the number of buildings and satellite dishes. Before we get started, it's worth considering how much that accomplishment means.

Now, the achievements of ESPN seem self-evident. Why wouldn't a cable sports channel offering sports news, sporting events, and sports-related entertainment 24 hours a day be an incredible success according to all conceivable measures—spectacular revenue, intense brand awareness and loyalty, market supremacy, and consistently strong year-after-year growth? Sports consumers, after all, are fanatics. Like addicts of less savory fixes, they can't get enough of what they desire. Throw more product their way—additional channels, new formats, a magazine, a web site, even sports they've never cared about before—and those fanatics will continue to consume whatever you're offering while their needs and numbers grow. What business, given such an easy sell to such an eager market, wouldn't be a success?

You could assign the achievements of ESPN to luck—the right place, the right time, the right untapped market—but that only brings to mind a quote from golf-great Arnold Palmer: "The funny thing is, the more I practice, the luckier I get."[1] Certainly, there was luck behind ESPN in terms of timing, opportunity, the right leadership at different stages, and the decisions made at several critical junctures. But nobody who learns the full arc of ESPN's story will evaluate all that and dismiss the amount of stamina, discipline, intelligence, hard work, risk-taking, and blood, sweat and tears that went into generating such luck. That's why the lessons of ESPN's rise to institution status and brand dominance are so rich.

The truth, of course, is that ESPN didn't stumble fortuitously onto an untapped revenue stream and then work like hell to develop its claim. Rather, the market for 24-hour, dedicated sports coverage on television didn't exist before ESPN created it. ESPN's founders, leaders, backers, and key employees generated that market by understanding the desires of people who follow sports like addicts and striving to fulfill those wants. They identified loose and disorganized fanatics—people with an unchanneled passion for the sports experience in many different forms—and turned them into loyal fans—customers focusing their eyeballs, water cooler conversations, and cable dollars on what ESPN is offering.

One reason the people behind ESPN were able to do that successfully is because they are fanatics themselves. That's the two-sided lesson I explore in more depth in this chapter. In my experience, other successful companies have also turned fanatics into fans—on the customer and employee side—but those organizations are as rare as they are noteworthy, and few have done it as well as ESPN.

In the interviews I conducted for this book, it was often said by the people who experienced the ESPN story firsthand that the company has gone through four distinct steps in development. I describe those steps so that ESPN's business decisions and accomplishments can be understood throughout this book in the context of the situation at the time. The nuances and details of the ESPN story are expanded on in later chapters, but here's a brief overview to establish the people, events, and time line we'll be following.

Ready When the Red Light Goes On

Every organization goes through very distinct, and often predictable, stages of development. What many have labeled ESPN's start-up began when it was conceived in 1978 and launched with venture capital funding in 1979. Those early, arduous years could be characterized as a constant scramble to patch holes in a leaky rowboat on a vast and unfriendly ocean while simultaneously endeavoring to discover an actual destination (and pretending all along that the rowboat is an ocean liner.) An ungainly metaphor, I agree, but one that anybody who has ever enjoyed the exciting, raucous, anxious, exhausting, sickening, inspiring, and rewarding time working at a start-up enterprise can probably appreciate, and may even fondly remember.

The vision and early energy for ESPN came from its founder, Bill Rasmussen, his son, Scott, and a few key backers and supporters. Rasmussen was a true sports fanatic who had worked in advertising before landing a patchwork of dream jobs in sports that combined sales, management, and play-by-play broadcasting. While working as the communications director of the WHA hockey team, the New England (Hartford) Whalers, Rasmussen gained experience producing sports television and events. Then, after a falling-out with Whalers ownership, Rasmussen found himself unemployed and anxious to see if the tickle of an idea he'd been carrying around for a couple of years could be transformed into a viable media business.

Rasmussen's original business concept was to fill the need for more local sports coverage in Connecticut. The Whalers had few of their games televised, and NCAA sports involving UConn (University of Connecticut) were popular statewide, but rarely available on TV. Technology, distribution and cost turned out to be problematic. A few conversations with local cable operators gave Rasmussen an awareness of how complicated and expensive it was to distribute original programming in discrete blocks of time. It was through those initial inquiries, however, that he stumbled onto the idea of broadcasting via satellite—still an extremely new and barely understood technology in 1978. Investigating further, Rasmussen learned first that satellite signals could be broadcast all over the country to local cable operators, and that this made more sense than distributing within a single state like Connecticut. The idea began to expand. In addition, Rasmussen was told that it was actually cheaper to broadcast for extended hours than in limited time slots. That data ingested, the opportunity it represented must have jolted Rasmussen with a sped-up heart rate. The vision of a dedicated national sports network was suddenly obvious and tantalizingly possible.

The satellite system Rasmussen encountered (more in Chapter 2) had only been commercially available for a few years but the channels HBO, Showtime, and TBS were offering movies and network TV reruns that way. In discussions with local Connecticut cable operators, Rasmussen learned that cable companies picked up those signals and distributed them to subscribers in a mild and not very effective way of competing for viewership with the big three networks—CBS, ABC, and NBC. Fox, you will recall, was not a player back then. In an example of one of those periodic moments when the dominant power misses the emergence of the next ferocious competitor, executives at the big-three network channels did not see cable or satellite as a threat; indeed, they hardly noticed the existence of this parallel system of broadcasting. Rasmussen made his pitch for an all-sports network to cable operators with all this in mind. Although the cable operators were skeptical of Rasmussen's idea for a dedicated sports channel and indeed skeptical of Rasmussen himself, he believed that if he could get his sports programming onto the air using a satellite, they would be willing to distribute those events to households with cable connections. This viewership was still a small market in 1979—only 20 percent, or 14 million, households in the United States had cable connections then—but the timing was absolutely right. Entrepreneurs who believed in the growth of cable—men like Ted Turner, John Malone, and Charles Dolan—were about to become moguls.

Soon, Rasmussen and his partners entered that feverish phase of a start-up when ideas suddenly begin to become real, and the demands of planning, selling, and building a business tumble together at an ever-increasing speed. They needed a name, financing, satellite access, programming, cable affiliates willing to partner with them, a business location, and experienced television production managers—all at once. They propped up their tent with multiple poles, shoring up one aspect of the venture with the tenuous commitment of a cable operator, satellite signal provider, sports partner, or financial backer, then raced across to bolster the other side before it sagged and collapsed. They did not know what they were doing until they needed to do it. They learned along the way, picking up information, ideas, and strategies when forced by each new crisis to make a decision or change course. They ran out of money, maxed out their credit cards, and avoided bill collectors. They bluffed business partners and cynical journalists, bringing skeptics along until the next deal arrived just in time and allowed the

7

journey to continue. They stretched the truth, and turned difficult and complicated plans into reality by proclaiming confidently, with a salesman's faith, that those plans would come to pass. Most importantly, they began to draw others in—those fanatics I mentioned—who may have doubted Rasmussen's ability to pull it all off, but never doubted the potential and excitement of the idea he was pushing.

The name was inspired. Cable operators, enamored with the success of the movie channels being distributed by satellite, wanted movies to be part of the offering. Rasmussen came up with the word *entertainment* as a compromise that was vague and inclusive enough to capture what they wanted to bring to viewers and still keep cable operators happy. The Entertainment and Sports Network, or ESP Network was the result. Within a few months, this was shortened to ESPN (reportedly by the graphic designer who thought it looked better that way) and the lettering was fashioned into the distinctive logo.

Despite the call for movies and TV shows, Rasmussen remained focused on showcasing sports events that weren't being covered by anyone else. Theoretically, they would be cheaper to run since no one else wanted to show them and would better resonate with niche sports fanatics. For example, Rasmussen and his partners knew that televised NCAA games would be treasured gems among avid college sports fans who had previously been unable to watch them, as they were outside the realm of the traditional channels.

From its original vision, to subsequent ideas, ESPN needed to find funding. Their first infusion of money came from a bizarre source, completely outside the New York—centered media or advertising worlds. Given the extent to which ESPN was violating all rules of conventional television wisdom, perhaps this should not be so surprising. In the search for financing, Rasmussen and his partners ran into Getty Oil, flush with cash and looking for investment opportunities. Rasmussen pitched his business plan to a Getty vice president named Stuart Evey, who was in charge of investments into noncore assets. Evey agreed to an initial $10 million infusion and soon exercised an option to secure ownership over 85 percent of the venture.

Evey was a character, an extreme version of the many strong, volatile, passionate, and excess-oriented personalities that ESPN attracted in its youth. He was a sports fanatic with a secondary craving for the media, show-business, and deal-making drug. Not surprisingly, he gravitated from the staid world of oil production to the flash of a sports television start-up and became fully immersed in ESPN decision making and operations. This generated turmoil in the leadership ranks, a series of power plays, ego fights, and turf wars that somehow managed to seem normal in the rushed day-to-day struggle to get the business off the ground. Rasmussen didn't like being overruled, discounted, and undercut, but money won out. As a result, the founders of ESPN would be evicted within a year.

The Getty money was desperately needed, however. In another nick-of-time event, Budweiser came through with a million-dollar advertising commitment, the largest in the history of cable. This was a cannon shot across the bow of the networks, cable affiliates, Wall Street, and Madison Avenue announcing that ESPN might just be for real. And in fact, between the Getty money, the Budweiser advertising deal, and a freshly inked two-year contract with the NCAA to broadcast games, ESPN *was* for real, just a few short months before it was scheduled to go live at 7 P.M. on September 7, 1979.

Trucks, cameras, a satellite dish, a studio, offices, programmers, and on-air talent—ESPN needed everything that a big network needed, but had almost no resources and no base of experience to draw from. The coup de grace in ESPN's prelaunch struggle was securing the services of Chet Simmons, then president of sports at NBC. Simmons, who had been involved in the launch of ABC's Wide World of Sports 20 years before, was waiting for a contract from NBC, and growing irked about being strung along. So he took a leap at a significant salary offer from ESPN even though he had already publicly dismissed the idea that cable sports could compete with the networks.

As the new president of ESPN, Simmons brought truckloads of sports television experience, big-league credibility, and—most importantly—extensive industry contacts. Starting with Scotty Connal, another sports executive, Simmons lured so many top executives and talent from NBC that ESPN in its early years was known by insiders as NBC North.

One industry hand was Bill Creasy, whose story is a good illustration of how and why talented people were drawn to the venture. Creasy had been one of the first graduates of USC's new telecommunication major in 1953, after which he worked in television, producing or directing sports events. For much of the 1950s, he was employed by a company called Sports Network Inc. located in Midtown Manhattan, in the business of renting production equipment such as trucks, cameras, and facilities. There, he got to know Chet Simmons because Simmons worked across the street for a rival company called Sports Programming Inc., which was later bought by ABC and turned into its sports department. Creasy's career began to soar when he became a producer of note in the CBS sports division, directing baseball games (including the Major League Game of the Week), football games (including the infamous Ice Bowl NFC championship game in Green Bay in 1967 and the first two Super Bowls), the Triple Crown, skiing in Europe, and NHL hockey in Canada.

Creasy took a four-year hiatus from sports production to head operations for the Oakland Seals of the NHL until the team was sold, then worked in horse racing before Simmons called in the summer of 1979 and asked if he wanted to get back into live television as ESPN's head of programming. Creasy felt the bug and was not afraid of working for a start-up with a man as respected as Chet Simmons involved. The offices in Plainville, Connecticut were a shock, however, to anyone who had worked with network budgets. On his first visit to the two-story commercial building where ESPN had set up, he saw that the entire first floor of the building was occupied by United Cable (which was later purchased by Comcast) and filled with rows of audiotape machines, like banks of IBM computers. Upstairs in a glorified attic space he found ESPN headquarters, a series of wooden picnic table-like desks crammed so closely together that one person couldn't stand up without the person behind wiggling out of the way. But it was live sports and it was exciting. ESPN offered Creasy a salary and he moved into the Plainville Holiday Inn in June 1979.

Construction work was ongoing at the site in Bristol, Connecticut where ESPN would set up its permanent campus. At the time, the programming facility amounted to a trailer and an outhouse. As the go-live date approached, Simmons, Connal, and Creasy put their heads together and scoured friendships and connections throughout the sports world to come up with any kind of programming that could fill the Sunday to Saturday grids—seven times the amount of sports programming the major networks were producing combined. At the same time, walls were going up, paint was being applied, a studio set was being built, and equipment was being installed and tested.

Doubts abounded, often in secret, occasionally in the open, and angry outbursts were common, but the pressure just made everyone work harder, obsessively focused on one imperative: Be ready when the red light goes on. A day out, Creasy started rehearsals on a script that wasn't even finished yet. An actual studio rehearsal wasn't possible until half an hour before ESPN was scheduled to begin broadcasting. Finally, with mere minutes to go, the studio was cleared, the first hosts of *SportsCenter*, Lee Leonard and George Grande, took their seats and the countdown began. When the red light went on, the signal was sent into the atmosphere to an orbiting satellite and, seconds later, back to homes across the United States.

ESPN went live with these words from Grande:

> If you're a fan, *if* you're a fan, what you will see in the next few minutes, hours, and days to follow may convince you that you've gone to sports heaven.

It was a message that sports fanatics could understand.

Yes, But We're Also a Business

The start-up stage did not end with the red light going on. The first *SportsCenter* broadcast was awash in technical difficulties, amounting to 30 minutes of amateur night. After *SportsCenter* and an NCAA preview, the signal flipped to a night-time, slo-pitch softball game in Milwaukee. According to Creasy, it *looked* like a night-time softball game in Milwaukee (with the unfortunate irony of being a contest between the Milwaukee Schlitzes and the Kentucky Bourbons, sponsored by Anheuser-Busch). The broadcast was a sign of things to come. The new network limped along through the fall of 1979 showing such noted sporting events as wrestling, hurling, Australian Rules Football, and men's volleyball games between South Korea and Japan. Yet, ESPN, in what was typical of its evolving culture and brand, exhibited a mixture of self-mocking humor and overt passion for sports in attracting viewers to odd events while also attracting attention to the channel. The brand message may have been unorthodox, but it was working: ESPN was serious about sports but not serious about itself—at least not publicly.

The leadership also evolved rapidly. The organization cycled through its first two top executives, taking what it needed from each before moving on. Bill Rasmussen, the founder, who had done so much work conceiving the enterprise, attracting other fanatics, and sacrificing his personal ownership stake to obtain desperately needed financing, was out. The next president, Chet Simmons, a terrific programmer who had lent his name, experience, and connections to a struggling start-up that otherwise would have been lost in the media wilderness, had one too many conflicts with Getty Oil's Stu Evey. Simmons left ESPN to take on what might have been the only other sports job you could imagine being even more daunting: the first commissioner of the United States Football League, launched to compete in the same market space as the mighty NFL.

After Simmons departed, Stu Evey cast about for ideas for the next head of the company. Creasy, in an advisory capacity (a role he would assume more overtly in years to come), along with McKinsey and Company, put together a list of three people. Evey would end up choosing one of them, appointing Bill Grimes, then a senior vice president of ESPN, as the new president in June 1982. Grimes was one of those sports fanatics who understood the ESPN brand well. He also had a way with people that was refreshingly enthusiastic and infectious, helping the culture stay close as the organization grew.

Internally, the imperative was for more programming and distribution. Rapidly, top management built relationships with leagues and cable affiliates. Meanwhile, young programmers were constantly on the phone, calling anyone they could think of for tapes of recent games—softball, lacrosse, badminton, whatever they could get their hands on—struggling to fill those Sunday to Saturday grids. The hard work was paying off and viewership and critical reviews were becoming more respectable if not impressive. From a business standpoint, however, ESPN was in brutal shape. Getty's initial $10 million had long since disappeared, and an additional $20 million was burned through without the warmth of any profit. Something urgently needed to change.

In their understandable concern, Getty retained McKinsey & Company to analyze the enterprise, see if there was the slightest hope for its future, and bring some actual reality into the business plan. From every standpoint, this survival stage was a critical juncture and a turning point for the better. The pressure to perform financially brought the sports fanaticism into a new balance, and a new understanding, embodied in operational discipline and attention to the bottom line. "Yes, we all love sports, but we're a business, too." The message was never overtly part of the vocabulary of the culture, especially with the rank-and-file where ESPN remained all about the sports fan. But if ESPN was going to stay on the air and continue to grow, it needed to achieve the kind of performance levels it praised nightly in the exploits of top athletes and championship teams.

The transition from the survival stage to the ramp up growth stage occurred when the McKinsey plan was operationalized. I talk about the revolutionary character of that change in the next chapter; it put ESPN into a clear leadership role within the cable industry. By the tail end of 1983, four years after the business was launched, ESPN had become the largest of the cable networks, surpassing even the mighty HBO and the upstart CNN. With the promise of future profitability and with potential that was becoming impossible to deny, Getty saw an opportunity to unload the business (and take some profit from its investment) while television industry suitors saw the chance to obtain a valued asset and correct a major mistake in their assessment of the sports viewer market. ABC bought the major share of the business from Getty in 1984, and the remainder from Texaco, and ABC itself was acquired by Capital Cities in 1986.

In the meantime and subsequently, ESPN began to grow in revenue and sway by obtaining valuable programming rights with college football, the America's Cup yachting race, the NFL, MLB, the NBA, the NHL, and NASCAR. The network that had started with softball, badminton, and Australian Rules Football became a significant player, almost overnight, in the very profitable world of mainstream American sports, and a serious competitive threat to the sports offerings of the major networks at the same time.

Roger Werner had been a member of the McKinsey team in the early 1980s when he was in his mid-thirties. Soon after, he was tapped by Bill Grimes to become a senior vice president. He had a brief stint at ABC Sports following the acquisition of ESPN in 1984, then returned to succeed Grimes as president in 1988. His tenure was short—a mere two years—but he continued to build the business aggressively and with strategic acumen, concentrating heavily on the relationships with cable affiliates to create the distribution channels while another top executive, Steve Bornstein, expanded the content offerings. That tag team approach has been a mark of ESPN leadership ever since.

Bornstein took over from Werner in 1990. The next eight years were a story of spectacular growth. In my observations of successful companies over the years, I've seen that kind of trajectory (where it's lasted, unlike the dot-com bubble) only a few times. The enterprise survives an early and sometimes extended period of low growth or outright struggle by sticking to its mission, building its capabilities, and refining its practices. The initial payoff is an uptick in growth that looks promising, but not extraordinary by any means. Nevertheless, beneath the surface of that modest rise, the output of so much hard work, focus, and right-thinking strategy compounds wildly, like the accumulated interest on careful long-term investments, leading to a sudden spike and an extended phase of explosive growth.

Author Seth Godin calls that lull before the rocketship ride "the dip" (see Figure 1.1).

According to Godin, a lot of great business ventures experience the dip before seeing the acceleration of success that emerges when the effort, attention, and investment of resources pays off. This extraordinary leap is so rare because most organizations and individuals give up during that phase when results lack proportion with the effort put in. In the cable industry, ESPN needed to put so many pieces in place that real growth was not possible for many years. Without satellite time, sports partners, cable affiliates, talented hosts, experience in programming, and revenue—all patiently and diligently built up over time— ESPN could never have seen those efforts accumulate and compound. This is another reason why competitors find it so hard to emulate ESPN's success: The dip eliminates those who are unwilling or unable to face an extended period of scarcity and struggle, or impatient shareholders who want quarter after quarter results, factors that often drive short-term focus, and thus organizational fragility that we are all witnessing today. By the time ESPN worked through its dip, it gained so much traction, capability, and revenue that it began to see abundant fruits of its labor.

To the point, during the 1990s, as it finally made money, ESPN blew open its borders in the United States and expanded internationally

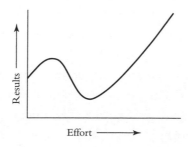

Figure 1.1 The Dip

with over 20 international television networks across 180 countries, tapping global advertising sales in the process. The television experience was replicated on the airwaves as ESPN Radio Network was launched in 1992 and gathered up affiliates to become the largest sports radio network in the country. With revenue, ESPN was suddenly in a position to acquire its own sports assets and market its brand in many different ways, including merchandise. They would purchase Ohlmeyer Communications (OCC) and Creative Sports, and later merge the two to form ESPN Regional Television. Other new programming outlets came next. ESPN2, a second sports channel—in a big flip-off to those who had once questioned a single all-sports channel—was launched in the fall of 1993, as were The ESPYs, a sports award ceremony that recognized sports talent and achievement in an Academy Awards-style celebration. A third channel, ESPNEWS was launched in 1996, providing nonstop news and highlights, while ESPN Classic was purchased and broadcast by ESPN in 1997, proving that not only did the fanatics love sports enough for multiple channels, they even loved watching games that had been over years before.

Concurrent with this growth, ESPN began to market and advertise itself more aggressively and confidently. A web site, sports pagers, home videos, video games, CDs, a credit card, books, a merchandise store, a chain of interactive sports-themed restaurants, and a magazine were some of the offerings that became part of ESPN's effort to utterly lead the mindspace of sports. Popular new shows ranged from the X Games to the Skins Game, which was part of the OCC purchase. Cumulatively, ESPN's programs and channels achieved record numbers in ratings and viewership while generating more advertising revenue than the big three networks, and taking in the additional revenue that a cable channel makes through its affiliate fees.

In 1995, Capital Cities/ABC was acquired by Disney, giving Disney an 80 percent controlling interest over ESPN. The new ownership situation did not end ESPN's growth trajectory by any means, but it signaled the beginning of a different and fourth stage in development. Although ABC was the asset that industry watchers focused on when they debated Disney's strategy and future, Michael Eisner, the chairman and CEO of Disney, saw things a little differently. ESPN, according to Eisner, was the crown jewel in the acquisition, and worth "substantially more" than the $19 billion Disney paid for the entire ABC holdings. While ABC was the trophy and the asset Disney would have to work hard to integrate, ESPN was the desired prize, quite a reversal of the relative standings between network and cable channel.

Digging the Moat

Indicative of the new relationship between ESPN and ABC, Bornstein became head of ABC and chairman of ESPN in 1998, a move that was simultaneously up and out. His hand-picked successor, George Bodenheimer, became the new president of ESPN. Within four years, Bornstein left ABC and the lines of sight between Bodenheimer and Disney were clear.

Disney and ESPN. Two aggressive organizations with extremely powerful brands, highly defined cultures and successful approaches to doing business, each focused on distinct sectors of the demographic spectrum. What could have been a complicated, challenging, threatening, and even crippling period of integration and rebranding simply wasn't. Quite surprising to me as someone who consulted a lot in the post mergers and acquisition space, Disney essentially let ESPN do what it was doing so well. We'll examine that story more fully in Chapter 6. Instead of faltering or retooling, ESPN dug the moat around the sports fan, secured its brand, and entered a market leadership phase without pausing for breath. It has continued to grow in rankings, revenue, viewership, program offerings, networks, and countries.

Yet, the likelihood of stumbling was high. Media empires have had their foundations shaken in the past 10 years. The landscape has been reshaped by new technology, new money, and new visionaries, as well as by the reassertion of "old" visionaries, old technology, and old money. The late 1990s, in particular, were a paralyzing distraction for many organizations. Some media entities were dazed and confused by the need for an Internet strategy, and many top organizations lost talent to Internet start-ups or reconfigured their culture and compensation structure to bribe workers to stay. ESPN remained on course, relying on the passion of its fanatics—inside and outside—to stick to the enterprise and its offerings, while carefully navigating the ups and downs of developing an Internet presence and managing to keep its digital offerings tightly bound to the ESPN brand. Indeed, while there are more ways to access sports information, entertainment, and merchandise than ever from ESPN, there is no confusion or divergence from the brand. Analysts talk in theory about cross-platform opportunities for organizations today, just as they used to talk about the ideal of synergy ten years ago. But ESPN is an unheralded case study that illustrates how such a strategy evolves organically while actually meeting customer needs and turning a profit.

What about competing with ESPN head-on? After all, ESPN had come from nowhere to conquer sports. That was the poetic irony to the ABC purchase of ESPN—the network that labeled itself "worldwide leader in sports" was drawn to the sports brand of ESPN. For years, ABC cobranded sports with ESPN. Following the Disney acquisition, however, there was no longer a reason for political correctness and ESPN's more powerful brand soon swallowed ABC Sports whole. But if ESPN could overwhelm ABC, someone else could surely overwhelm ESPN? And yet, even though TBS, Fox, and Comcast have taken runs at ESPN's market share with various strategies, so far no other network or web-based challenger has come close to replicating ESPN's success. The brand leadership in sports and sports-themed entertainment, the coverage of major events, and the revenue from advertising and cable fees has created a moat within which ESPN sits secure. ESPN has even fought off brand-intense threats to its key male demographic from outside sports and television.

Indeed, no other television network, sports or otherwise, is as profitable as ESPN. Disney does not make the raw numbers public, and it would be unethical for me to report on financial or strategic matters I learned about in confidence as a consultant, but I can quote the public record. ESPN contributed an astounding 33 percent to Disney's total operating income in 2008.[2] ESPN is one of the top recognized brands in the United States. Every day, the average American devotes 54 minutes of his or her time to ESPN offerings, and the combined reach of the organization's various programming outlets has exceeded 100 million. Significantly, ESPN's diverse portfolio of offerings (including 4 channels and 40 business entities) has insured it to the typical risk that a network faces with a single channel or a narrow band of prime time programs. No matter what happens in sports, ESPN is still the delivery vehicle of choice for fanatics.

A recent quote from Don Ohlmeyer, the widely respected television programmer and long-term producer of Monday Night Football, describes the power of ESPN well. According to Ohlmeyer, "ESPN is the most profitable network in the history of entertainment and communications."[3] Not just sports, not just cable, but television. Something about this organization's leadership, culture, ownership, operations, and marketing has enabled it to thrive and grow and imprint its unique brand like few organizations in any industry. It's the GE, the McDonalds, the Wal-Mart of television, and its management and organizational story is largely unknown.

On the Hiring of Fanatics

From the beginning, ESPN offered sports fanatics something they could get nowhere else: round-the-clock and constantly updated highlights, information, sporting events, and sports punditry. In recent years, it has become apparent how good the Internet is at parsing people's interests into distinct niches. Before there was an Internet, the only place sports fanatics could go to get all their sports needs fulfilled was ESPN. And even after the arrival of the Internet, ESPN remains the first access point for most sports fanatics because of the establishment of that brand. Remember, a brand is not a slogan or marketing scheme: It's the organization's values and personality or culture engaging in a relationship with the customer. And that relationship succeeds or fails in the long run based on how well promises are fulfilled.

If ESPN was built to reach the sports fanatic and engage that passion, what about the people drawn to the organization as employees? How direct a link has there been between sports fanatic employees and sports fanatic customers? As so often happens in such matters, there's the legend and there's the truth. The legend makes a great story and an easy bullet point in a presentation. But understanding the truth and its shades of gray is more instructive for how a great business really builds its fanatical brand.

As I stated in the introduction, legend is that ESPN *only* hires people who are sports fanatics, and has done so since the beginning. The story goes that Scotty Connal, Chet Simmons's first right-hand man, was emphatic about it when he interviewed prospective employees. His most important question to a job candidate was: "What part of the newspaper do you turn to first every morning?" Answer anything but the sports section and the interview was effectively over. Give the right answer, and Connal dug in more deeply. What's your favorite team? Give me some stats. What's the most painful sports moment of your life? What's the best memory? Name some bench players on your championship team. Unless you knew sports at the most detailed level, you were not really a fanatic and you didn't belong at ESPN.

When I asked people about the truth of that legend, I got some confirmations and some qualifications. Yes, it happened, Connal really did hire that way and there was even a production manager who continued the Connal tradition. Al Jaffe did much of the campus recruiting for production employees for many years. From early on, ESPN was one of the dominant television distractions of university life, like David Letterman, the Simpsons, *South Park*, or Jon Stewart during various eras. Sports-oriented students watched ESPN, talked about it, and plenty with ambitions for careers in media or television programming wanted to join it. So when Jaffe used questions to assess their degree of fanaticism, those who answered right qualified for the money rounds during which other attributes—intelligence, integrity, passion for work—were evaluated.

Still, when I continued to ask whether ESPN hired only sports fanatics, I got more nuanced answers. Some thought it was a critical part of ESPN's culture, others thought the practice functioned in some departments but not others, while still others viewed it as overblown or off the mark. I thought it was important to dig in because employees constitute culture. If there's not a pure line of sports fanaticism threading the DNA of all ESPN employees and leaders, does that undercut the arguments about the robustness of the culture and brand? Is ESPN just another company where some people are passionate about the product, others temporarily take on the passion to succeed, and still others are indifferent or even cynical? What's the reality and what's the myth?

The distinctions start with the departments. On the financial or administrative sides of the enterprise, the answer is no—being a sports fanatic is not a requirement, although many of the individuals in those departments that I know absolutely love sports. Perhaps their own company transformed them in ways that have yet to reach their consciences? Sports is in the air and it certainly comes up as a topic of interest, but it's not the resounding passion for everyone. This has been true since the beginning. In the early years, those in the trenches of "operations" were just employees who happened to live in northern Connecticut; while the top managers were either finance and accounting types who could have worked in any industry counting widgets, or those with experience in television specifically and sports only incidentally. Similarly, on the sales and marketing side of the business, as in sales and marketing anywhere, product and business relationships are key, and sports are only a passion that some may enjoy and others may be relatively indifferent to.

In production and programming, however, there is a much more blatant sports obsession. Perhaps this shouldn't be too surprising. People who want to be in sports television are naturally drawn to the greatest sports television venture ever. That level of passion is what Scotty Connal and Al Jaffe were testing when they conducted interviews. The results are not surprising. The hallways and cubicles in the production side of ESPN are jammed with sports fanatics. Sports conversations are ongoing. A passion for games and events is palpable. Sports knowledge—details, statistics, memories, analysis, assessments, joys, and sorrows—saturate the air and can be felt in the tingle on the back of your neck.

But even in programming there are degrees of dedication to sports, and many of the top ESPN programmers are sports fans but hardly sports fanatics. They like their own teams, they like some sports more than others, but they wouldn't live and breathe sports as an all-consuming lifestyle if it wasn't for the whirlwind demands of the enterprise. Among the top leaders of the company, that same variation holds true. Founder Bill Rasmussen was an outright fanatic, a man who wanted into sports in any way, shape, or form and when he couldn't find the right means, went out and built it. The critical Getty liaison, Stu Evey, was as much a fan as anyone in the stands at a big game and was suspected by some of the professional TV executives of being a little star struck by the big name athletes, a notion he disputes emphatically. Likewise, Roger Werner, the most cerebral, calculating, and purely business-oriented president of the company, talks calmly and dispassionately about sports in a business call, but others have described how passionate he is about outdoor sports and racing when he lets that other side of himself show. Perhaps it shouldn't be surprising that Werner has been the founding executive of two other sports channels, the Outdoor Life Network and Outdoor Sports.

The presidents who followed Werner had a love for sports, but I never I got the impression that their love reached the level of "fanaticism." Steve Bornstein likes games and competition and the good stories that come from sports, but he likes them through the filter of programming—what's good TV, what would be better TV? I don't know whether Bornstein would follow sports as intensely if he wasn't in the business. George Bodenheimer talks sports with ease and interest as a way of breaking the ice with business colleagues and clients, and he certainly understands the power that sports holds in many lives, but I've never noticed an overwhelming passion for sports in him, other than his intense love of golf, Tiger Woods, and those New York Football Giants.

So, if even the top leaders of ESPN have been a mixed bag when it comes to sports fanaticism, is the overriding theme a myth? In

Bornstein's view, sports fanaticism was never an imperative at ESPN, but was considered to be a given. Chances are, you had some degree of sports love if you wanted to work at ESPN where sports and sports-related entertainment was the brand and the only product, and the hours and the intensity were and remain brutal. In other words, sports fanatics basically self-selected for their fit within the organization. Indeed, Bornstein has always insisted that, rather than an interest in sports, "brains, ambition, and integrity" were the vital components in those hired or promoted because those are qualities you can't educate into people, nor can anyone fake them in the long-run. Like Herb Kelleher at Southwest Airlines, who made a habit of hiring for attitude and training for ability, Bornstein believes you bring your smarts, your hunger, and your personality to work with you every single day regardless of the ups and downs of the business or your personal life.

If Bornstein personally has any fanatical interest outside of day-to-day business, it is for television programming, and that's a love shared by many others. In its first year, ESPN may have looked scrappy and second-rate to the experienced sports producers of NBC, but to Bornstein, coming from an underfinanced public television operation, it was as though he'd arrived in heaven. There was equipment just laying around in hallways that he could only have dreamed about accessing back at his old job. What's more, he'd finally found work in which he got paid to watch television. Bornstein thinks that television itself is the drug that attracts and hooks talented people. "I've never met anyone in the media business who left voluntarily. It's a very exciting and fun business to work in and there's a lot of psychic compensation associated with doing something you enjoy that much."

Those kinds of comments were frequent among both old guard and new guard leaders at ESPN. Geoff Mason, who has been the organizing force behind the scenes of some of the great sports events of the past 40 years, recalls sitting on the porch with Don Ohlmeyer when both were just starting out, newly married with young families, plotting their future careers. Ohlmeyer was a television director and Mason a television producer. They both loved what they were doing and wondered how long they could keep the good times going. The bet was that the television business was not going to get any smaller and somebody would always need programs directed and produced. Looking back, Mason says, "We had no right to be that correct." Both men, primarily in sports, rode the television rocketship to places and experiences they would otherwise have had difficulty reaching. More recently, Mark Shapiro, an extraordinary programmer who launched, while still in his late twenties and early thirties, many of ESPN's most distinctive offerings, experienced the same kind of career trajectory. Television and entertainment are industries that reward talent and ambition. The glamour of the television business as much as the sports product has been the lure for bringing the best and the brightest to ESPN.

And yet, you can't discount the role of fanaticism in ESPN's success. I've never seen an organization over that many years maintain an employee and executive base that has been as driven, as able to sustain brutal schedules, and as eager to take on the latest urgent project as the people at ESPN. That fanaticism is the energy behind ESPN's survival phase in the 1980s, its period of extraordinary growth in the 1990s, and its ability to dig the moat around its brand dominance in the 2000s. But where does the fanatical energy come from? Money hasn't been the motivating factor. When Bill Creasy was hired, few people in television had his kind of experience, but salary was barely discussed because almost no one in television made any money then. That thriftiness still holds at ESPN today, as if the company is still a struggling up-and-comer. Plenty at ESPN earn less than colleagues in similar type organizations. Even the top executives, well paid as they are, do not secure the kind of outsized compensation packages fairly common in high performance organizations today. Given the intense scrutiny around executive compensation today, ESPN perhaps was ahead of it time once again. So what, if not sports fanaticism, is the source of that tremendous energy and drive?

When he talks about the keys to leading a successful organization today, George Bodenheimer often says, "Hire people with passion, they will always over deliver." That's been a core competency at ESPN, where there is a history of hiring bright, ambitious young people on their first, second, or third jobs out of college and giving them more opportunity for having an impact and achieving advancement than is typical in established organizations.

If there has been a typical employee it is someone who is ambitious, extremely aggressive at tackling what needs to be done, and utterly inexperienced in the traditional organization, structure, and hierarchy of a bigger company. The old adage about Type A leaders, that they are the kind to ask for forgiveness, not permission, has held true at ESPN, except rarely is anyone told that forgiveness is necessary.

Each day can bring a crisis. You might come in planning to do one thing, but by the time you arrive at your desk in the morning three more urgent matters have been added to your list. There sometimes seem never to be enough people, but although complaints about this have sometimes been frequent and even bitter, everyone knows that lacking enough people is actually a good thing, because if you have enough people that means the business is stalled.

Most have responded to the demands because of the many-sided leverage ESPN had and has. Sports is a business and a product that is part of the social conversation. Everyone knows ESPN. Your family and friends are curious about it. You get lauded for being part of it. And ESPN offered all that psychic compensation, the center of the universe feel, as well as the rewards of achieving great things. When ESPN was a fast-growing start-up, fanatics came to it because it was on the threshold of becoming the biggest thing in sports. When ESPN really took off, fanatics came to it because it was on the brink of becoming the biggest thing in media. Then, after ESPN achieved all that, fanatics continued to come because ESPN is the only field worth playing on. With all that growth, there have always been clear paths for very fast progression. Even today, the atmosphere is one in which everyone is vying for more responsibility, more recognition, bigger titles, a larger impact on what the organization produces. Success means running faster and faster. Sometimes you pause, take a breath, and question what you are doing with your so-called life, but then comes the next crisis and the next opportunity, and you just run all the harder.

It sounds difficult and stressful, and despite the recent efforts of Bodenheimer to make the atmosphere more conducive to enjoying family life or maintaining some aspect of work-life balance, ESPN is still an extremely demanding work environment. But people are drawn there for the glamour and the opportunity, the lure of television and the addiction of sports, and despite the personal challenges, they tend to love it. More often than not, when I talk to former ESPN employees about their experiences, they're proud of their accomplishments, they marvel at the pace and quantity of work that was required, and they volunteer a wistful comment: "It was the greatest time in my life."

The Astoundingly Simple Principle

In front of the camera, ESPN has made a specialty of featuring enthusiastic sports fanatics as broadcasters, anchors and commentators. Talent like Chris "Boomer" Berman and Dick Vitale exhibit with every word, exclamation, and grimace the infectious, unbridled love of sports typical of the raving sports fan. You get the feeling they're fans first and journalists second. And that seems to be alright with the viewers at home.

On the other side of the television screen, the dedication of viewers has been the result of all the hard work and the good decisions made about the culture, the brand, and the business strategy. Sports fanatics were the network's early ambassadors and long-term torch holders. Through the way it provides its offerings, ESPN has a visceral connection with its customers. What's more, that same connection extends to many of the athletes they cover. Inside a lot of professional athletes and coaches is an obsessed fan, juiced up on competition and the drama of winning and losing. I can think of few other companies that do as good a job of creating an atmosphere of fun and excitement for its people, its customers, and its talent. Maybe Southwest in the airline industry, Starbucks in the consumer goods space, or Apple and Google in high tech. But it's hard to surpass ESPN.

"Serve fans." That's what John Skipper, the founding editor of *ESPN The Magazine* and currently the corporation's Executive Vice

President of Content, calls the "astoundingly simple principle" at the heart of ESPN's success.[4] I believe that "serve fans" is the mission, central value, and critical metric that has allowed ESPN to evaluate all its decisions, charge forward in the changing landscape of communications and entertainment, grow by many magnitudes beyond its original premise, and stay steady through multiple leadership and ownership regimes without the firm hand of a legendary founder.

"Be ready for the red light" is the production discipline behind delivering quality live programming in a professional, entertaining, and moment-capturing way. "Yes, but we're also a business" is the fiscal and operating discipline necessary to restrain costs, generate revenue, fend off competitors, and enable growth. "Digging the moat" is the strategy ESPN used to solidify its brand dominance. And "Hiring fanatics" is the means by which ESPN has identified and channeled the energies of the types of people who are not content to merely serve out time but want to throw their full creative potential into their work and achieve something extraordinary.

But "Serve fans" is the overarching mantra. While that sounds like "customer focus"—a very common bullet point in many corporate mission statements today—I believe it is different at ESPN, where the imperative of serving the fans has a distinct tenor and urgency. I've heard the expression in formal board meetings, intense closed-door office arguments, and reflective discussions on golf courses and yachts. It's the ultimate touchstone when decisions are being made, whether those junctures are about enormous investments of resources and brand equity or relatively minor choices in editing, hiring, or budget allocation. Bodenheimer is known for always asking the question, "How is this going to help us serve fans better?" The question has the effect of cutting through the confusion and the egos and the noise to clarify the priorities and focus everyone on the desired result. The great consulting firm McKinsey and Company, which I've have had the pleasure of serving as long as I served ESPN, refers to this notion as "the central question." Everyone knows the central question at ESPN.

That mantra has been with ESPN since its inception, as part of the corporate DNA, even before it was articulated. Serving fans is the reason ESPN was formed and the mission that people feel when they are drawn to the organization. As I will discuss in subseqent chapters the mission of ESPN is beautifully articulated today:

To serve sports fans wherever sports are watched,
listened to, discussed, debated, read about or played.

How much simpler and cleaner can you get than that? ESPN has fashioned its fanatical brand around this clear concept. The organization embodies the passionate sports fan, someone who is joyfully enthusiastic about competition and sports drama, hungry for more information and fun, and eager to watch and relive the moments that make sports special. The enterprise has been successful because there are millions of sports fans out there just like that, and ESPN is incredibly adept at delivering what they want.

CHAPTER ONE KEY POINTS

"Serve fans or customers"
It isn't about the enterprise, it's about the customer. All your business decisions must be genuinely made through the filter of that preeminent consideration.

"Hire fanatics"
You need the energy of true believers to sustain a venture that goes beyond the ordinary. Conventional rewards will not motivate such people. They will be moved by a sense of mission, an us-versus-them mentality, and strong connection to the passionate customer.

"Be ready when the red light goes on"
Fanatical passion helps an original and compelling idea form but the most formidable challenge in launching a new business

is bringing the vision into existence. By making an audacious but attainable commitment to begin operations at a specific deadline, ESPN was able to harness the energy of that urgency and overcome many pitfalls, potential delays, and overwhelming doubts. The organization never forgot the lesson of what urgency can accomplish.

"Yes, but we're a business, too"

Congratulations, you've successfully launched your new venture and your idea has come to life. But can you sustain it? Even the most compelling idea needs to meet the test of reality. Once an achievable strategy is in place, a day-to-day focus on business discipline is required to stick to the plan. No vision is reached in an instant. Many dreary months and years must be endured before the plan proves out. Plenty of organizations and individuals falter and lose their focus during that dry period. The payoff comes to those who keep the discipline.

"Digging the moat"

A fanatical brand is one that establishes an unassailable relationship with customers. That means delivering on the core promise to serve fans in every possible way, while taking up all the open space in a market.

Chapter 2

THINK LIKE AN INCUMBENT, ACT LIKE A CHALLENGER

At ESPN, I saw organizational culture developing in real time. I arrived nine years after launch, when the survival phase was still transforming itself into the enterprise capable of ramped up growth: ESPN beginning to become ESPN. But this transformation was not an easy chemistry experiment with clear instructions and expected outcomes. We were all feeling about in the dark, ESPN as a young company, me as a young consultant, both uncertain as to how the many variables would influence the organization's growth and direction. Nor did the priority list often allow for big picture thinking. The leadership at ESPN was dealing with so many dynamic and constantly shifting challenges, crises, and opportunities at any given moment that it was always easier and more expedient to devote 100 percent focus to the matter at hand.

But you can't grow culture on purpose or by design. Culture is the way a group of people adapt to the world. It's formed out of the possibilities of an environment and its boundaries, as well as the amalgam of values, stories, myths, and informal rules that spell out how people are to behave most of the time. In their breakthrough book, *Corporate Cultures*, published over 25 years ago, Deal and Kennedy state that strong cultures help employees "by knowing exactly what is expected of them, and therefore will waste little time in deciding how to act in a given situation. In weak cultures, employees waste a lot of time just trying to figure out what they should do, and how they should be doing it" (p.15). As a student of anthropology and organizations I knew all that to be true, but watching ESPN grow and change I was struck by the degree to which the limitations of its early circumstances became the crucible in which its strong, dedicated, even fierce culture, was forged.

ESPN didn't have enough money to compete on a level playing field with other media ventures. Its backing came from outside the industry. It lacked the long-term presence of a strong visionary founder. It had little access to the big events that make sports must-watch TV. It was a small cable channel competing against multi-billion dollar networks. It needed to broadcast its programming over a second-tier system. It was stuck up in Bristol, the boonies of northern Connecticut. And yet somehow, each of these detriments became assets as the ESPN culture evolved.

To a certain extent, this was about turning weaknesses into strengths, while capitalizing on the underdog feeling that was reinforced every day by their humble surroundings. This is something I think all resilient people and organizations do by instinct and temperament, like the high-achieving CEO who overcomes a childhood affliction such as a stutter, dyslexia, or ADD and makes of himself someone with uncommon levels of energy, focus, and determination. But more than overcoming its limitations, ESPN embodied them. Those detriments and obstacles became ESPN's defining character and way of doing business. If you happened to catch any of the interviews of Michael Phelps, after crushing several Olympic and world records in the XXIXst Olympiad, you heard a young man state that every time he was bullied, made fun of, or doubted, he only became stronger and more determined to win . . . the same spirit found in the heart of the ESPN culture.

In this chapter, I describe some of the critical events and circumstances that enabled ESPN to become ESPN.

Insecure Overachiever

In some business circles, among those who have been bested or outmaneuvered, ESPN has a reputation for arrogance. Like Microsoft, Starbucks, or Wal-Mart, it's the giant that always gets its way. But when you get inside the company and meet the executives and staff on their own turf, defenses down, you can be surprised by their humbleness. A strong streak of insecurity is a major part of the organizational character.

I noticed that streak—what McKinsey calls the "insecure overachiever"—early and often, and I heard echoes of it when I talked to people about the origins of the company. Bill Rasmussen had a salesman's bluster. He convinced everyone that a dedicated sports network was not only a great idea; it was absolutely going to happen. But there was always inner doubt. The lack of money, talent, deals, and time were brick walls the express train could slam into at any moment. But every morning, the founders, backers, and key executives needed to go out into the world as if all was on track. The flip side of this imposter syndrome is hubris, a drive to become bigger and better than everyone else. Not surprisingly, ESPN has this kind of psychodynamics, or what I call "organizational schizophrenia" to spare. The best example I can use to illustrate that point comes from a leadership exercise.

In one of my first major activities at ESPN I worked with the top 20 executives, who had gotten 360 feedback from their peers, superiors, and direct reports, to see how they measured up against the organizational mission and values that Steve Bornstein developed with some counsel from me. After the feedback data had been collected, I met with each executive for about an hour to go over the results, give them my take on the data, work out an action plan, and come to agreement about what each executive needed to focus on to leverage strengths and shore up weaknesses. The aggregate data was interesting because certain themes came through clearly, so I designed some training specifically to bolster the most critical needs.

According to Bornstein, one of ESPN's strategic imperatives was teamwork. As a savvy leader, he wanted to leverage the underdog spirit, but wanted to ensure that it was focused outwardly, against the competition, not inwardly against one another. As he put it in the list of value statements:

> Our success has always been dependent upon people working together as a *team*. To sustain our success and competitive advantage, we must communicate with one another openly and honestly, assist each other in time of need and vigorously support the team building effort.

And yet, teamwork was a slightly weak or underappreciated capability among the executive leadership group. All were ambitious and smart, but they did not yet work well across silos or divisions, a phenomenon common in companies that experience rapid growth, and are therefore focused on their individual enterprise. Some of that may have been due to the nature of the industry as well. Television, as a business, has more than its share of political infighting and go-it-alone egoism. It's a rough game where success can often be measured most clearly by the failure of others. ESPN didn't have that kind of problem—there was too much of an outcast mentality among those drawn to the company to engender such Byzantine behavior—but Bornstein believed the organization wouldn't achieve its long-term goals if teamwork wasn't reinforced and rewarded going forward. It was critical to establish that capability now, while the organization was poised for ramped up growth. Many organizations have "teamwork" as a value in their Mission statements, but few truly embrace it, measure it, and reward it when it happens. When competing in an intense business environment, the power of committed people working together can defy odds, and as someone who was a fan of team sports, Bornstein understood this deeply.

In their bestselling book, *The Wisdom of Teams*, Katzenbach and Smith argue that leaders need to be very clear about what type of team structure would best drive desired results of an enterprise. If you are a "working group" of assembled professionals, then one might argue that there is no need to support teamwork aggressively. A golf team may be considered a working group—yes, they are a team, but there is little, if any, interdependence or true synergy that would be realized if team members tried to work together. (And let's not forget that working together as a team is not easy; it takes enormous effort.) However, if you are a basketball or soccer team, you cannot compete, regardless of the individual talent, if you fail to work together as one unit. The sports examples here are numerous, but just think of the U.S. Olympic basketball team of 2004; a ton of individual talent that never came together, which resulted in the sum being far less than the value of the parts, not even coming close to the Dream Team of former years, or more recently, the gold-winning U.S. team of 2008, coached by Mike Krzyzewski (better known as Coach K).

I heard management guru Tom Peters once state that people "Treasure what you measure." Unfortunately, so many organizations say they value one thing, but reward another. Given that much of what I do with organizations is help them identify, clarify, articulate, and, most importantly, measure their values, I am constantly in search of best practices in this area. Well, years ago I came across an article that provided great insight into this issue, entitled, "On the Folly of Rewarding A, While Hoping for B," written by Steve Kerr, the past Chief Learning Officer of GE and Goldman Sachs. The bottom line is that you should never claim that something is a core value unless you teach it, measure it, exercise consequences when it's not embraced, and reward it when it is.

When you're trying to teach, and ultimately prove, the value of some attribute or strategy to a group of smart, accomplished, intensely busy executives, the standard approach is to find some 30-page Harvard Business School case study, hand it out as homework, and then meet to discuss. I realized that at ESPN, that kind of academic, instruction-based style would not have been met with enthusiasm by the executives. Therefore, I resorted to using an entertaining film as a case study to make the same point about the importance of teamwork and harnessing the "underdog" spirit. The film I chose for the ESPN executive team was *Hoosiers*.

When sports fans debate great sports movies, there are few who don't include the 1986 movie *Hoosiers* on their all-time top ten list. Starring Gene Hackman, Barbara Hershey, and Dennis Hopper, the film chronicles a small-town Indiana high school (the fictional Hickory High School) as it captured the state championship in 1951. One of the great underdog stories of American cinema, I think the film still feels powerful and gritty because it captures the raw vulnerability—those crazy hopes and gut tightening anxieties—of the little guy. There's no way Hickory High School should win. They don't have the elite resources, the elite athletes, the elite institution or fans—but through relentless practice, shrewd strategy, and a sense of mission, they come to believe in themselves and they end up defeating their mightier opponents.

At ESPN, *Hoosiers* hit home even harder than I anticipated. The points about teamwork were clear and easy to pull out. But the movie seemed to illustrate another, deeper theme that everyone at ESPN absolutely felt and fundamentally believed. The ESPN executives identified strongly, almost viscerally, with the underdog. When the Hickory High School basketball team gathers in the locker room for a team prayer before entering the court to face an intimidating, all-state opponent for the championship, the preacher reads from the Bible (1 Samuel 17): "David, reaching into his bag and taking out a stone, slung it and struck the giant Philistine on the forehead." The executives at ESPN saw themselves as David. They viewed ESPN as the little organization no one thought would succeed. They understood the anxiety of the underdog role, they carried the grudge of being "miss-underestimated," and they relished the thought of being able to take on the big networks and shock the world.

As the film and the story demonstrates, the right leadership made all the difference. Getting individuals to work together, to leverage their talent (SKILL) as well as their spirit (WILL) is the very focus of leadership. The coach played by Gene Hackman had come from a more rarefied atmosphere (like many of the executives at ESPN who had come from ABC and NBC) and he had a chip on his shoulder about feeling outcast. But he also knew how the players at the big schools thought about themselves and prepared for games. He had a mixed bag of talent to work with in his own players, but the performance and character he was able to draw out of those kids put the team over the top.

For the ESPN executives, this was all very inspirational and the showing of *Hoosiers* was an event many mentioned to me as significant, even years later. As recent as a year ago, George Bodenheimer had mentioned to me in passing that we should consider using *Hoosiers* again to train the next generation of leaders at ESPN. The way people talked about it made me realize that it had felt to them as though they were watching the ESPN story rather than the story of some Indiana basket-ball team. ESPN was the underdog and the world-beater at the same time. It was "Us Against the World"; at the same time, it was "We're Better Than They Are."

Bornstein regularly articulated that idea in a typically competitive and aggressive way. "We need to think like an incumbent and act like a challenger." For some reason, when I break that statement down I find it hard to recreate its power. Bornstein's view was that ESPN needed to hold two contradictory realities to be simultaneously true. ESPN was the scrappy underdog—undermanned, underfinanced, underestablished, off in the hinterlands, banging relentlessly on the door to achieve access, acceptance, credibility, and profit. This was no pretend leadership act, but something deep in Bornstein's personality that also reflected ESPN's attitude. In *the Taboos of Leadership*, I observed that Bornstein believed that running ESPN was his own great good fortune, and there but for the grace of God, he'd be pumping gas somewhere back in Ohio. He wanted the people at ESPN to never take their success, sta-tus, and achievements for granted. It was all extremely precious, and could be snatched away in the blink of an eye.

At the same time, no matter what circumstances it found itself in, ESPN needed to believe that it was the worldwide leader in sports, that it had a better model, better leaders, better production teams, bet-ter ideas, and better programs than its competitors. It needed to think of itself as the incumbent already occupying the superior market position, and make decisions accordingly.

Out of such barely resolvable tensions, mindsets and personalities are formed, although they are schizophrenic at times. As an incumbent, ESPN acted like one of the big boys from day one, bold enough to do anything they could do, just as well as they could do it. As a challenger, ESPN took risks and was constantly creative, opportunistic, and inno-vative in how it conducted its business. This meant that out of necessity, it deviated from the start, taking chances, trying new ideas, seizing on whatever worked and turning it into an asset, moving quickly on to the next challenge.

Frequently, in the 1980s, I was told that the attitude was, "No one's watching us anyway, so who cares if we fall on our faces?" That was part of the organization's swagger, creativity, and sense of fun—all communicated to the viewer on the television screen by the enthusiastic and self-mocking hosts. The unstated corollary of this cavalier kind of talk was "Why shouldn't we take a chance and swing for the fences?" Psychologically, this gave room for the risk taking so vital to ESPN's success, a drive to try what others hadn't thought of before or had backed away from for various reasons. It also spoke to the desperation of the underdog who has nothing to lose and is bold enough to try and actually win the damn game despite all doubts, inside and out.

A Beacon in the Sky

Fundamentally, ESPN's role in the media world was formed by its first radical decision: to distribute its content via satellite. While that may seem obvious today, if you think about cable television and satellite signals as a radical new technology, not a ubiquitous part of the way we get home entertainment, you can imagine what kind of media revolution began in the 1970s. A helpful comparison can be made by thinking about the Internet. Before the World Wide Web, when communicating via e-mail and over electronic bulletin boards was limited to computer geeks, only a few visionaries saw the possibilities of a totally wired world. Twenty years later, business and life has been transformed in most ways imaginable. Cable did the same thing to television. ESPN, out of necessity, was at the forefront of that radical shift, deviating from the start.

The late 1970s was the critical time period, but cable television had actually been around since the 1950s. It was invented in rural Pennsylvania, where traditional television signals were difficult to receive because of interference from nearby mountains and forests. By erecting a tall cable tower or antenna at a high point, signals could be received from far away and then distributed to local homes that were literally wired to the central antenna.

From a few dozen cable providers and a few thousand homes nationwide in the mid-1950s, the system expanded and even began offering programming that was not available on the major networks. Recognizing the potential competitive threat of this parallel system, the television networks lobbied in the late 1960s for tighter restrictions on cable operators. The FCC responded by putting a freeze on the growth of new cable offerings. The talk was about protecting consumers, but the reality, of course, was about protecting a monopoly. That's a common tension between established market leaders and outside innovators.

Networks were right to fear cable, but they couldn't stop the advance of what was becoming a compelling and cost-effective technology. In 1972, Charles Dolan (whose lucrative company Cablevision supplies the New York City area today and owns Madison Square Garden, the New York Rangers and the New York Knicks) launched HBO, a pay channel that showed movies and sports events to cable subscribers. HBO was originally broadcast using microwave technology, but satellite technology was always in the plans and held the promise of nationwide distribution. Running out of money, Dolan would soon lose control over HBO to his primary financial backer, Time Life Management, much like Rasmussen lost control of ESPN to Getty Oil. Time installed the young Gerry Levin (the CEO who later brokered the Time Warner merger with AOL) as the new head of HBO. The network was the first to broadcast via satellite.

It's amazing to think about it, but satellite technology had only been around for little over a decade. In 1957, when the Russians launched Sputnik, they gave it a radio transponder to exchange signals with Earth—that was the beginning. NASA launched its own satellite system in 1964, in time to broadcast the Tokyo Summer Olympics. Other systems from other countries followed, but in 1975, RCA American Communications launched a commercial system called Satcom 1. HBO bought time on that system and on September 30 of 1975, it broadcast the pay-per-view production of the famous Ali-Frazier heavyweight title match from the Philippines, the so-called Thrilla in Manila. With such an auspicious beginning, no wonder sports found a home on satellite.

Through satellite the market for television viewers suddenly opened and expanded. Millions of people in the United States and abroad could receive a television broadcast via satellite signal, and channel capacity increased exponentially allowing for much more programming. You'd think the race to dominate this new medium would immediately take off, but a few more years passed before the magnitude of the potential was widely understood. Ted Turner was one of the first. His Atlanta-based WTCG ("Watch This Channel Grow") was broadcast nationwide in 1976 and became known as the first superchannel, specializing in sports and classic movies. The name was changed to TBS in 1979. Turner's next venture, the 24-hour all-news network CNN, began broadcasting in 1980. Like HBO, TBS and CNN would later be bought by Time Warner.

Bill Rasmussen learned about Satcom 1 during one of his first meetings with local cable providers in Connecticut. When they suggested he consider satellite as a medium, he bluffed as though he knew all about it, but soaked up every bit of information they could provide. Then he got on the phone with a salesman from RCA American Communications and arranged a meeting in a rented boardroom. Getting a channel broadcast on satellite meant leasing the rights for a satellite's transponder. Rasmussen learned two critical things from his meeting: first, that leasing a transponder for 24 hours per day of programming a month was cheaper than leasing for just 5 hours per day; and second, that RCA had three 24-hour transponders available at $35,000 each per month.

That price was steep considering the state of ESPN's finances, but seemed like a bargain given the mission to provide sports programming. Hedging their bets, Rasmussen applied for one transponder and let the two others go, while committing himself to getting the financing in order within 90 days. Obtaining the transponder rights was a remarkably democratic process: First come, first served. As it turned out, however, ESPN had gotten its order in just in time. Six weeks after the meeting with RCA an article in the *Wall Street Journal* about the new technology led to a rush of inquiries. Major media organizations like Time, Walt Disney Productions, Warner Communications, and 20th Century Fox were shocked to learn that an unknown entity named ESP Network had gotten in on the satellite boom before them. Not surprisingly, within a year, transponder rights that had cost ESPN $35,000 a month for five years were going for many millions.

Because of satellite technology, cable television stood on the precipice of great change. We can debate which is more important, the medium or the message, but once the medium was established, the need for message or content was clear. A terrific boom in programming soon arose. And ESPN was one of those programmers. Perhaps it was luck that the network had been at the right place at the right time. But Rasmussen and Evey recognized the potential of the technology that had fallen into their hands and seized the opportunity. Let's not forget that they were in a position to win. You don't throw a Hail Mary pass when you're down 40–0. You need to have a chance at the game winner to make the long-shot worth trying.

Business strategists often talk about the scalability of an idea. What's the size of the potential marketplace, can it be expanded, and is the service scalable? When ESPN was conceived, the founders had Connecticut and (maybe) the rest of New England in mind. They knew that local sports would find rabid fans in that region. But they immediately realized the concept could be expanded anywhere. A broadcast wasn't limited to Connecticut; it could be aimed at Texas, Colorado, California, and Minnesota, too. In this, ESPN's timing was also excellent. The nationalization of local sports conveniently matched a larger trend: the increasingly transient nature of our economy. But while people may move from coast to coast and city to city, emotional attachments to things like sports teams remain strong over a lifetime. Just like McDonalds or Starbucks can taste good no matter where you find their products, watching CNN in your hotel room in Dubai can be a comfort and watching your alma mater compete in an NCAA basketball game when you live 3,000 miles away is a tremendous luxury. ESPN enabled sports to become free of local boundaries and accessible anywhere. It should not be overlooked that advertisers, connected to a specific region or team, could suddenly reach an entire nation, too.

Just as the Internet boosts small businesses today and enables them to compete with larger entities, satellite offered ESPN the chance to be a major player in an industry that had been dominated for decades by only three networks. For a pittance, ESPN was able buy a beacon in the sky that bathed the richest nation in the world with its programming, 24 hours a day.

The Ultimate Road Trip

The second most critical factor in ESPN's formative beginning was the haphazard decision to situate its headquarters in Bristol, Connecticut.

Bristol had been a center for clock making a century before, but that was about the extent of its historical significance until the arrival of ESPN. The good citizens of Bristol might dispute the characterization, but a disgruntled ESPN broadcaster struck a nerve when he famously described Bristol as a terrific town to look at through your rearview mirror. Given all the possible locations in America, Bristol was the last place in the world most executives would deliberately plan a future media empire.

For the first generation of established executives, managers, and broadcasters recruited to ESPN, this was not an insignificant impediment. Those taking the jump were usually mocked by their major network colleagues with scorn and glee. "You're going where?" This fed the "us versus them," David and Goliath, Bristol versus New York and Los Angeles mentality. And it reinforced the belief that "nobody thinks we can do it, nobody has any respect for us," which was channeled into a desire to make the product better than what the networks were offering. But it also smacked of the truth. Bristol really did seem like the edge of the world. Steve Bornstein, arriving from the wilds of Ohio, said it was like going to Iceland, some dark faraway place you'd only heard of and never imagined visiting. There was nothing to do there but work and life outside work was miserable. Imagine you're in the media industry, you love the glamour and buzz of it all, and you're used to living in Los Angeles and New York. Those are great towns because you're surrounded by terrific night life and culture. When you leave the office, you've got 10,000 different things you can do to entertain yourself and your family. When you go to a bar, you run into colleagues from other networks and you start talking about the business, and opportunities turn up, and you think, as you swirl the ice in your glass, maybe the grass is greener on the other side of the fence. Now imagine, instead of New York or Los Angeles, you're living in Reykjavik, and when you go into the bar no one even speaks your language except the same guys you were sitting next to at the office, a half hour before. That's what it felt like in Bristol.

On the other hand, maybe that's a great way to draw the most out of people in terms of performance and build a hell of a tight culture. Thinking about it, I'm reminded of some of my own early consulting days. The road trips were hard. I was away from my family, my dear friends, and the comforts of my own home. I was locked into some alien organization with a group of people I barely knew, putting in ungodly hours trying to meet some unreasonable deadline. But out of those hours, camaraderie formed. The barriers came down. I got to know people. We solved some problems together. And afterwards, we had a shared experience in common, a touchstone for reconnecting instantly, and a contact we could call on without hesitation. Living in Bristol and working at ESPN was like the ultimate, never-ending road trip. As my dear Dad always said, "when shit happens and times are tough, remember, you will always have great stories to tell." And culturally speaking, stories are an inherent part of strong cultures, and ESPN has it's stories.

In Bristol, there was nothing to do but work, and there was no end to the work to be done, so people stayed at the office long after anyone under normal circumstances might have headed home. ESPN was small then, just a few hundred employees, so everyone knew everyone. Most of the young people brought on board were single and in their mid to late twenties. For many, it was their first job out of school. Few had spouses or children to worry about, so it was nothing to work 70 to 80 hours, 7 days a week. That was the demographic most susceptible to the lures of the nightlife in big cities, but there was nothing like that in Bristol except for Hamps, which later became the White Birch Bar, a kind of saloon in a tumbleweed-rolling town.

With no nightlife to distract and no families to go home to, what was there to do but work? Young people who joined the company were in for brutal hours and nonstop stress, working from early morning until as late as midnight, almost always for six and often for seven days a week. The work didn't pay well, so most of those young employees lived with multiple ESPN roommates in crowded apartments, catching a few hours sleep late at night before heading back to work in the morning. The only distraction outside of sports and television was partying. Given the average youth, the distance from family, and the unrelenting pressure of the work, when they partied, they partied hard, and created some great stories.

One of the downsides, particularly in the first decade of the company, was that the testosterone-laden atmosphere—so much sports, so many young college grads, such hard partying—could make ESPN a difficult environment. This is most apparent with the challenges many women have faced handling everything from unintended bias in a male-dominated workplace to outright harassment. But for men and women alike, the stress, pressure, and demands of the work, coupled with the isolation of Bristol, accounted for a lot of unhappiness and loneliness in those early years.

At the same time, ESPN, cognizant of the demands of the enterprise and believing genuinely in the mission, created an atmosphere that was comforting and familylike while also rewarding performance, talent, effort, creativity, and desire. There were informal parties and formal parties, summer picnics, and short trips. The camaraderie and tight connections came naturally. "It was the timing of it all," Rick Barry, the executive who first introduced me to Bornstein, said. Barry was rare among the young people in that he'd already had his share of life in blue-chip corporate America, and wanted no part of such experiences again. ESPN was the opposite of that. It wasn't a pampered or coddled environment like Google or Microsoft have now, with their campuses that provide for every luxury and desire in order to attract and keep young talent, but it was an atmosphere of tremendous opportunity and egalitarianism where hard work, commitment, and merit were rewarded, by management and peers.

The isolation, the semiforced camaraderie, and the unrelenting work-hard-play-hard tradition generated outstanding results. As Geoff Mason described the first generation of producer employees, "They were kids right out of college who would do anything to get the job done. They didn't have two nickels to put together, they were living in northern Connecticut, and they were putting up terrific shows with fewer cameras, fewer dollars, fewer tape machines, and cheaper mobile units than the big networks. They made up for all the disadvantages with unbelievable effort and creative energy."

Interestingly, there was a strong sense of ownership among that nucleus of early employees. That ownership wasn't financial at all—the pay was low and there were no shares to be financially vested in—but individuals, regardless of title, tended to take personal responsibility for improving things that needed to be brought up a notch, and they behaved this way without being told to and without ever receiving formal recognition. They picked up paper if they saw it on the floor, fixed errant fax machines, made sure coffeepots were filled, and straightened signs. They were devoted to their company and treated it as if they were its stewards, making decisions about operations as if their own money was at stake. Later, many of these same people formed the top leadership at ESPN.

As the company started growing and that original group of young people got older, they began getting married within the company, and they bought their first houses close by, so the sense of community strengthened. Even 30 years later, the hours are still brutal, and the intensity of the work continues to amaze, and the lack of distractions must help that focus remain strong. You have to love what you're doing at ESPN to survive. The potentially random decision to start up in Bristol has been leveraged, by design or accident, to enhance the culture and generate the high performance. But Bristol is no longer a far-flung outpost in the media galaxy. "You work in Bristol?" is now a question of curiosity with a tone of respect and envy. ESPN executives don't have to travel to New York or LA to convince partners and clients to make decisions; instead, people willingly travel to Connecticut. Bristol itself has grown into a pleasant, family-oriented bedroom community with many amenities that make it a very comfortable place to live.

Who would have expected that in Iceland?

Fast, Cheap, and (Occasionally) Out of Control

Experienced hands from established businesses or media companies who joined ESPN in leadership positions were soon struck by something missing:

Rules.

No one decided to forego rules because that was the way to free up innovation and leverage creative energy. Rather, no one really knew where they were going or what the venture would become. ESPN came from nowhere and its destination was uncertain. Moreover, everything moved so quickly that there was no time to contemplate the niceties of policy, regulations, or work flow. I heard that is what it was like at Google before the IPO, when the organization was staffed by young people racing into the future, barely pausing for breath. Old hands brought on board in top executive positions added some steadiness to the rudder, but the loose, creative bustle of the culture was already part of the DNA.

Jim Allegro, who came over as a seasoned executive from ABC to ESPN in the top finance position to "supervise the kids" after ABC Cap Cities bought the young company, put it this way: "It wasn't network TV. It didn't have any rules. If you wanted a policy you wrote it. There were no volumes of guidelines from 1903 you could consult and make a decision by. That was the negative side of ESPN and that was the beauty of it, too."

No rules meant a lot of things. First, it meant that the hierarchy, the chain of command, the line of authority—whatever you want to call it—was loose, flexible, and often distracted by whatever urgent crisis had hit the fan on that particular today. The negative side of that was that standards of conduct, reporting, decision making, budget allocating, and discipline could be random, poorly considered, chaotic, and contradictory. This got ESPN into trouble frequently, in areas ranging from negotiating production contracts to dealing with workplace environment issues to meting out discipline. It also interfered with the smooth achievement of work goals. Projects were chronically underfunded. New projects were frequently launched without taking the care to allocate the right resources. People suffered terribly trying to figure out how the hell to get things done.

But no rules also meant that anyone could do anything to accomplish something so long as the results were top-notch. This kind of Darwinian chaos made quality and performance a miracle that was rewarded with heady advancement. The best programmers, producers, cameramen, sales managers, secretaries, editors, and accountants survived, thrived, and emerged from the wild jungle as leaders who guided others in learning how to work fast, cheap, and (occasionally) out of control.

On the production side, this is known as guerilla TV. The networks, when they covered a major sports event, were like organized battalions in which every soldier has a role, the group deployed carefully and strategically in a well-planned and highly financed campaign—Napoleon marching on Moscow. ESPN, thinking like an incumbent but acting like a challenger, did everything with smaller crews, under harsher conditions, with fewer cameras, phone lines and trucks, with less money and less time and more energy and spirit, while still somehow achieving the quality of a major network production.

Bornstein hammered that idea home at every opportunity. Coming from public television he thought ESPN had more than enough resources and equipment already, so it wasn't necessary to imitate the bloat of the networks to achieve the same results. For Geoff Mason, used to producing top quality television under the best circumstances money could buy, this new way of making programs was a total shock. "I remember talking to Howard Katz (a senior executive, who later became president of ABC sports under Bornstein) about doing the U.S. Open golf tournament. He showed me the few cameras we had, and I swore and said, wow, we're lean and mean here." Katz just laughed. Starting to understand, Mason asked how many business phones they would have in the on-site production trailer, expecting five or six, but Katz told Mason there would be only one. Mason said, "You can't do a &#$@! golf tournament with one business phone!" But Katz insisted that they could, that it had always been done that way. "And that turned out to be one of the most valuable experiences of my life," Mason noted. "I'm convinced that's why ESPN is so successful today. They realized they didn't have to go out and spend a ton of money and waste resources to look good. You could make up for that with hard work, good planning, and efficient operations. That had never really been done before in sports television. Unlike everyone else, ESPN didn't throw money at the product, they threw young, hardworking people who were totally dedicated to getting the job done."

ESPN lore is filled with stories of projects, many of them huge in scale and effort, that were accomplished on the fly, with limitations in resources and time that would have killed any chance of success at a major network. There's a war-story sense of pride and amusement in relaying how harsh the conditions were, how outlandish the demands, how improbable the prospect of success. When ESPN Radio was launched, for example, the idea was originally conceived when ABC Radio approached ESPN to provide brief tidbits, 30-second spots at most, during breaks. Jim Allegro had an idea for going a little further than that, and Bornstein let him run with it. Allegro went to John Walsh, the former editor of *Rolling Stone* who had become ESPN's production guru, and said, "Maybe we can start a whole radio network." Walsh agreed it was a good idea and therefore it should be done. Such things can take years to germinate and develop, but 60 days later ESPN Radio was on the air with 16 hours of weekly programming, 8 hours on Saturday night and 8 hours on Sunday. This was an incredible feat. Everything about the radio network had to be built from scratch, including the studios. Two studios were needed, and the plan was to stack one of top of the other, but when the steel buildings were delivered, it was realized that the weight of the second studio would crush the first. So a second studio was built out of wood, and they got the structure completed just in time for the first broadcast to air. That night, Keith Olbermann, one of the hosts who had agreed to support the new venture, led his broadcast with a scoop he'd gotten that very afternoon. That was the kind of luck and timing ESPN made for itself again and again.

One of the traditional elements of television production that didn't work with the ethic of Fast, Cheap, and (Occasionally) out of Control was unions. ESPN doesn't like to discuss this fact, but maintaining a union-free environment has been absolutely critical to its way of doing business. I'm speaking about it now because I believe that while such a subject is taboo for business executives who are sensitive about public perception, it's a taboo that needs to be busted. No part of this story is meant to be anti-union; but it is meant to reflect the reality of the competitive environment ESPN faced.

An unanticipated side benefit to locating in Bristol was the initial ability to stay clear of unions. If ESPN had been established closer to New York City, there's no way the unions would have allowed camera crews, studios, and trucks to be deployed without union membership. By the time ESPN had established itself, an entrepreneurial culture focused on results rather than working hours or salary had set in. Despite attempts by union organizers to gain members, the ESPN rank and file recognized that their ability to produce 8,000 hours of quality programming a year, given the limitations of time, money, people, and equipment, would be negatively impacted by union rules. Perhaps this aversion had something to do with the overall youth of the employees. Part of the draw to ESPN was due to the fact that advancement at major networks was so limited by the system of seniority. Union rules dictated that time served took precedence over performance, over making something spectacular happen despite all the odds.

ESPN was able to work with freelancers and talented young non-union employees because of the great industry connections and experience of its leaders like Chet Simmons and Steve Connal. They had a network of thousands of freelance camera operators and people with trucks for rent and crews willing to moonlight on the side. They could get trucks and crews deployed cheaply anywhere in the country with a flip through the Rolodex.

Other networks could easily be hamstrung by the unions. Their costs were too high, and they were often forced to drop their best people and keep their least productive whenever a downturn occurred. When jobs needed to be eliminated, it was the youngest, newest workers—not coincidentally, the ones who were most aggressive, energetic, and hungriest—who were shed first, leaving the stodgiest, least technically up-to-date people in place. ESPN employees were used to doing whatever was necessary to get a quality product on the air, and they didn't care to be rewarded by seniority.

ESPN leadership was not a passive bystander on this issue. Of course, it had a point of view and worked hard to sustain a working environment where people knew they would be cared for by upper management. It did so not only because cheaper production costs and more flexibility let it do better work, but also because it believed that it knew best how to treat its own employees. Nonunion does not necessarily mean working conditions are worse. Successful organizations have proved that it can sometimes mean conditions are better. Southwest Airlines avoided unions at many levels because it established trust between employees and management. Employees believed they would be treated fairly, so they didn't need outside representation. Similarly, Costco is applauded in the press and in terms of share price for its unusually generous stance with employees. Compared to Wal-Mart, which has underperformed Costco significantly in recent years, Costco employees are pampered with high wages and benefits and a long-term employment plan. Despite this attitude and proven approach, Richard Galanti, CFO of Costco, laments the presence of unions at Costco. As he put it, "We wish they [the union] weren't there because we don't feel we need a third party to talk to our employees."[1] Good managers can understand this sentiment. Bad managers use it as an excuse.

Regardless of any stance you might take on the union issue, the overall theme of fast, cheap, and (occasionally) out of control was a critical force that helped create ESPN's culture and way of doing business. The early president/programmers like Simmons and Bornstein knew what was possible in production and what was not. They knew you could make really good TV with less money and resources. Would they have held the line so strongly if resources weren't stretched so thin? Although I think it was in the personality of Bornstein, especially, the point is academic. The resources were finite, and very limited at that. There was money, but not enough to waste. And if you wanted to keep making new things, stuff that hadn't been planned for six months earlier, you needed to maintain that spirit of entrepreneurialism and guerrilla TV as a way of being. The sense of ESPN's mission and potential was so strong that everyone from the rank and file to the experienced outsiders responded to that call. At ESPN it wasn't about the high-priced announcers or the cushy amenities on road trips or the cool technology, it was about the integrity of the sports event. After all, that's all the fan cared about.

Did it last? ESPN generates enough revenue and has enough resources today to do whatever it wants. But no company, especially a large one, can shoot from the hip in quite the same way forever. In recent years, more rules and regulations have been put in place. Behavior that was once part of the boisterous out-of-control atmosphere has been seriously curtailed, though I think that's also part of the overall trend of changing workplaces everywhere. The hours are a little saner, or at least balance and family time are more prized and encouraged. At the same time, the ethic of fast, cheap, and (occasionally) out of control remains strong. It's part of the organization's way of thinking about itself and what it does to fill all those programming hours.

When the Model Doesn't Work, Turn it Over

Despite the us versus them mindset, the beacon in the sky, the fortuitous location in Bristol, and the fast, cheap, and out of control approach to quality programming, ESPN didn't make any money until it figured out how to stop giving its product away.

Getty Oil had expected to break even on its $10 million investment into ESPN within two years. But by a year in, Getty had spent about $60 million and ESPN was burning through another $30 million per year. So Getty called in McKinsey and Company to assess whether there was any hope for the asset called ESPN or what its liquidation value would be if the pieces were sold off as scrap. As I mentioned in the previous chapter, Roger Werner, future president of ESPN, was part of that outside team of consultants. The McKinsey group looked at ESPN, the possibilities of satellite and cable as a medium, and the sports television marketplace in general, and drew some startling and harsh conclusions. Yes, cable was a growth industry that would steadily penetrate the American television marketplace. Yes, sports television was a growth market and there was room for an organization to distribute the extensive programming that ESPN was offering. And yes, ESPN was viable and could become a significant media entity. But it was going to take another 5 years and $120 million. And it was going to require flipping the industry business model to do it.

According to Werner, "We felt that at the rate cable was being built and subscribed to, over a five- to ten-year horizon, a large universe of paid TV homes would emerge and an all-sports service could command a meaningful share of viewership in that universe. We also felt that ESPN could sustain that market share on a given level of spending. But the cost side of the business had to be modeled carefully."

Simply following industry convention, ESPN had adopted the broadcast network model. The long-standing traditional approach to television distribution was for networks to pay affiliate stations to show their programs, and earn all their revenue from advertising. The big four networks, ABC, NBC, CBS, and FOX, still conduct business that way today. But ESPN would never survive, Werner believed, if it pursued an advertising revenue driven model exclusively. "We questioned the long-term viability of that and pointed to the need to challenge the fundamental assumption and explore the possibility of developing a second revenue stream." To obtain that second revenue stream, Werner advocated that ESPN stop paying affiliates to carry programming and start charging them for the privilege.

Any media executive would swallow hard at the audacity behind such a reversal. But for ESPN, a three-year old cable channel based in Bristol, Connecticut, such a plan seemed particularly bold, if not outrageous. Perhaps it took an outsider to see what industry insiders, particularly at the major networks, were blind to, but the McKinsey vision was prescient. Fortunately, Stu Evey from Getty and Bill Grimes at ESPN agreed and convinced Getty Oil to double down yet again. The McKinsey group switched its focus from assessing the business model to executing the strategic and tactical operating plan. As the primary architect, Roger Werner was lured onto the executive team as chief operating officer to lead the implementation.

That was when luck came to ESPN in another particularly nice piece of timing. In the fall of 1982, after only a year in operation, the plug was pulled on CBS cable because it had already lost $30 million. Coming from one of the trumpeted industry leaders, this was a terrific shock and wake-up call, and caused the many dozens of smaller publicly traded cable operators to lose significant market value as their share prices took a nosedive. In the press, there was a frenzy of speculation that cable itself was doomed and the 200-channel universe was never going to happen because the promise of original independent programming could not be fulfilled.

"It was at this point," Werner says, "that we saw an opportunity. I felt that we could go to the industry and say, guys, if we can't reverse this flow, if we can't change our business model and get paid a nominal fee as opposed to paying you guys a nominal fee, we're going to go out of business, too. And you may as well face the music and deal with it now."

The job became convincing cable operators that flipping the business model would be good for all parties, that it was in fact not just a viable plan for ESPN but a necessary one for the health of the industry. ESPN's primary argument was that it could no longer afford to provide the sports programming that cable operators' customers were becoming hooked on if the payment system wasn't reversed. But this "stop me before I shoot myself" kind of logic could only take ESPN so far. The more convincing case was that all cable channels, not only ESPN, were suffering under the conventional way of operating. The limited revenue obtainable via advertising on niche channels was stifling the growth of cable in general. If the model was reversed, more cable channels would get into the game, providing more programming and handing cable operators a more attractive lineup to lure television subscribers.

Of course, that kind of visionary perspective requires a certain generous and visionary mindset to appreciate and align with. An equally persuasive point of view was that cable operators, despite a setback at CBS and a temporary dip in share price, had a good thing going already. Reversing the flow of fees to a cable channel just to keep it alive was like signing over a paycheck to a desperate used car salesman. Within the cable industry, there were some fierce opponents to the idea and some who got it. In particular, John Malone, then chairman of the cable group TCI, and Bill Daniels, one of the pioneers of the industry and an enthusiastic sports fan who was a founder of the USFL, realized ESPN was right and became advocates with their colleagues inside the business.

Using the leverage that the current five-year distribution contract with affiliates was expiring in two years, ESPN proposed new rates going forward. Those cable operators who signed on immediately were offered a gradual progressive rate over the life of the next two agreements. Those who didn't sign up would be stuck with whatever prevailing rate the market could bear when the current agreement ended in 1985. The discussions were often ugly and heated, edging to threats of lost distribution and lawsuits. By the end of 1983, ESPN had a few deals in hand. By the end of 1984, most of the industry had been converted to the new model. Turmoil in the cable industry continued as hundreds of small independent operators were consolidated by a few bigger players. The 1984 Cable Act that deregulated the industry further accelerated the churn of consolidation and investment. Communities and households all over the country were rapidly being connected and more programs than ever were being developed. By 1985, ESPN had finally become profitable, meeting the schedule McKinsey had set for it when it concluded its study five years before. Most impressively, it achieved profitability without sacrificing on its mission to serve the sports fan with quality programming. In fact, it enhanced that mission because profitability was the catalyst for new programs, groundbreaking deals with the major sports leagues, and an expanded number of channels.

The impact of ESPN's flipping of the cable model can't be overstated. Not only did it save ESPN, but it helped progress the variety of channels, programs, and information sources we have access to today. The idea of a cable company paying affiliates to carry its broadcast seems ludicrous now from an operating perspective. But I'm not sure that revolution could have been started or even conceived by someone already vested in the traditional way of doing business. Radical innovations that change industries almost always come from outside those industries. McKinsey needed to conceive it, a backer from the oil industry needed to see the sense of it, and a desperate outcast operation from Bristol needed to implement it.

Naturally, the other cable channels, many of which we enjoy and take for granted today, like MTV, A&E, Discovery, and so on, followed ESPN's lead and began charging cable affiliates a nominal fee. There was nothing nominal about ESPN's fee, however, in the decades to come. From the initial 5 cents per month charge, the fee quickly became 20 cents a month, and the executives at ESPN, surprised at the success of what they were doing, found themselves wondering how much higher it could go. The dual revenue stream from advertising and affiliate fees was the holy grail. Steadily, as the revenues led to better programming, and the programming led to more subscribers, higher ratings, and higher fees that could be charged to advertisers, that circle of profitability continued to expand. From an astounding 70 cents per month, per cable subscriber in the early 1990s, Bornstein and Bodenheimer were able to raise affiliate fees to an industry-rocking $3 per month in the late 1990s. No other cable channel even comes close to that universe of profitability.

To describe the significance of that achievement Bornstein relies on a metaphor used by Warren Buffett. "We dug the moat around ESPN." By driving affiliate fees higher than those of any other competitor, ESPN has put a serious impediment in place that secures its position as the most popular and profitable cable channel, if not the most profitable entity in the media industry.

Happy Accidents

In business, as in life, unfavorable circumstances can hold us back or they can be turned to our advantage. The disadvantages, the outsider status, the sense that everyone in the industry was incredulous about ESPN's prospects in the early years, got under the skin and became the us versus them mentality so intrinsic to the culture. Even many of ESPN's cable affiliate customers were aggressive about constraining the organization's growth. The various leaders at ESPN used those threats and that chip on the shoulder to focus determination and commitment. Every dollar saved was a badge on the wall. Working faster and doing whatever it took to produce the best results was the self-rewarding goal in an industry dominated by union regulations, seniority, and complacency. The desperation was palpable because the employees really did believe they were on a mission to serve sports fans and they really did understand that the venture was vulnerable to failing. As Roger Werner puts it, "The kind of commitment I asked our people to make was to succeed or go out feet first in a pine box. There was no middle ground. We knew we needed to do certain things to survive and be the leader in this business, or go home. It was all or nothing."

Surviving, at every stage, meant doing things differently. Securing a satellite transponder because traditional broadcasting was too expensive, locating in Bristol because it was off the beaten track, using two cameras instead of five cameras because that's all that was necessary, flipping the long-standing business model because it was in the way. When you deviate from the start, that reflex gets into your corporate DNA. W. Chan Kim and Renee Mauborgne document this phenomenon well in their international bestselling book, *Blue Ocean Strategy: How to Create Uncontested Market Space and make the Competition Irrelevant.* The strategic deviation of Southwest Airlines, Cirque du Soleil (see Figures 2.1and 2.2), American Express, and Amazon provide just a few other great examples of companies that were built on a traditional

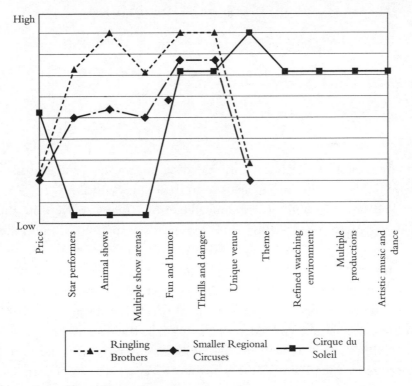

Figure 2.1   Circus Entertainment

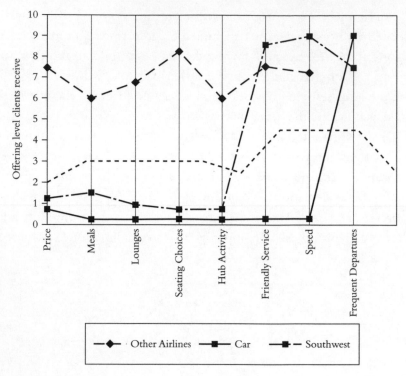

Figure 2.2 Airline Industry

based business model, but incorporated significant differentiators in the beginning to set themselves apart from their competition.

I've been around other companies—big, major players in their respective industries—who were trying to adapt and lead in new ways, but failed because they'd never done it before. They didn't have the instincts, the fortitude, or the cultural experiences to draw on and make the effort a success. At ESPN, however, time and again at meetings I heard executives outline their plans for the business and their programming ideas, and I'd think to myself, this can never be done. But ESPN has risk taking, creative problem solving, and defiance in its bloodstream. (See Figure 2.3.) If anyone whispers that something can't be done, that doubt becomes a rallying cry, almost as if it's the proof that it needs to be done.

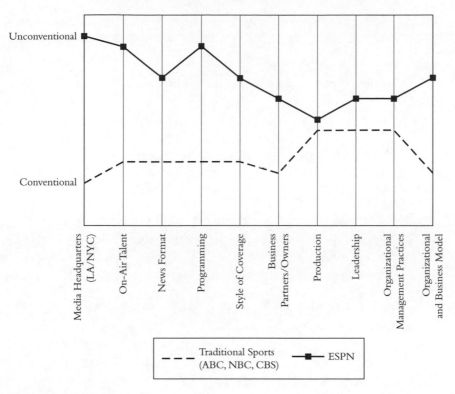

Figure 2.3 Sports Media

Looking back, it seems there were so many happy accidents, so many unlikely circumstances that allowed ESPN to survive and succeed. But the only common basis you can assign to those many moments of survival is the character of the culture and the determination of the mission. To deliberately transition from start-up to an almost unassailable position as industry leader and institution is extremely rare. Very few companies make it. To get there, ESPN needed to think like an incumbent and act like a challenger. Most start-ups avoid interjecting big company practices like a virus out of fear that such approaches will dampen the creativity, flexibility, and spirit that makes the start-up special. But ESPN leaders recognized that given the rate of growth and the vision, they needed to develop the capacity to be an industry leader from the beginning, and execute with sheer brilliance. As Larry Bossidy and Ram Charan state in *Execution*, "execution" is not the only thing that leaders need to get right, but without it, nothing else matters.

Then they went ahead and did it, and boy, do they have a hell of a story to tell!

CHAPTER TWO KEY POINTS

"Let insecurity drive achievement"

Every person and every organization has its weak spots. Some avoid confronting weaknesses, and never grow. Great leaders and organizations work on their insecurities head-on, and let that drive their passion for achievement.

"Make teamwork more than a value statement"

If it is clear that working together as a team is truly necessary for the success of an organization, then there needs to be *training*, measurement, consequences, and rewards associated with the value. Avoid articulating anything as a value if you do not have any intention of holding people accountable.

"A little organizational schizophrenia can be a good thing"

It has become cliché, but if you are going to be the best, you must believe you are the best, all the while working as hard as you can to become the best. This is critical for leadership. Yes, it's a tough balancing act, but the art of leadership lies in being able to instill a confidence within the organization while maintaining a constant drive to improve and develop. ESPN is the best organizational example I know, just as Tiger Woods is probably the best example of an athlete maintaining both contradictory perspectives.

"Deviate from the start"

To achieve incredible growth and success in an established area requires thought about where you can be distinctively different.

Otherwise, the ramp-up time and cost to compete against an established player is just too much. Southwest Airlines was different from the start. They changed many things about the way airlines are operated. Apple is now a major player in the crowded cell phone business, where they did not even exist two years ago. They pulled this off because the iPhone was a deviation from the start.

"Follow your values, and challenge the rules"

Rules can be useful, but they can also be stifling to an enterprise. The larger an organization becomes, the more it will need rules, but be careful. If an organization is clear on its values, it can afford to relax on rules, and be fast, cheap, and occasionally out of control.

"When the model doesn't work, turn it over"

Some organizations are so invested in the process, and systems, they lose sight of what they are seeking to achieve. Frederick Taylor, the father of scientific management, said that "the *system* you currently have is perfectly designed for the *results* you are currently getting." If you are not happy, or can't live with current results, you need to change the current model.

Chapter 3

THE RIGHT LEADER AT THE RIGHT TIME

With the spotlight on the broadcast talent, the sporting events, the programs, the commercials, and even the role of the company within the cable industry, executive leadership remains the untold story at ESPN. How has ESPN managed to grow and prevail over a 30-year period with six different presidents (actually one, Stu Evey, had only the title of chairman) and five different majority ownership groups? There's no Bill Gates, Michael Dell, Larry Ellison, or Howard Schultz at ESPN. In other words, unlike many companies that have experienced explosive growth over one to two generations of existence, ESPN has not been driven by a strong ever-present founder. As a result, I've always been struck by how remarkable it is that the mission, values and strategy of the enterprise have remained so consistent and focused. Lacking a strong and charismatic founder-figure, many organizations struggle with the leadership and succession question, rarely getting it quite right. Somehow, the leadership at ESPN has stayed on track and always charging forward without the constant hand of a single extraordinary individual who has the vision, drive, and unique industry know-how to carry the business over a number of transition periods.

Instead, over its life span and four stages of growth—Start-Up, Survival, Ramp Up, and Institutional, depicted in Model 3.1—each top leader at ESPN has brought an original personality, unique and distinctive strengths (or what McKinsey refers to as "spikes"), and a clear set of strategic and personal tools to the job that seem, in hindsight, to have perfectly matched the needs of the organization at the time.

When I reverse engineer how this was done, I can only come up with one simple explanation: The people making the key decisions

MODEL 3:1—SMITH'S STAGES OF ORGANIZATIONAL AND LEADERSHIP DEVELOPMENT

Stage 1: The Start-Up

MAJOR CHALLENGES
- Developing a compelling vision and business case
- Securing supporters—financial, staff, and consumers
- Establishing early wins
- Identifying key talent who are connected
- Maintaining confidence in tough times

REQUIRED LEADERSHIP SKILLS
- Visionary, high energy
- Salesmanship
- Resourceful
- Innovator
- High tolerance for ambiguity

ESPN LEADERS
- Rasmussen
- Evey
- Simmons

Stage 2: Survival

MAJOR CHALLENGES
- Developing the long-term strategy
- Identifying new opportunities for growth
- Identifying new sources of revenue
- Leveraging strengths
- Minimizing weaknesses
- Developing first generation professionals into second generation leaders

REQUIRED LEADERSHIP SKILLS
- Strategic
- Opportunistic
- Content/technical expertise
- Follower development
- Team development and leadership
- Patience

ESPN LEADER
- Grimes
- Werner

Stage 3: Ramp Up Growth

MAJOR CHALLENGES
- Maintaining risk taking while avoiding major mistakes
- Aligning all employees (putting the right people in the right places)
- Identifying growth opportunities other than organic (mergers, acquisitions, partnerships, etc.)
- Refining and expanding policies and procedures without becoming too bureaucratic
- Developing preemptive strategies to maintain position against competitors in the marketplace

REQUIRED LEADERSHIP SKILLS
- Systematic thinker
- Solid management
- Negotiator
- Operational
- Motivational
- Thinks outside the box
- Developing or refining mission and values

(Continued)

(Continued)
- Raising the performance bar
- Industry expertise
- Relationship builder

ESPN LEADER
- Werner
- Bornstein

Stage 4: Institutional

MAJOR CHALLENGES
- Maintaining top talent
- Engaging all employees (getting people to commit to and be excited about their jobs)
- Expanding and protecting the brand
- Appropriate community involvement
- Maintaining internal humility while exercising bold leadership externally
- Having fun

REQUIRED LEADERSHIP SKILLS
- Culture carrier
- Public ambassador
- Big picture
- Globally minded
- Inspirational
- Leadership developer
- Listener
- Empowerer
- Delegator

ESPN LEADER
- Bornstein
- Bodenheimer

regarding the next leader were worried more about what was good for the organization (and the sports fan) than how to perpetuate their own personality and style. Although this sounds like common sense, in my experience, it's pretty rare. Most leaders are unwilling to hand over power to someone who does not look like the face staring back at them in the mirror. And many boards shy away from selecting the internal candidate who lacks established credentials but carries the culture and organizational knowledge in spades. Instead, they often reach outside the organization for someone who has earned the glow of success in another company, and then they find that intangibles don't always carry over. What's more, there's a tendency when picking leaders to swing significantly from one set of desired attributes to another and back again, a kind of AB BA pattern where the charismatic inspirational CEO is followed by the detail-oriented manager and so on.

If there's a leadership personality at ESPN, it resembles a mosaic of characteristics, strengths, and insecurities that you can trace, almost like you decode a genome, back to the leadership ancestors. Every one of the top leaders has left a distinct personality mark on the organization that remains part of what makes the business successful today. There are no blank years or missing limbs on the family tree. And I imagine that for a leader, making that kind of contribution is extremely satisfying. We all want to know that a piece of ourselves is going to live on after we die. Ernest Becker, in his classic book *The Denial of Death* (1973), labeled this phenomenon "Heroic Transcendence," where the heroism transmutes the fear of death into the security of self-perpetuation.

Let me describe the leadership story at ESPN and you can see for yourself how it all fit together and continues to perpetuate.

The Pioneers and the Settlers

We romanticize the people who came before us and founded a country or established a business, but if we met any pioneers in person, outside the colorful history books, we'd probably think of them as a rough, sharp-edged, or uncivilized bunch. That's true to a degree of some of the early leadership at ESPN. I'm not in the business of whitewashing the truth. I think we're grown-up enough to understand that it's possible for our leaders to have some personal weaknesses to go with their personal strengths while still being very effective at what they do. And the stories of ESPN's early years would certainly make for some colorful reading, but this isn't a kiss-and-tell kind of book. What I want to describe are the skills and attributes each of those leaders brought to an intense and rapidly growing business in order to figure out what made it all work.

The initial leadership group was a dynamic trio, almost chemically unstable, and prone to explosions. It included founder Bill Rasmussen, the hustling salesman and boundless sports fanatic; Getty executive Stuart Evey who oversaw the organization as the representative of the primary investor; and sports television industry insider Chet Simmons. The atmosphere during the brief but tense start-up period was filled with arguments, exchanges of condescension, and a whirlwind of constantly churning activity. Leadership experts talk today about the importance of team building and the benefits of going into an entrepreneurial business with people you like and respect. None of that seemed to matter at ESPN. It's possible that each of the three men despised one or both of the others, or at least discounted the value of what they brought to the equation. But it's also true that each brought skills, connections, and personality traits that were absolutely vital for the survival of the enterprise. Everyone suffered. All the niceties of camaraderie and the experience of a supportive place to work was subsumed by the urgent needs of the business and a vision that beckoned.

It's hard to imagine how they managed to stay bound to the same idea without a single strong leader, but somehow they did despite the occasional left hand not knowing what the right hand was doing. Bill Rasmussen was the classic salesman-entrepreneur, driven beyond the normal realm of obsession to realize a dream, willing to overextend himself, bluff, or hustle his way past obstacles, while overlooking many critical business necessities (like sufficient revenue) that would have stopped a more realistic or calculating person. ESPN's salvation, that infusion of $10 million of Getty's money, was also the beginning of Rasmussen's end. He'd be out within a year and a half. And although he saw a fairly decent financial return for his personal investment of ideas and will, he might have been a billionaire had he managed to hang onto his equity stake and sustain his position as founder-leader. It's hard to imagine someone not being bitter about an outcome like that, but Rasmussen doesn't read or sound like a disappointed man. Those who knew him back then speculated that he was hurt by not even having a going-away party; however, the most critical sentiment one can find on record is when he mentions in his book, *The Birth of ESPN*, that " . . . I lasted about a year. The standard 'offer' didn't work very well with [me, so I eventually] succumbed and 'resigned'" (p. 239). Ever the optimist, he seems humble about it, proud and a little in awe of the vision to which he was able to give momentum. And, of course, as a salesman who's always thinking in a forward direction, Rasmussen has had other projects to keep him busy since, though nothing comparable to ESPN.

Besides his dream and his fanatical passion for sports, Rasmussen's legacy to the organization was his ability to scramble and make the impossible happen. That's not so uncommon for an entrepreneurial start-up, but ESPN has never lost that ingrained sense of how to jump-start new projects quickly and still produce quality results. While an established organization might hesitate, move more slowly and cautiously, conserve its energy, and carefully get all its pieces in place before acting, ESPN has continued to launch many of its big ventures by the seat of its pants, with (perhaps unnecessarily) limited resources and unreasonable deadlines as well as great gusto, almost like a salmon swimming upstream, flinging that big muscular body up and over a waterfall.

Having seen that approach work more than a few times, I believe there's sound logic behind the madness. CEOs at sizable organizations have confided in me how difficult it can be to bring an established and comfortable executive team up a few notches in urgency and encourage them to accomplish something extraordinary. Complacent, cautious, risk-averse behavior can dominate in established corporations, and moving fast and being aggressive is a rare strength. I think ESPN, by retaining its "us versus them" start-up mindset, is able to generate and channel a heightened level of desperation whenever necessary—a valuable capability in a world where standing pat can mean getting passed. When ESPN goes into new project mode, the activity may seem to an outside observer like chaos filled with frenetic anxiety; but within ESPN there's comfort with the panic, a genetic familiarity with tackling the "big hairy audacious goals." The people at ESPN use desperation and urgency to get the adrenaline flowing and the resources focused. Doing so, they accomplish something significant without turning it into a financial boondoggle that can cripple an arrogant market leader.

Rasmussen, as I mentioned, did not play well with Stuart Evey, but few could. As the man who decided that ESPN was worth Getty's dollars, Evey was not a hands-off angel investor, confident in the abilities of the management group that had drawn him in. Instead, he recognized that Rasmussen, or at least the ESPN business plan, needed as much professional support as financial. He provided the financial backing without hesitation. He knew exactly which levers to pull at Getty to get more money, and was expert at framing the early struggles of the organization in a way that inspired enthusiasm about the ultimate outcomes. What's more, he did all this at significant risk to his own career. As a representative of the primary investor he probably should have been more discerning and skeptical about ESPN's abilities to execute the plan. Without Evey, there's no way ESPN would have survived. Any media-based investor would have pulled the plug.

The professional support Evey offered was a bit more complicated. His entry into the management group shifted the source of power to himself. Even Rasmussen, whose name had been on every deal and contract, realized that Evey's money made him boss. Evey was intrusive, opinionated, forceful, and domineering, but he also cared deeply about what the product looked like and he wanted to ensure that ESPN did more than survive—that it would actually become a significant player, a championship caliber business. As such, he did what Jerry Jones or Daniel Snyder, the owners of the Dallas Cowboys and Washington Redskins respectively, have frequently done in the NFL world. He went out and bought the best coach and the most talented players he could find. At every opportunity, he bolstered the ESPN team in terms of its administrative and its production talent. And then, like Jerry Jones, who often seems unable to leave well enough alone, Evey liked to come down from the owner's box at tense, critical moments, patrol the sidelines, cheer the team on, and offer his own opinions about how to play the game. That kind of support is a complicated blessing at best. You need it because you need the money and the talent and the energy. But as a professional, you just want the amateur coach to stay off the playing field.

Between Rasmussen, who continued to act with the blithe authority of the founder in charge, and Evey, who stormed the sidelines and praised, threatened, and cajoled any who got in his sights, it must not have been easy for Chet Simmons to do his job as the television production expert. Simmons was smart about negotiating ultimate operating authority for himself. He obtained the title of president, helping to push Rasmussen off to the wings. But how stressful, disorganized, amateurish, and haphazard this whole start-up cable channel must have seemed to him! Simmons came from the pinnacle of the sports media world, where he helped start ABC Sports and *Wide World of Sports*, and later became president of NBC Sports. He was used to the most credentialed talent, the top sporting events, the almost unlimited budgets, long-settled employment and services contracts, and the best equipment. He had led an organization with established ways of doing production, firm and clear policies, and the ability to throw resources at any urgent crisis. It must have felt as though Bob Nardelli, after years as president of one of GE's divisions, had left not for market leader Home Depot, but for some Internet start-up with bizarre funding embroiled in amateur hour. And don't forget, this particular start-up wasn't located in Silicon Valley, New York, or Chicago, but in Bristol, Connecticut, the middle of absolutely nowhere.

Simmons likely had plenty of second thoughts, but little time for them once the work began. His industry experience and steady hand couldn't have been more critical. He gave instant legitimacy to

ESPN. Because of him, talented industry figures like Bill Creasy, Jim Dullaghan, and Scott Connal brought their considerable production abilities to Bristol. Together, that conglomeration of know-how and connections enabled ESPN to find the freelancers, and the trucks, and build the production trailer and the studio set. Simmons was a terrific programmer in his own right and he, more than anyone, enabled ESPN to look like a real network from the beginning. He launched ESPN, in the basic sense of the word. He got it off the ground.

But Simmons, like Evey and Rasmussen, had his weaknesses, too. Simmons, although a principled, honest, and loyal executive and a terrific programmer, was not universally thought to be the most gifted administrative executive. To be sure, I do know several current executives who felt he was a great mentor and speak very highly of him to this day. Rosa Gatti, currently SVP of Communications, told me that he had amazing patience working with young employees just out of college, and like the legendary Jack Welch of GE, would always write notes to employees with praise or a question. However, by most accounts, his interests and experiences didn't stretch in the "bottom line" business direction. He knew how to manage producers, programmers, sponsors, schedules, talent, and events, and was completely dedicated to quality television; but he didn't have the same sharp instincts for building the business, managing the bottom line, negotiating the best deals, or developing the talent in the back-office. When he left Bristol three years after launch, partly to find relief from the frequent conflict with Evey but also to seize an incredible opportunity to become the first commissioner of the new USFL, nobody (except perhaps Evey) thought that was a good thing for ESPN. As they say on the Bristol campus, "As the Dish turns. . . ."

There's a certain adventurous satisfaction in being a pioneer. You explore a new world. You get shot at by hostile natives. You carve out and claim territory, and plant a flag in your new dominion. Back home, in the civilization you came from, everyone thinks you're crazy. The land you're calling an empire is a bug-infested forest with no amenities. They see the hardship of that place and wonder why the hell anyone would put themselves in such a situation. You see the limitless potential.

Unfortunately, soon after pioneers have reached a new land and established a toehold, they either die off or are too worn out to see the more civilized developments come along. It's left to others to carve the wooden beams and erect the first buildings, establish law and order, and start getting rich. And that is where the settlers come in.

The Settlers Are Coming . . .

William (Bill) Grimes was the next president, and the first of the new generation of settlers at ESPN. Of course, he'd been there from early on but he was a different kind of leader for the organization, a professional manager, and one it would need to survive as a business.

Unlike Rasmussen, the sports fanatic, or Simmons, the sports programming professional, Grimes's experience in the media industry at CBS for 14 years had been in sales, human resources, and management. A director of HR before heading up CBS's AM and FM radio stations, he was hired at ESPN on the recommendation of the consulting firm, McKinsey and Company. McKinsey's belief was that ESPN needed a serious infusion of bench strength in the area of general management, so Grimes was recruited to serve as the firm's first chief operating officer.

Although such a series of roles and experiences might suggest a dry personality compared to the flashy, tempestuous, passionate types who preceded him, Grimes was anything but. He was, to use a term not in anyone's vocabulary at the time, the high EQ type. He had an infectious enthusiasm for the organization and the work they were doing, and he gave the impression that he couldn't believe his own luck in being tapped to be part of the enterprise, let alone running it. He had that rare ability to be high energy while also connecting easily at the personal level with the people around him. He seemed to love everybody and was genuinely inspiring.

At the same time that Grimes was a people person, he was also an empowering leader. He didn't micromanage, but put people in charge of their projects, trusting in their abilities and supporting their success. For a company that was rapidly growing beyond the capacity of its human capital, this was exactly the approach that was needed. Young, inexperienced but talented and extremely hungry programmers and bean counters were needed to grow into roles of great responsibility under high-pressure circumstances. They knew they would never have gotten a sniff at such opportunity back in the real world, at an established insurance company or major network, and so they were grateful, but also in over their heads. Grimes, through his open-mindedness and his nonjudgmental nature, created an inclusive environment in which it was safe to be creative and take risks.

It must have taken a special personality or force of will to shelter the people in the organization from the financial pressures it was under to perform. Nobody outside the top ranks talked about ESPN as a business, always as a product and service to the fans. Even as the organization became more corporate and established, Grimes continued to support the principle that you should not be afraid to take chances. If things didn't work out, you just admitted defeat and moved on rapidly to Plan B, executing better the next time. Rather than fretting about failing, he made you feel it was better to go out with guns blazing.

Grimes instilled a never-say-die kind of determination, but a lot of flexibility, too. He encouraged fast decisions, fast action, and fast course corrections whenever they were necessary. There wasn't a lot of deliberation and hand-wringing going on. But as success came to ESPN, there started to be a lot of fun. On the critical side, Grimes's ability to resist micromanaging could also be described as a lack of attention to detail. He was a consummate salesman, always encouraging, and that was probably healthy for an organization in which failure, risk, and pressure were in abundance, and young talented people needed to feel the psychic rewards of getting a win once in a while, or they'd probably jump off a bridge.

The Calculating Strategist

Bill Grimes left ESPN in 1988 after five years as head of the organization, a time in which it transitioned from start-up to growth. Grimes left to head up another exciting new network, the Spanish-language

Univision. He carried his enthusiasm with him, announcing that his first order of business upon assuming his new role would be to learn Spanish.

Under Grimes's stewardship, ESPN had begun to instill solid business practices into the working culture. The thriftiness, attention to the bottom line, and eagerness to do a better job with fewer resources than the competition were all in place before Grimes, but Grimes headed the company when those practices began to be ingrained as corporate policies and processes. It was also during Grimes's tenure that ESPN flipped the business model on the cable affiliates, secured the rights to major sports like the NFL, and was sold by Getty and bought by ABC.

There was a force behind Grimes, however, who was probably even more responsible for establishing the business practices and the capacity for revenue generation. That was Roger Werner. Werner was on the McKinsey team that assessed ESPN's viability as a business and made recommendations. He stayed on at ESPN to see them implemented. When Grimes was named president and CEO, Werner was tapped to take Grimes's previous job.

Their partnership was a successful mix of personality types and skill sets. While Grimes was the salesman and people person, Werner had ice in his veins. He was analytical, execution-oriented, and fearless about going for what he wanted, whether that was a contract with the NFL or a deal with the cable operators. Although the affiliates came on board with ESPN's proposed reversed fee structure under Grimes's tenure as president, it was Werner who headed the team that engaged in the rough, bare-knuckled negotiations and scratched and clawed out the deal that ESPN needed.

When Grimes's tenure continued into its fifth year, there was no more room for Werner to move up or assume additional responsibilities, so he was asked by the Cap Cities ownership team to become the COO and executive vice president at ABC in preparation for taking on an even more senior role. But the work wasn't a whole lot of fun. Unlike ESPN, with its growth trajectory and wild west excitement, ABC was broken and needed to cut costs, shed people, and reconfigure itself with smaller ambitions. Then Grimes left ESPN to enter another business. While there was no one at ESPN with the total skill set to lead the organization at that moment, Werner was still intimately familiar with the business and aching for the opportunity to run ESPN. He was part of the team that had mapped out ESPN's five year turnaround plan and seen it through. He had a tremendous sense of pride and authorship in that accomplishment. He knew the executive team and considered them friends. From cost cutting and layoffs at ABC, a return to ESPN was not just a relief, it promised to be a lot of fun.

McKinsey doesn't hire dummies. No surprise, Werner's predominant attribute as ESPN's leader was his intelligence. Whereas Grimes felt the need in his gut for an inclusive, creative, risk-taking culture, Werner was the type who understood the value of that intellectually and saw that it was encouraged because it gave the business a desired capability set. He thought in terms of quantifiable measures and communicated strategies, action items and negotiating stands using tough, no-nonsense business language. Grimes's soft, high EQ touch was great in a leader, but it was best saved for the office where it could be applied to the talent, the employees, and the owners. The cable operators and league representatives played rough, and Werner was hardheaded enough to beat them most of the time. He wasn't blind to the gifts and needs of others. He just used them in a more calculating way to achieve his objectives. He spotted the executive potential of Steve Bornstein in the programming department, for example, as well as George Bodenheimer in affiliate sales, and included them both in his swings across the country convincing irascible, intransigent cable operators they needed to stop losing money by starting to give it away.

Werner wasn't bloodless by any means. He loved sports, especially fast cars, water skiing, and motorboats, and he loved the ESPN product. Under Werner there was not so much activity in the way of acquisitions or growth of program offerings, but there was a heavy emphasis on building and leveraging the ESPN brand. He started the long-term thinking around many of the products ESPN would begin to offer, launching a marketing division, selling merchandise, making plans for

ESPN stores. Ahead of his time in terms of expanding the organization's market footprint, Werner took every opportunity to promote the business and the brand, evolving into a sort of salesman-in-chief, articulating what ESPN was doing and why, convincing customers to buy the signal and suppliers like the NFL or the America's Cup to bring their product to the network. He even had to sell the uniqueness and future potential of ESPN to various ownership groups as the stakeholders continued to turn over, making frequent presentations, explaining the growth potential, heading off challenges to the cost side of the business that would have crippled the ability to achieve the goals. Selling the business, and growing the business, that's how Roger Werner spent the 1980s at ESPN.

He didn't, however, make a lot of money for himself. That was the downside of being a professional manager in a company without publicly traded shares and a series of owners who were always setting up the business for sale. By the end of 1990, Werner looked up from his hectic job as CEO and gazed around the country at his peers in the business. He had been instrumental in bringing ESPN from a $20 million hole in the ground to a $2.5 to $3 billion business, transitioning it from an entity industry insiders laughed at to the most profitable programming network in cable. But while many of his peers were growing rich on their personal stakes in their own businesses or the companies they ran, Werner's net worth was disproportionately pale in comparison. In November of 1990 he left ESPN, after a brief but eventful period as president, and a longer influence as one of the significant architects.

The Programmer-in-Chief

When Roger Werner left, his replacement was his second in command, the then current head of programming, Steve Bornstein. Depending on who you talk to, Bornstein was either immediately announced as Werner's designated successor, or had to sweat for a few days while he lobbied hard for the job, demanding it really, and the ownership group at Cap Cities/ABC considered their options. Regardless, Bornstein understood without doubt or hesitation who was right for the organization at that time: He was.

Like any human being, Bornstein has his strengths and weaknesses, but in Bornstein the overall impact of his character is unusually intense and disturbing. By "disturbing" I mean that, whether you like Bornstein or not, you will be unsettled by him, and depending on the intensity and duration of the connection, you will be thrown off balance temporarily or permanently changed. There is no walking away from Bornstein without being marked by the experience. He has a demanding, intelligent, impatient edge to his personality that can be disconcerting while simultaneously acting as a powerful draw. You want to please him and excel for him, and you certainly don't want to sound foolish in front of him. Bornstein's gruff, exacting style practically makes him the dictionary definition of an old-school leader. And yet, although his take-no-prisoners approach to dealing with employees and adversaries alike has left plenty of bodies strewn behind, he also engenders and offers intense loyalty and caring while bringing out the absolute best in people in terms of performance, creativity, sharp thinking, and achievement. It's that mix that keeps people enamored of him, even as they are occasionally hurt, frustrated, angry, and bewildered.

Bornstein had been involved in sports television production as a student at the University of Wisconsin in Madison. From there he'd moved to Columbus, Ohio where he worked at the remarkable Qube TV network. Believe it or not, Columbus was the hotbed of cable TV innovation in the 1970s, generating such stalwart channels as Nickelodeon and MTV. But Qube, which you have probably never heard of unless you grew up in Ohio, was the most leading edge network of them all. In fact, Qube's approach then seems downright science fiction-like today.

Qube was interactive cable. It offered a whopping thirty channels for customers to watch, of which ten were broadcast channels, ten were pay-per-view channels, and ten were interactive. Qube was launched by Warner Communications to be an innovative competitor with all the other hundreds of cable operations in the country. A remote control box with rows of buttons was connected to your TV with a wire. Five of the buttons allowed viewers to answer questions posed on the interactive channels. Those varied from opinions on topical news stories to selections of favorite bands. You could register for education programs that way and even play interactive games. All of this before the arrival of the household computer or digital technology.

Although Qube was a hit with customers, the technology and especially the building of the two-way cable infrastructure was too expensive to enable profitability. So Qube went by the wayside like other great television inventions of the time, including Telstar and Atari. However, it's pay-per-view system, which covered Ohio State University football games and boxing bouts, was exceptionally popular and probably drove the penetration of Qube in the Ohio market.

In 1978, before the launch of ESPN, Bill Creasy and another producer named Jack Schneider visited Qube in Columbus on behalf of Werner to see about producing OSU football games. Dressed in their expensive suits, Creasy and Schneider looked like slick New York media men visiting the backwaters of Ohio. Bornstein, then a slightly overweight Jewish kid in his early twenties with an oversized afro, was the executive director at WOSU television and in charge of sports production which they supplied to Qube. Creasy, it was well known to Bornstein, had produced the first two Super Bowls. Schneider basically announced that he and Creasy were going to take over football production and started demanding the equipment and staff they would need to do the job. But Bornstein, though expected to fall into line, pushed his glasses up and told them if they wanted to produce the games they could do it all on their own, or they could hire WOSU to produce the games and split the fee. He dryly added, "Sir, with all due respect, you're getting one camera and one truck."

Encountering that hard-nosed attitude and blunt toughness, Bill Creasy fell in love. Always on the lookout for talent, when Creasy started work at ESPN, he immediately hired Bornstein for $27,000 a year to become a programmer. He put him up at the Holiday Inn in Plainville, Connecticut, where Bornstein would live for more than a year. For Bornstein's part, Bristol was like an alien nation, the closest movie theater 45 minutes away. The amount of top equipment and resources, compared to college television, was a revelation, but the lifestyle was miserable. He'd never worked harder in his life. He didn't know anybody outside of work. If he wasn't broke, and if he could have found any other job, he would have made a run for it. Creasy was so worried about that possibility he made Bornstein call him regularly to check in when he left Connecticut on holidays.

As for the job, Bornstein became very good at it, very fast. When he arrived, three months into operations there were four people programming the network. Within three more months, the channel was running 24 hours a day. ESPN had one big contract with the NCAA but nothing else steady. Many of his hours were spent on the phone, calling various colleges to see if they'd played hockey the previous night; if so, had anyone recorded it, and if so, would they mind throwing that tape into a FedEx bag and overnighting it so ESPN could air the event the next day? Sometimes scheduled programs didn't go on because the receptionist left a package on the pile on her desk without realizing the contents were meant to fill a few hours of air time.

In a few short years, Bornstein had risen to become head of programming for ESPN, the first executive to be given those responsibilities. Within 10 years of starting at the company, he was named president at the age of 38. To everyone at ESPN, older, younger, more experienced, fresh on board, there was no question Bornstein should hold the position. He was a force of nature in terms of personality, and he was already considered one of the brightest programmers of his generation. This fact was later confirmed when he became the recipient of the prestigious Vanguard Award for programmers, one of the highest honors given by the National Cable and Telecommunication Association.

During his time as president, ESPN launched its radio network, the X-Games, its ancillary marketing division, its online presence, its research division, the ESPYs, and lots and lots of original and established programming. ESPN expanded internationally, reaching more than 120 countries in a few short years; and it expanded its number of channels, launching ESPN2 in October 1993, ESPN News, ESPN Classic, and the V Foundation for Cancer Research, named in honor of the late Jimmy Valvano. The growth was unbelievable and the organization became dominant in a way no one would have expected. Under Bornstein, the couple hundred million in profit generated by Werner reached the billion mark.

Organizational observers are sometimes guilty of attributing too much influence to an individual leader with strong charisma when it comes to the growth and success of a business. But it would be hard to overstate the impact of Bornstein's leadership on the drive, creativity, and resilience ESPN showed over the years under his watch. Talk to anyone, past or present, at ESPN, who experienced a Bornstein meeting and you will hear the same kinds of things. The brilliant mind and visionary outlook; the sharp and often devastating probing questions; the sense that as he listened to your pitch—and you were always trying to make your case with Bornstein—he was either bored, or he was calculating how wrong you were; all of it topped by the relief and pleasure when, hours, weeks, or long months later, he quoted your points from memory, and articulated them better than you had done with the notes in your hand, and used them to make something important happen. The questioning and the doubting was about challenging you to have passion for your position and pushing your thought processes. If you could fight for it, state it well, and back it up under relentless pressure, then Bornstein respected your point of view, and he respected you.

It kept you off guard, and it kept you trying to do better next time. You knew you needed to be more prepared than you were in other situations. Even during the most casual encounter, you needed to be ready to provide a valuable insight or piece of information. For example, whenever I would run into Steve in the hallway or men's bathroom, I would throw out the ever-conventional greeting, "Hey, Steve, how are you doing?" His response was always the same. "I don't know. What have you heard?" The first time I heard this reply, I laughed and said, "That's a good one Steve, I haven't heard that before; so how are you?" He *didn't* laugh, and repeated his reply, with a qualifier; "We are paying you all this money, Doc, to know the company and help us, so what in the hell have you been hearing?" I then realized that he was seriously seeking information. He was always after data and input and new ideas, and when he seized on something it could be so sudden you didn't always understand the significance. Then it would dawn on you, and you'd be running after Bornstein to catch up.

On the hard side of doing business, Bornstein had equally prominent strengths. As a negotiator and a deal maker, he was as savvy as a poker player. He read people easily, whether across a boardroom or a restaurant table, and quickly gauged their weak spots and needs, thereby securing better concessions. Like all fierce competitors, he liked winning for its own sake. He stopped for nothing when going after an objective, and he was often rough around the edges while doing it. When assessing data, he had an instant grasp of numbers and could spin situations around, look at them from different perspectives, and do calculations in his mind that others hadn't considered, and then offer an elegant solution. He made bold, risky, innovative decisions quickly because he seemed to sense that speed, as a mode of working, not only got ESPN ahead of the competition but also kept the creative and performance tensions on maximum throttle. I'll never forget one night having dinner with Bornstein and Bill Creasy in Manhattan. Bornstein ordered a steak well done, with steamed spinach on the side. When our food arrived, the waiter had not brought the spinach. From the look on Bornstein's face, the waiter realized he had forgotten something. He rushed back a minute later with the spinach, only to hear that Bornstein no longer wanted it. The waiter apologized profusely with the age-old restaurant excuse: "I'm so sorry, Mr. Bornstein, we got slammed just when I put in your order." Bornstein looked back, and simply said, "That's not my problem, it's yours." This was one of Bornstein's favorite restaurants, and we would go back many times over the years, and I must say that they never forgot his steamed spinach again, regardless of how busy they may have been. That is what Bornstein does: Somehow his demanding character is palpable, and it pushes people to be at their best, raising the performance of everyone around him, even while he pushes himself harder still.

There was no letting up for Bornstein, but there was a softer side. If you were close to him, he made sure you knew you were one of his prized possessions. He could be warm and sincere, and he made sure people realized there was a line between the personal and the professional. Outsiders or new entrants to the executive ranks could be shocked at how Bornstein and the people around him talked to each other, berating ideas, shouting back rebuttals, arguing with total emotional investment and a lot of volume and invective. But all that was left behind at the door, and friends stayed friends. Business was business. You didn't take anything personally (or at least you tried not to). If you didn't have a thick skin, you couldn't last, because under Bornstein's tenure there was a sort of perpetual war going on, with everyone fighting for their point of view and position. After work, you had drinks and laughed it off. That's where Bornstein showed himself to be a genuinely caring person, and that's why people cared for him so much, and were fiercely loyal to him.

Bornstein cared about the people around him in another way, too. He wanted to see them develop. It was Bornstein who suggested that we bring the people practices of major Fortune 50 companies into a company that still played like a start-up. He was preparing ESPN to grow into itself.

I got the go-ahead to conduct satisfaction surveys with the employee base, which would then be followed by a group meeting in which those employees could provide Bornstein with feedback on how well the company was doing with respect to its mission and values. The idea was to give people a chance to speak, in a safe environment, about areas where the company was still falling short. Of course, nothing was safe with Bornstein. Having enough experience of that already, I instructed him to listen silently, take notes, and just say thank you at the end of each presentation. "Don't forget your reputation," I told him. "You're intimidating. If you take it personally or come off as defensive, this part of the training is going to be a failure. No one will feel comfortable in presenting their ideas to you." He shook his head, and smiled.

It was a bit like telling General George S. Patton to practice sensitivity. I knew the first session was starting rough when Bornstein refused to take notes. He didn't need to take notes because he had a steel-trap memory, but it would have been nice to dilute the impression he gave of listening with hostile attention. Instead, he sat there with his arms crossed and his mouth in a frown, growing increasingly uncomfortable until he could no longer hold back. He put his hand on my arm to keep me from saying anything, and admitted to everyone that I'd told him not to interrupt, but he needed to make things clear. And then he proceeded to debate statements and defend positions on the grounds that the employees may not have all the critical information needed to suggest a compelling change. There were pressures and concerns that they were sheltered from, and if they wanted to criticize they ought to know what those were.

That was a lesson I thought about for years and which became the gist of my book, *The Taboos of Leadership: The Ten Things No One Will Tell You About Leaders and What They Think*. You couldn't hold Bornstein back and his force of will made it difficult for those around him to compete for oxygen. It sure was difficult for me to encourage people to continue to be open with Bornstein in those sessions! But at the same time, Bornstein wanted people to know what he thought, why he thought it, and why it was the right thing to do. He believed leadership was not a democracy, though it should encourage free speech.

He stretched my thinking again when it came to personal development plans based on 360-degree feedback. I explained to Bornstein that the feedback needed to be completely anonymous and strictly confidential. No one would be privy to the results except the recipient. That was and is the industry standard for doing 360-degree feedback exercises in corporations. I knew that if people believed that Bornstein had access to the feedback, I would be perceived as a spy and they would be less than candid about their perceptions.

Bornstein, in his typical way, made me get out of the ivory tower and join the real world. At an organization that really needed people to step up to the leadership roles they were being offered, personal growth wasn't a nice-to-have intervention, it was essential for results. As CEO, Bornstein didn't feel he could abdicate in this area any more than he could let budget or strategy sessions go by without comment. Bornstein wanted that data, not to trap or trip anyone, but because it was valuable to him for knowing exactly where his people were at and what they needed. I provided him with my "cost benefit" analysis of such an approach, and he provided his, and we came up with an interesting compromise. (Funny thing; he would often influence me in my area of expertise, but I never recall influencing him about programming sports....Hmmm?) The compromise was this—I insisted that the first year would be strictly confidential, after which we'd give a one-page summary of feedback and areas to work on to each person's direct manager and to Bornstein. He agreed, still griping. But this gave people a year to work on their areas of development. And boy, did they focus on making positive changes. Knowing the feedback would be opened up a year later provoked a big step-up in performance along the lines of the mission and values.

My firm (Leadership Research Institute) still conducts feedback that way today. It was a lesson in how leaders wield power and influence to achieve desired results. It may have been tense, stressful, and a bit more messy than I'd hoped, but it illustrated that stretching one's capabilities is best done under real-world conditions when there are real consequences at stake. For Bornstein, nothing was done theoretically. Everything mattered. And if you were going to do something, you'd better have a purpose, a measurable outcome, and an undeniable will to win. That's how he led ESPN and I think the results show that his approach had unparalleled impact.

The Kinder, Gentler Leader

Bill Grimes had Roger Werner. Grimes was a people person with a high EQ. Werner was analytical, strategic, and sales-oriented. When Werner became president, he balanced his business strengths with Bornstein's programming brilliance. That pattern of having a strong second to complement the skills of the first-in-command continued with Bornstein. His second was George Bodenheimer, who brought relational skills second to none and vital sales acumen to the top office just when marketing and growth, and maintaining the culture, became as critical as programming. Bodenheimer was soft-spoken and a phenomenal listener with personal integrity you could feel, all skills that made him an easy confidant for those who wanted to think through challenges and prepare in advance of meeting Bornstein. The two men supported each other (in terms of skill set and personality) as well as I've ever seen in organizations.

When Bornstein decided to leave ESPN for the top job at ABC, there were a number of outstanding internal candidates ready for his job. That spoke well for Bornstein's focus on leadership growth and development. Like Welch at GE, he'd built the bench strength of the executive ranks to the point where he could be replaced from a number of directions. Around that time, the jockeying started, as it naturally does. Many of those potential candidates were a lot like Bornstein. They were competitive, aggressive, willful, and accomplished. Bodenheimer was far more understated. He listened more than he talked. He was deliberate and humble rather than impulsive and brash. But if he was occasionally underestimated as a good corporate soldier because of the impression those qualities gave, Bodenheimer was very clear internally about what he wanted and how he wanted to get it. I'll never forget walking from the ESPN office in Manhattan with Bodenheimer around that time. We stopped at a red light, and he looked me in the eye and confided his aspirations for the top job. "You know, Tony, I want this thing, and any advice you can give me would be appreciated," he said. The intention and desire was impressive. You couldn't be a top performer at a company like ESPN without having the *skill*. But Bodenheimer was declaring, in his understated, quiet, off-line way, that he also had the *will*. Leadership is never easy. The closer you get to it, the more you realize it's not for everyone. You need to want to grab it and take it. In his own way, Bodenheimer made that desire clear, and he was very upfront about communicating it.

Like me, Jim Allegro, the long-term CFO turned adviser, was one of several voices that Bornstein turned to for advice around the process as much as the people. I won't reveal anything on the people side of that selection, but Allegro advised Bornstein that to make succession work he needed to do two things: He needed to identify the person who had the skill and will the organization must have to be successful going forward; and he needed to introduce that person to the hierarchy so that when the transition arrived, people didn't say, "Who the hell is that guy?" Allegro was another who believed that Bodenheimer, though very different from Bornstein, would be perfect for the job. He encouraged Bornstein to facilitate and create as much exposure as possible for Bodenheimer, so that the senior execs at ABC and Hearst could learn more about the man they might be getting at the helm when the time came.

Some people lead out of necessity. Some people want to lead because of the power and the ability to assert their will. Some people want to lead because it means they've beaten others to the brass ring and all the treasure that may provide. And some people want to lead because they love a place so much, they can't envision someone else at the helm. For Bodenheimer, the urge was almost paternal. ESPN was like his family. He had a strong emotional feeling for it, he understood it well, and he wanted to nurture its potential and further its success story.

I suppose that shouldn't be too surprising. Like Bornstein, Bodenheimer was at ESPN from the beginning. However, Bodenheimer was hired not as a programmer but as a mailroom clerk. Yes, he literally started in the mailroom. The production trailer was spartan then, no filing cabinets or dividers. Bodenheimer would open the door to bring in the mail and get yelled at by the producers for allowing the wind to send loose documents flying. "Shut the damn door, George!"

Bodenheimer didn't stay in the mailroom long, though. Soon he was tapped for his people skills and turned into a salesman. He quickly became a rising star on the sales and marketing side of the company. Then, at a very young age, he was given his first position of note at ESPN's Denver office where he managed top affiliate accounts like

United Cable and TCI. It was a tremendous amount of responsibility and pressure, but Bodenheimer did an incredible job. He was instrumental when Werner was selling the idea of flipping the business model to the major cable operators. Bodenheimer worked those connections subtly, deliberately, and with great effect, convincing affiliates of the merits of the switch with a calmer voice, making allies while the hard and often contentious negotiations between Werner and the cable operator holdouts were going on in hotels and boardrooms.

As president, Bodenheimer's personality shift was a nearly complete 180 from Bornstein's. It strains credulity to describe the leader of one of the top high-performance businesses in America this way, but it's true and everyone who has encountered Bodenheimer's personality attested to this: Bodenheimer is calm, reassuring, but purposeful. He's a great human being who exudes trust and integrity. You quickly think of him as a brother or a father-figure. You know without a doubt that he has your best interests at heart right away. When you're in his presence, you talk easily about what you're thinking and, even more surprisingly, about what you're feeling. You think about raising your guard because this is corporate America and who really trusts anyone? Then you realize there's no need. A true gentleman who is friendly, warm, never in your face, always even-tempered, well-mannered, and likeable. What could be viewed as a salesman's easy way with people is nothing so fleeting or shallow. A wonderful blend of humility and power, Bodenheimer, who has been named "The Most Powerful and Influential Person in Sports" (*Sporting News*, 2004, *Sports Business Journal*, 2008) has navigated ESPN through very competitive waters and remained on top, while still having the capacity to remember where you left things when he sees you much later. He asks about the concerns you had with your family or situation. He follows up or tracks you down with brief notes from his BlackBerry just to check in. You know how precious a CEO's time is and the casual grace of it all makes the gesture that much more impressive.

For an organization that had always been tense with the highly revved throttle of performance, urgency, and pressure, Bodenheimer's touch was a relief. The pace of ESPN had always eaten its employees alive. Anyone who was drawn to the company was more than willing to give all they had and more. But Bodenheimer was the first to start talking about the need to balance work demands with family life. This was particularly appropriate because the original core group of employees had now grown up and had families of their own, and the times, too, were changing; new employees had different expectations, even as they expected at ESPN to still work like hell. Unlike some CEOs, Bodenheimer never served up politically correct double talk designed to stave off criticism. He practiced what he preached. He created windows for his family time and stuck to them, and he expected other people to do the same. Sometimes employees like to impress their bosses with the ungodly hours they keep. If Bodenheimer got an e-mail from the office at 4 A.M., he'd let that person know the urgency was not warranted. When it was, however, he told you. But he picked up the phone and did it the old-fashioned way.

None of this should make you assume that life at ESPN had become easy. Bodenheimer also expected top performance, but he laid out his expectations for it in a different way. When ratings began to slip, and several people argued that it was simply because of the fragmentation going on within the business, Bodenheimer didn't buy it. He certainly understood the fragmentation issue, but challenged the programming department to raise the ratings. It was unacceptable to him that ratings were in decline. He made ratings a priority, and so there would be no other questions about any of the business priorities, he had them all printed on laminated cards that each executive would carry. As you might have guessed, ratings improved.

Bodenheimer is not one to peer over shoulders and dig in on every data point; he truly empowers his employees. He's a delegator. Given the size and scope of ESPN today, there's probably no way a CEO could be anything but, except Bodenheimer makes the approach work. He's smart and secure enough to know what he doesn't know, be it the complex aspects of satellite technology or the ever-changing dynamics of the online business. So he lets people do their jobs with integrity and passion and he evaluates the results. He has the right demeanor and disposition to bring the best out in others. People enjoy working for him, and for different reasons than with Bornstein they bring him their A game. If you want a real life example of what Jim Collins calls a "Level 5 leader," someone who "builds enduring greatness through a paradoxical blend of personal humility and professional will" (*Good to Great, 2001*), then take a hard look at George Bodenheimer. He is as effective as any top executive that I have ever worked with.

While Bodenheimer is notable for evolving the atmosphere at ESPN, that doesn't mean the organization has lost its teeth. Bodenheimer brings out the pit bull in others. People want to fight for him. It's an interesting phenomenon, almost as though his calm demeanor brings out the best, and when need be, a fierce intensity in others. I think this response is actually shrewdly managed. Bodenheimer may be a natural consensus builder and somewhat conflict-averse, but he knows the value of conflict and tension internally, inside a business, and externally in negotiations. When an idea or a decision needs to be thoroughly hashed out, Bodenheimer may not always lead the discussions like Bornstein did but he always knows who to have in the room. He picks conflicting viewpoints and passionate personalities and throws them together to get a full hearing. He chooses people who pick fights to participate. The meetings in Bornstein's time were not that different in aggressive tone and passionate debate than in Bodenheimer's, but the focus of conflict is dispersed and Bodenheimer is the sage and deliberate decision maker.

Externally, the same thing goes. Mark Shapiro, who served as one of Bodenheimer's chief lieutenants for five critical years before leaving ESPN, is more in the Bornstein mode. He's aggressive, competitive, and ambitious. It's not enough for Shapiro to win, he needs to do back flips on his rival's grave. These were terrifically valuable qualities to have in someone Bodenheimer relied on to drive performance in the programming side of the business and in negotiations with key partners. But Bodenheimer was also sensitive to limits. Shapiro tells a terrific story about the negotiations with one of the major sports league partners. Four men in a room, the commissioner of the sports league and his assistant across from Bodenheimer and Shapiro. Negotiations were proceeding well, with clearly defined wish lists on each side. Then Shapiro realized the league was trying to influence the television schedule to limit the number of playoff games in the package and reduce the overall value to ESPN while still raising the price. It was a clever move, but not something done with the best intentions. Shapiro caught them at it during that critical moment of final negotiations and he pounced.

His voice rising, his incredulity showing up as sarcasm, Shapiro took a fierce and aggressive stance about not overpaying. He pressed his points ruthlessly using the league's own data as proof of the guilt. Bodenheimer sat back and let Shapiro do his work, watching the momentum of the negotiations turn and the deal begin to drift toward ESPN's advantage. All was accomplished. ESPN won. But Shapiro took it too far and continued to humiliate the commissioner's number two for the amateurish attempt to overcharge ESPN. As Shapiro put it, "I had already killed the prey but I kept going back to see if there was a little meat left on the bone."

The meeting wrapped up, and the results were very good for ESPN. Shapiro was high on the conflict and the victory. It was late at night. Shapiro and Bodenheimer drove back to the office parking lot to their respective cars and were about to part company when Bodenheimer started to talk. Shapiro knew right away he was in trouble for having gone too far in the meeting, but Bodenheimer put his arm around his shoulder and made him listen in the right way like a father talking to a son. As Shapiro recalls, Bodenheimer said, "You did a great job tonight. That was smart, quick thinking. It was a great catch that saved us money. But when you win a point, you don't need to go back. The point's over. You embarrassed that guy in front of his boss, and the commissioner saw it. And I'm telling you, you did some long-term damage to your relationship with the commissioner tonight. That's his guy and you knocked him down hard. And you didn't need to do it. When you win, you win. You don't need to pump up the score."

The truth of it was proved out. Shapiro's relationship with the commissioner was rocky for the next few years. But more important for Shapiro, he learned something about being a leader, an effective executive, and a human being that he'll never forget. And the lesson came courtesy of a boss who cared enough about him as a person to look beyond the cost savings and the competitive victory and teach him a little about life.

Bodenheimer is the perfect leader for ESPN right now because he honors the institution and brings out the best in people. I thought of George when I read a commentary on the late, great Tim Russert in *Newsweek*[1] (June 23, 2008): "Rather than try to reinvent himself as he grew up and went from worldly triumph to worldly triumph, Russert never lost his sense of place, or his love of tribe" (p. 33). Like Russert, George is the ultimate "culture carrier." He's refined the mission of ESPN to embrace the need for diversity, international growth, and the intense focus on the fan. He stays rock solid on the values of the company and he creates an empowered environment where people know they can come to him with ideas and solutions so long as they meet those values and objectives. The company's early move into high definition television was an example. Bodenheimer, like many CEOs, had limited technical foresight in that area, but the people who did knew that the mission of the business is to serve fans and that high definition signals were how fans wanted to see their sports events. So Bodenheimer green-lit their proposal and another successful evolutionary tract was launched. As Bodenheimer puts it, "Every day I walk into the office and it's George, what are we going to do about this? Can I get more on the budget? Can I get less on the budget? It never stops, and it never should stop because that's business. I don't have all the answers. But I'll tell you what I do have. I've got 5,000 diverse people who are passionate about what they do, who are very motivated, who have expertise in a wide variety of things our company does, and who know exactly what our mission is. And I view my goal as empowering each one of those 5,000 people to do what they do best and help lead the company. They might not have all the experience yet but they're passionate and they're ready to go, so we let them go. I've found at ESPN they rarely let you down."

That's a textbook statement about what leaders are supposed to do in today's organizations that are global, diverse, innovative, rapidly changing, and non-hierarchical. The difference is, George Bodenheimer has the skills and personality characteristics to actually lead that way.

Myths of Leadership

I think it's easy to get mystical about leadership, to generate alchemical formulas to explain its wondrous power. The reason is simple. Leadership is confusing and messy as hell. It comes in many different circumstances and personalities. So we want to distill it. I do the same thing, but I have examples from lengthy firsthand experience to fill my data base. Consider the leadership succession at ESPN. All the presidents had strong personalities very different from each other; each had different "spikes," and each was dealing with very different circumstances in an organization as it moved rapidly from wild start-up to struggling entity to a business with established credibility to an institution that influences an industry. How do you engineer a leadership path like the one experienced by ESPN? How do you know a young guy in Ohio with big hair has the stuff to run your company one day and churn out billions in revenue? How do you find the top echelon special package of capabilities exhibited by someone like George Bodenheimer in the mailroom?

The answer is you don't and you can't. But you can create circumstances and a corporate culture in which leadership thrives. Make no mistake, leadership is always necessary when it comes to successful organizations. It's what distinguishes them from the organizations we don't hear about. We can all think of teams of very talented performers, loaded with "stars," who lacked a great coach and never made it to the championship because no one was able to harness the combined greatness and synergy of the diverse talent. And we also know of the great coaches, who took a group of players absent of "stars" and created stardom for the team because of their talented leadership (for a great example of this, read Michael Lewis's *Moneyball*).

97

As I mentioned at the beginning of this chapter, ESPN is different from many vital organizations with personality in that it has never had a single dominant leadership personality, in its infancy or throughout its life. Southwest found Herb Kelleher, an icon of unconventional management. Howard Schultz was the reason Starbucks, an undistinguished chain of coffee stores, became a world colossus. Dell Computing is the imprint of the personality of Michael Dell. Same goes for Microsoft with Bill Gates and Apple with Steve Jobs. There are so many examples of dominant companies with dominant leaders that it seems like a prerequisite of success. But ESPN proves you can have shifting leadership and a series of personalities and styles and still win. Indeed, as struggles with the transition from founder-leader to next generation show, the ESPN approach to leadership can be a long-term competitive advantage.

Part of how ESPN managed this was the strength of its core mission and values. Those were not just words at ESPN, they were real. ESPN drew its fanatics—people who wanted to be in sports or sports television—and they embraced and carried the ESPN code. It's a living example of what Jim Collins and Jerry Porras call in their book, *Built to Last*, a "cult-like culture." ESPN is a cult. It's members are fierce about protecting and promoting its interests.

It fits, then, that ESPN's leaders have always been heavily invested emotionally and in terms of years on the job at the company before taking over. Of course, Chet Simmons was the one exception who came from outside the organization, but that was when ESPN had no history to draw on. Bill Grimes had served as vice president before being tapped as president. Roger Werner was an instrumental member of the McKinsey team that assessed ESPN's business model and changed it. Then he was brought on as Grimes's number two to execute that shift. Steve Bornstein had been with the company since the first few months as a programmer, phoning small colleges and begging for game tapes, then was groomed by Werner on the business side and taken with him to negotiations that were critical to the organization's future. George Bodenheimer started in the mailroom in the first year and drove talent to and from the airport when a gopher was needed. He saw the organization from different angles in affiliate sales and spent years at Bornstein's side running the company and making important decisions before being given the top job. Today, as president and CEO, he's also the employee with the most seniority.

In other words, ESPN didn't have one founder-leader, it had many. Those people were involved in the company from its earliest days, grew up in it, loved it, and understood how to press its buttons and achieve success. Somehow the ownership resisted the common urge to bring in outside help at the top levels, and ESPN always grew from within. Of course, it had world-class talent to draw from because it attracted the best, the brightest, and the most passionate. But that's how a culture stays strong and true.

Perhaps because any cult of leadership was trumped by the constant pressure of urgent business needs, ESPN also did a remarkable job of complementing the strengths of the top executive with important lieutenants. I've only mentioned the successive leaders in this chapter, and I would be remiss if I didn't make the point that all great institutions are marked by great leaders throughout their ranks, and ESPN is no exception. In fact, like many of the great companies, such as IBM, P&G, GE, Goldman Sachs, and McKinsey and Company, ESPN has become a leadership factory, attracting, developing, and most importantly retaining some of the most effective leaders in the industry today. Still, I was always struck by the way Werner's technical strengths were complemented by Bornstein's, Bornstein's by Bodenheimer's, and now Bodenheimer's by his top lieutenants. It is impressive that each top leader sought out skills and personalities that didn't always mimic their own, but looked beyond the mirror for the diverse attributes the organization absolutely needed at the time. This swinging back and forth between people who are very different from each other has never been disruptive because they are culture carriers who have provided ESPN with the tools it needs at any particular time to continue to excel. Finally, in terms of advisors, ESPN has never been shy about seeking trusted outside counsel, not only from consultants like me and my late dear colleague Don Hurta, who were made to feel like part of the family, but also from former ESPN insiders like Bill Creasy, Jim Allegro, and Geoff Mason, who still have their pulse on the culture, the personalities, and the needs of the business.

The leadership story of ESPN seems unlikely from a distance but the more closely you examine the moving parts, the more you understand why it worked. Leadership is a process that involves many people working toward a common vision. But leadership does not just happen or surface when a group of people get together in pursuit of a vision. Instead, an individual stands up who recognizes the need and has the ability to intentionally influence others to pursue the goal to their full potential. Creating a rich and diverse pool of people with such characteristics, providing them with responsibilities and pressures that stretch and grow them, and carefully grooming them by exposing them to the realities of the decision-making culture at the top has worked for ESPN in keeping its founder-leaders ever vital.

CHAPTER THREE KEY POINTS

"Every stage of an organization demands a different type of leadership"
If you have ever studied Situational Leadership (Hersey & Blanchard), you know that every stage of an individual's growth demands a different type of leadership style. So, too, is the case with organizations. A start-up company needs a different type of leader than a mature, established company. To be sure, the different leadership approaches and style can come from the same leader. According to my old partner, Marshall Goldsmith, in his best-selling book, *What Got You Here, Won't Get You There* (2007), the key is to assess what the organization needs at each stage, and adapt accordingly.

"Exploit your leadership strengths, and surround yourself with other leaders who compensate for your weaknesses"

Effective leaders leverage the hell out of their strengths, and are always working to minimize their weaknesses. They also realize that some weaknesses will never become strengths, and thus they surround themselves with others who compensate for their deficiencies. As Marcus Buckingham wrote in *Now, Discover Your Strengths* (2001); it is easier to "pull out that which was left in" than to "put in that which was left out."

"Don't be fooled by the myths of leadership"

Given the popularity of leadership books and leader biographies, many have come to believe that you must fit a certain profile and possess a certain personality to become a great leader of an enterprise. Nothing is further from the truth. Who would have thought that an African American woman from scarce means would become one of the most powerful media executives of all time (Oprah Winfrey, CEO, Harpo Productions); or that a computer geek from Seattle would lead the most successful software company in the world (Bill Gates, Chairman, Microsoft); or that a folksy grandfather from Nebraska would lead the most successful investment firm (Warren Buffett, Chairman, Berkshire Hathaway Inc.); or that a wild and crazy, whiskey-drinking lawyer from Texas would run the most successful and admired airline in the industry (Herb Kelleher, Chairman, Southwest Airlines). Bottom line, keep your eyes and ears open—you never know from whence your next great leader will emerge.

Chapter 4

CREATE YOUR OWN GAME

First *SportsCenter* set, 1979. Pictured on set are George Grande (L) and Bob Ley.
Source: ESPN.

SportsCenter's modern set circa 2000. A behind-the-scenes look at ESPN's
SportsCenter with Trey Wingo at the desk.
Source: Rich Arden/ESPN 2000.

Early ESPN camera at Iowa State. Signage circa 1980.
SOURCE: ESPN.

Dick Vitale and Bob Ley on ESPN's *College Basketball Report*.
SOURCE: Tom Ford.

Early ESPN billboard on Route 229, Bristol, Connecticut, directly across the street from ESPN.
SOURCE: ESPN.

An ESPN cameraman is shown taping a sailboat during the America's Cup race.
SOURCE: ESPN.

NFL fans above an ESPN HD banner at a 2003 NFL preseason game: New York Giants at New England Patriots.
Source: Rich Arden.

ESPN's *Monday Night Football* truck at Giants Stadium, East Rutherford, New Jersey—August 2008.
Source: Lorenzo Bevilaqua.

ESPN's *College GameDay* at the Rose Bowl. (L to R) Mark May, Chris Fowler, Lee Corso, and Kirk Herbstreit—January 2006.
Source: Scott Clarke.

Anthony Smith with fellow V Foundation board members, sportscasters Lesley Visser (sports commentator, CBS and HBO) and Peggy Fleming Jenkins (ABC sports commentator, 1986 Olympic gold medalist in women's figure skating), at the annual Wine Celebration in Napa Valley.
Source: Author's personal photograph.

Anthony Smith and Steve Bornstein at the Super Bowl in San Diego, 1998.
Bornstein took over as ESPN president in 1990. During his eight-year tenure,
ESPN set out to become the worldwide leader in sports, or, as Bornstein put it in
the ESPN values statement, "the premier sports channel."
SOURCE: Author's personal photograph.

ESPN CEO George Bodenheimer and Anthony Smith at the 25th anniversary
party in NYC. Bodenheimer took over as president of ESPN in 2003. In
Bodenheimer's era, the strategic mission changed somewhat to reflect both
Bodenheimer's passion to preserve the corporate culture and ESPN's new
circumstances.
SOURCE: Author's personal photograph.

SportsCenter veterans, Bob Ley and Chris Berman, join Bill Creasy, the first head of programming for ESPN, and Anthony Smith at the 25th anniversary party in New York.
SOURCE: Author's personal photograph.

Satellite dishes at ESPN's headquarters in Bristol, Connecticut. When satellite communications became available, ESPN snatched them up, mere weeks before the bigger competitors caught on. ESPN elected to go with satellite broadcasting and went national and 24 hour.
SOURCE: Author's personal photograph.

ESPN's campus in Bristol, Connecticut.
SOURCE: Author's personal photograph.

ESPN presidents at the ESPN 25th Anniversary—New York City, September 2004. (L to R—Back) Bill Rasmussen, William Grimes, Chet Simmons. (Front) Roger Werner, Steve Bornstein, George Bodenheimer.
SOURCE: Author's personal photograph.

ESPN was built on the idea that sports fanatics could not get enough televised sports coverage, no matter how much was offered to them. But how to fill a 24-hour time slot, seven days a week, 365 days a year? The networks, with all their money, resources, and established industry relationships, didn't even consider the possibility. Sporting events—meaning, by and large, NFL football games, Major League Baseball games, and such notable occasions as heavyweight boxing matches and the Olympics—were serious spectacles that demanded a marshalling of forces reminiscent of a military invasion. They were not tackled lightly. Conversely, daily sports news coverage was a paltry regional affair, in which a scant few minutes of highlights were sandwiched between local news and weather. What's more, the general conversation about sports in the media (and presumably the public) was seasonal and had strict limits. During baseball season, the talk was of baseball. Only mad followers in dark rooms followed off-season baseball rumors over the "Hot Stove." Likewise, no one apparently cared about the NFL after the Super Bowl cheers ended until the season started up again the next fall.

The TV program that edged closest to the sports fanatics' ravenous hunger for extensive coverage was *Wide World of Sports*. Launched in 1961, it initially showed track and field events at U.S. colleges. After the franchise was sold to ABC, the young Roone Arledge was installed as producer and something interesting and creative started to happen. Arledge had a simple but effective strategy: Obtain cheap broadcast rights for the kinds of sports that no one is watching on TV and bring them to a lucrative American marketplace. Viewers got bowling, wrestling, ski jumping, log rolling, demolition derbies, and (my favorite) speed skaters hurling themselves like amphetamine-spiked jackrabbits over a row of wooden barrels and crashing into bales of hay. The sports may have been ridiculous, outlandish, and barely interesting, but *Wide World of Sports* took it all seriously, and somehow the sonorous, anticipation-filled voice of legendary sports broadcaster Jim McKay made those contests riveting to watch.

There was, in any event, not much else showing on a Saturday afternoon. Indeed, even mighty ABC struggled to fill its several hours time slot once a weekend with a straight face and a reverent tone. You would have been crazy to think an entire channel could be filled with the stuff. Still, ABC's *Wide World of Sports* had a sense of mission that would have felt familiar to people working at ESPN or watching the channel years later. The show's introduction—"Spanning the globe to bring you the constant variety of sport. . ."—could have been describing ESPN's own mission. And the ABC franchise, overtly or not, provided a blueprint for how a struggling off-in-the-wilderness cable channel could make a serious run at the sports media market.

When it launched, ESPN had an energy, a brashness, a hipper sense of humor, and certainly a desperation that ABC lacked. It looked on the established market of sports television and saw it dominated by staid and slow-moving providers. With the audacity of the insecure overachiever, it attacked that marketplace from many different angles at once, all those small bites eventually amounting to something like a school of piranha attacking. ESPN understood that there were hundreds of sporting events every week not being covered that some people wanted to see, or at least could be convinced were worth seeing. Maybe those viewers didn't constitute a national audience as a single entity, but they were dedicated fanatics who would bother cable providers for ESPN and find the channel on the bulky TV converter sitting on the coffee table.

Even so, as an industry outsider and a start-up with limited backing, ESPN could barely afford coverage of those events the networks weren't bothering to follow. So it employed a mixture of tactics to find and/or develop programs that were affordable and yet would satisfy sports fans' hunger. Where coverage did not exist, ESPN produced it. When games were not available, ESPN created them. Where the major networks dominated, ESPN attached itself like a parasite. Whenever there was a big event that all the networks were part of, ESPN squeezed itself in somehow, the unexpected Thanksgiving dinner guest greedily reaching for a turkey leg.

Serving the Underserved

With no league contracts and nothing mainstream to show, ESPN started its broadcasting with the bizarre, the outlandish, and the unremarkable. Any event related to sports was worth putting up on the screen, from Australian rules football to Canadian 3-down football, from slo-pitch softball to cheerleading competitions, from boxing to pro wrestling. One of Bornstein's favorite finds, and something that no one would have previously imagined as a sport, was the running of the bulls in Pamplona, Spain. I guess we should credit ESPN for the number of American college students who now see getting drunk and running from a crazed bull as a foreign travel rite of passage.

How bad was ESPN's programming predicament? Geoff Mason was the head of NBC Sports in Paris preparing for the Moscow Olympics when ESPN was launched. He'd worked for Chet Simmons back in New York when Simmons ran NBC sports, so he called Simmons in Connecticut to wish him luck in the new venture. "You've got a hell of a challenge," Mason noted. "What kind of events are you looking for?" Simmons paused, chuckled, and answered, "Long ones." They needed anything to fill the time slots; the longer the events, the more frequently they could be repeated, the easier the programmers at ESPN could breathe. Mason joked about establishing an Indy 2000, four times as long as the Indy 500, and letting ESPN have the rights. Simmons laughed and said he wouldn't turn it down. "If you can get that done, I'll make you a senior VP." In fact, flag-to-flag coverage of auto racing—what we're so used to with NASCAR today—was an ESPN invention. As Steve Bornstein puts it, "We did it because we had to fill 24 hours of programming. Nothing brilliant there. A 500-mile race took up three and a half hours and putting that on was a hell of a lot easier than coming up with three different one-hour programs."

That's what ESPN was like in those first couple years. It was a radically open-minded approach to content. Getting programming—any programming—was the job of the young producers like Bornstein, always on the phone, always looking for videotapes. It didn't matter if the game was a few days old, ESPN would throw it on the air as soon as the tape arrived, as though it were the most critical sporting event in decades. Treating sports seriously was not only a core belief for ESPN programmers, in those days it was a practical necessity. As with programming, production also fell on the shoulders of young kids who didn't have two nickels to rub together and who had fewer cameras, fewer tape machines, and cheaper mobile units than even the lowliest team at one of the networks. Nevertheless, when they produced a game, they threw all their intensity and creativity at it and began to build ESPN's capability to put on a solid show. The vigor and the energy was something you could almost feel. ESPN didn't have the money or the technical resources to match the big networks (and, as I've argued, still tries to emulate that hardship today as a means of getting itself going) but it was convinced it could look as good as the networks. It didn't in the early days—it wasn't even close—but it believed internally that it could, and that attitude was something the networks didn't appreciate or take seriously until it was too late.

Actually, the patchwork approach, however desperate and demeaning it might have looked to an experienced network executive, wasn't as haphazard as it seemed. There was a strategy behind the mad scramble, and Roger Werner articulated it well; "I think one of the smart things the company did in the early days was look at the marketplace and ask ourselves: Where can we build consumer franchises that are really unique and where none of the big competitors are playing to any significant degree? And from that kind of analysis and thinking, we carved out a lot of new territory." That's what spawned *SportsCenter* and generated a college football and basketball franchise that still exists today and led to new stand-alone channels like ESPNU. It was the kind of thinking that enabled ESPN to recognize that the motor sports fan was woefully underserved in the 1980s until ESPN launched a franchise that was truly unique and helped make NASCAR a national phenomenon today. With the same mindset, ESPN looked at the popularity of weekend fishing and outdoor life programs and saw another consumer segment where it could cover some time slots and draw in the underserved. Woven together, the patchwork of cast-off events, delayed games, and unusual markets began to form a wide tapestry.

There were those, however, who did not believe the world of loosely defined alternative sports was sufficient for an American sports network to survive. Steve Bornstein, Roger Werner's successor, was one of those who felt that traditional "stick and ball" sports programming was an absolute necessity someway, somehow. "If all you're selling is beach volleyball," Bornstein said, "you're not going to make it."

In that sense, ESPN's first contract with the NCAA to cover college sports like football and basketball was an early life preserver. Bill Rasmussen negotiated the contract with the NCAA executives in Kansas the year before ESPN launched. The inviting proposal from ESPN declared the start-up's desire to complement NCAA coverage rather than compete with the networks. ESPN wanted to extend the football coverage to more schools and cover all the bowl games. Even more daring, ESPN was ready to commit to covering Division I, II, and III events from September through June, promising highlights and feature shows during the off-season summer months. In return for being given the privilege of promoting NCAA aggressively in such a manner, ESPN would increase its payments to the NCAA based on the number of overall monthly subscribers.

Those were all bold claims for a cable channel that had yet to broadcast a single hour of programming. But Rasmussen applied his salesman's confidence and enthusiasm in the vision he painted for the NCAA executives. To back up his promises and assure the NCAA of the demand for the ESPN product, Rasmussen put together a live telecast of a University of Connecticut basketball game and broadcast it via satellite with a banner message to viewers: Wherever they were watching, whatever their reasons for watching, contact ESPN and let them know if they wanted to see more. It turned out that rabid UConn Husky fans across the whole country tuned in, and, yes, they did want more.

Communicating that desire to the NCAA negotiators helped Rasmussen convince them that satellite cable, whether or not ESPN was the main programming provider, had significant potential to expand their market. It wasn't merely the coverage of unheralded colleges and unsung sports that would benefit the NCAA. Through satellite coverage ESPN was offering a chance to reach underserved sports fans everywhere—all those ardent alumni and passionate followers spread throughout the country.

The potential of cable to reach diverse customers was yet another indication that sports was no longer a regional affair, and that interest in even local sports events had gone national. When consultants assess new businesses and proposed product launches, one of the first questions that comes to mind is whether the product or the approach is scaleable. ESPN believed that underserved fans and undercovered sports events were a potentially significant market when drawn together by a new technology and a new perspective and attitude.

The NCAA Basketball Tournament was a case in point. The Division I college basketball championship tournament had been established in 1939 and had been a national television event dating from 1969, when NBC televised the championship game and a number of the earlier regional contests. But in 1982, ESPN began broadcasting the opening rounds of the then 48-team elimination tournament live. What's more, because ESPN did not have regional affiliates, it broadcast those early rounds nationally. In keeping with its need to fill programming hours, ESPN also rebroadcast games later the same day, sometimes more than once, assuring that the best games were seen widely. The NCAA tournament was already a national television phenomenon, but without a doubt, ESPN's extensive coverage contributed to the mania and popularity of what soon became known as March Madness—something that CBS, to its credit, recognized and capitalized on, buying up the rights to full coverage of the tournament a few years later. While it was involved, however, ESPN drew attention and strong praise for the quality of its productions. In particular, the dynamic cuts ESPN made to other games in progress gave viewers a sense of the athletic drama taking place simultaneously on multiple fronts—in other words, a feeling for that madness.

Cheap and Under Control

While big league stick-and-ball games were the prime attraction of sports fans, such events were hard to get rights to, expensive to produce, and limited in duration. But ESPN learned early on that if it could create its own game, it could produce sports programming much more cheaply and control the destiny of that franchise.

The best example of a stand-alone ESPN franchise is *SportsCenter*, ESPN's news and highlights sports roundup. *SportsCenter* was the first program anyone who happened to be watching ESPN on September 7, 1979, would have seen. For years, it didn't amount to much. In fact, we need to forget what a dominating sports program *SportsCenter* has been for the past 20 years to realize how daring or even foolish and offbeat it seemed at the time.

The gamble of developing its own sports news program appeared particularly crazy because ESPN had very little access to sports news. The start-up venture lacked rights agreements with the leagues or the major networks, so there were no highlights it could show. The producers, filling what must have seemed like endless minutes of airtime, compromised by throwing any visual highlights they could access up on the screen. They covered news about softball games and bowling tournaments and tractor pulls as though they were major events. And other tricks helped, too. When it came to the big four professional sports leagues, ESPN may have lacked clips of the previous nights' games, but it could still throw the score up on the screen and talk about the drama and the significance and the ramifications and nuances. In fact, the anchors were encouraged to talk sometimes at great length, making up the narrative occasionally as they went along.

And not only did they talk, but they talked with a certain attitude. There was a passion for sports in the conversation, but always with a sharp wit as well. The anchors, as ESPN started to feel solid on its own feet and more comfortable with its outsider status, began to sound like whip-smart kids in the back of the class who lobbed insightful room-cracking jokes toward the teacher in a way no one could quite get angry about. The attitude communicated was, "What do we have to lose—no one's watching anyway?" *SportsCenter* anchors, commentators, and reporters demonstrated their love for sports in their detailed, knowledgeable, passionate discussions and debates, but they also demonstrated through their sense of humor and irreverence that they didn't take themselves seriously as sports journalists, nor did they take ESPN seriously as a business entity. Behind the scenes, this nonchalance was belied by the intense work ethic and the high production values. But the easy grace and cavalier talk was an endearing way to encourage viewers to look past the production faults and the programming weaknesses and connect, instead, with ESPN, the fellow sports fanatic, the knowledgeable friend at the office water cooler or down the hall in the college dormitory.

Such unscripted, personality-driven conversation is commonplace in cable television today for a very good reason. Facts and news details are brief exchanges of information that only hint at the stories underneath. To explore the full drama of something like a sports event, you need to talk about those facts and evoke the story line and even talk about the talk of others. As opposed to the actual events, the talk of news coverage is limitless in scope. Think about it. Today, any single political event or newsworthy story can generate endless discussion on cable television right up until the next big event happens. We call that punditry, and it's a distinct feature of the media age we're now living in. Out of necessity, ESPN understood this well and early, and its anchors, reporters, commentators, and subjects filled the air with the national conversation of sports. Monday Night Football may have been showing on ABC, and the World Series may have been on CBS, but the honest, irreverent, and energized talk about those events was going on at ESPN.

Today, the anchors of local sports shows and sports talk radio programs emulate and indeed surpass their ESPN role models and forefathers in terms of brash tone and irreverent style. The mimicry is similar to the way airline pilots (according to *The Right Stuff* author, Tom Wolfe) have a bit of the relaxed southern drawl of legendary airman Chuck Yeager in their voices when they talk over the intercom to passengers, even if they were born and raised in Minnesota. But when *SportsCenter* was becoming established, the style that ESPN brought to its coverage was unique. It was as catchy and enticing as a new comedian like Letterman or Seinfeld. As ESPN became popular in college dorms and households across America, the expressions and tone of the broadcasters made their way into the cultural lexicon.

So where did ESPN get those anchors, reporters, and commentators? As usual, ESPN went outside the normal marketplace and got them cheap.

On-air talent is the face of any television channel, and as such, most networks invest heavily in that asset. Think of CBS, struggling to fill the evening news anchor role held by Dan Rather for 25 years. The decision was made to lure Katie Couric from NBC's *Today* show with a lengthy contract at $15 million per year. The money and the extent of the commitment were ample evidence of the importance the network put on that strategic decision. The hope was that Couric could become the new, rejuvenated identity of CBS News' flagship program. The big gamble, however, didn't work out. CBS News remained stuck in last place in the ratings and stuck with Couric.

As a start-up, ESPN didn't have the resources to hire a brand name broadcaster. But nor was that the organization's style. Instead, it invested in leadership on the business side, grabbing Chet Simmons from his role as head of NBC Sports. While viewers would never see Simmons's face on the screen, ESPN programming and production benefited immeasurably from his experience and connections. For its original *SportsCenter* anchors, though, ESPN used experienced veterans who were relative unknowns. George Grande was a local sports reporter. Lee Leonard, as one of Bryant Gumbel's cohosts on NBC, was more recognizable but no household name. Bob Ley was a college broadcaster and public announcer for a cable system in New Jersey. As such, they were inexpensive, replaceable, and versatile. What's more, they had great passion for and knowledge of sports and they were encouraged to make that kind of personal connection with viewers.

Chris ("Boomer") Berman was an even bigger and cheaper gamble of a hire, but someone who became a walking emblem of the culture and attitude of ESPN as it grew. Berman was a recent graduate from Brown University with an irrepressible passion for broadcasting and sports. He worked at a number of small stations for a few years after college before joining ESPN one month after its founding. In terms of youth, intelligence, sports obsession, and tirelessness, Berman was cut from the same cloth as the staff of bright young production people filling roles they could never have gotten at established networks. Berman saw his chance and seized it, and his booming personality was further amplified by the ESPN broadcasts. In the middle of high-density downloads on what was happening in sports, Berman interspersed rapid-fire nicknames for players, inside jokes, and raw shout-outs of appreciation for great plays. His enthusiasm was pure contagion.

But *SportsCenter* needed to evolve as ESPN found its footing. According to Bornstein, the program became something special and further established ESPN's credibility when John Walsh was brought on board in 1988, first as an editorial consultant and then as the managing editor in charge of all content. Bornstein emphasized the unconventional nature of that decision. "I hired a brilliant editor who'd never walked in a television studio before and was legally blind." Having enjoyed Walsh's company for years I can concur that the choice must have seemed radical. Walsh is an albino with a Santa Claus beard whose eyesight is so poor he needs to stand inches away from a television monitor to see the show he produces.

Walsh's background was not in TV but in print journalism, his most significant stint being at *Rolling Stone* magazine. When Bornstein brought him on as a consultant, he made no bones about what was important to ESPN. "I said to Walsh, 'Here's what you've got. *SportsCenter* is the only thing we don't pay rights for, so this is our most efficient financial vehicle, and I want you to turn it into the *Sports Illustrated* of television." Walsh wrote a treatise for Bornstein about what was wrong with the show. Bornstein hired him based on the quality of those observations and recommendations. ("His standards and disciplines," Bornstein claimed, "are as good if not better than most news organizations.") As the editorial head, Walsh immediately got to work on his own critique by overhauling the program.

Walsh knew *SportsCenter* was staffed by a group of dedicated fanatics working tirelessly, but he also felt they lacked a full understanding about the potential of the product. Walsh says, "They were getting highlights flown in to Bradley Airport [near ESPN headquarters] and someone would say, 'Hey, we got one! Let's put it on the air.' All they knew was that they had something they loved working on."[1] The producers of *SportsCenter* didn't know what those highlights could be.

Under Walsh's direction, *SportsCenter* changed. The first segment was no longer an unfocused affair but an overview of top news stories, just like the front page of a newspaper. Back-end segments of the show, increasingly creative in format, became regular franchises that dug in deeper or provided more debate and commentary on the top stories. Anchors could still bring their humor and personality to the *SportsCenter* news desk, but the news content of the information was more detailed, thorough, and professionally written and produced. Walsh had a nose for talent in his on-air personalities, and he brought many of the more memorable anchors to the organization, such as Dan Patrick, Keith Olbermann, and Mike Tirico. He also had a theory, proven valid in its success, that if he brought print-based sports journalists on board and turned them into on-air personalities, *SportsCenter* would benefit from their reporting acumen, and quality reporters would be seduced by the television exposure. *SportsCenter* turned many regional news reporters into household names, making them inside experts and commentators. Sports journalism has never been the same since.

SportsCenter was an original creation, made on the cheap, entirely within ESPN's control, and with a personality that relied on broadcasting talent but was not overshadowed by it. Most importantly, as Walsh understood, *SportsCenter* gave ESPN the opportunity to stamp its personality across all sports, even the major ones, beyond anything ESPN paid rights for, all while carving out a new market for underserved fans. Ratings soared, and *SportsCenter* became the crucial program sports fans needed to watch on a daily basis. The success gave ESPN new opportunities to capitalize on its cheapest asset. In 1991, Bornstein decided to start repeating the previous night's episode of *SportsCenter* the next morning, and several more times throughout the day. Instead of being turned off by the repetition, sports fanatics were elated. The highlights and wisecracks may have been the same, but now viewers could get their fix multiple times a day, often catching parts of the nightly broadcast that same night and again the following morning. *SportsCenter*'s opening jingle was a bell to all the sports world's Pavlovian dogs, inducing involuntary excitement and rapt attention. And it turned ESPN, a once derided start-up with no big game rights, into four letters that were synonymous with sports.

Crashing the Party

In addition to showcasing highlights and moderating the national sports conversation, ESPN learned how to attach itself to major sports at some oblique angle even when it lacked the rights for those games. For instance, ESPN may not have owned the rights to the nationally broadcast final four games of the final round of March Madness, but it could associate itself with March Madness by covering the early rounds every other network was neglecting. You could call this strategy "Inviting itself to the party."

In another example of that approach, Chet Simmons had what can only be described as one of the great programming ideas of the decade. He wanted to cover the NFL Draft. Young programmers like Steve Bornstein didn't even know such an event took place. Old industry hands and even NFL commissioner Pete Rozelle thought the idea was frankly ludicrous. The NFL owners had even refused ESPN's offer to cover parts of the draft in 1979 because they believed it was not worth following. But Simmons knew that ESPN's coverage of the draft was the perfect vehicle for the many thousands of underserved NFL fanatics out there whose college football acumen and hopes for their NFL teams made them interested in the draft. Simmons finally convinced Rozelle, Rozelle reluctantly convinced the owners, and ESPN was given the green light to go ahead and record the spectacle of NFL teams selecting college players, one by one, over the course of seven rounds in the off-season.

It was true that on the surface the NFL Draft didn't offer up much that was exciting. The extent of the drama involves football executives huddling over their paperwork, then slipping notes to the commissioner, who announces each pick with about 10 to 15 words. But around those words ESPN stoked up the drama. Which team was next, what were their needs, who would they pick? Viewers who cared about football—labeled draftniks by ESPN's Mel Kiper, Jr.—were so riveted over the course of those many hours that the NFL would soon move the event to the weekend to allow more people to watch. As a ratings hit for ESPN, the draft gave the cable channel credibility with NFL fans that would pay off big-time before the end of the decade.

Similarly, ESPN may not have had the rights to the Super Bowl, but starting in 1986 it decided it could still throw a Super Bowl party. Leveraging NBC's broadcast and the hunger of fans for more extensive coverage than the actual event allowed, ESPN sandwiched the Super Bowl with 15 hours of its own supplementary programming, including recaps of the season, last-minute updates for the game, speculation, and possible strategies, followed—once the game was over—by nearly endless highlights, debate, and discussions of what had happened.

And when there weren't enough parties to go around, ESPN realized it could host its own. In 1993, ESPN began hosting the ESPYs, or Excellence in Sports Performed Yearly awards, a sports counterpart to the Academy Awards, the Grammys, or the Emmys. Individual leagues had held their own awards ceremonies for years, offering trophies for most valuable player, best rookie, best coach or manager. But no such thing existed for the wide variety of sports in its entirety. ESPN claimed that territory smartly.

In its production of the NFL Draft, its Super Bowl coverage, and the ESPYs, ESPN showed that even if it was locked out of the mainstream sports world, it still had options available. ESPN could go ahead and start its own game. Such creative programming—stuff that the networks hadn't thought of, wouldn't touch, or couldn't afford the time to cover—was the way to establish a presence in sports everywhere.

Paying to Play

Even though ESPN was cheap and oriented toward cast-off programs, party-crashing schemes, and productions it could develop and fully control, it also proved to be unafraid of spending big money when it considered the payoff worth the risk. An early sign of that attitude showed up in 1987 outside the world of stick-and-ball games when ESPN produced the America's Cup. Four years earlier, ESPN had made a quick decision to broadcast coverage of the final stage of the venerable yachting race at Newport, Rhode Island. To its delight, underserved sports fans in the yachting world watched in significant numbers and called ESPN with adamant demands for full coverage. ESPN, never hesitant to fill programming hours with extended events, let the yacht race videotape roll and got its highest weekday afternoon ratings numbers ever. By the time the 1987 America's Cup came around, ESPN had gained the rights to this overlooked franchise and presold all the ad time.

Geoff Mason produced the 1987 America's Cup, this time hosted by Australia, as his first assignment for ESPN. As an experienced television sports producer, he believed that getting a mini-camera and live microphones on skipper Dennis Conner's yacht—the popular American favorite—would be critical for capturing the excitement and drama of the competition. Conner, however, wanted $100,000 for the privilege of having his progress filmed. Mason explained the situation to head programmer Steve Bornstein. Bornstein convinced Roger Werner to give Conner the money he wanted for having the camera installed. Then, in typical ESPN fashion, Bornstein let Mason know the next day that they'd found a sponsor to cover all of Conner's costs.

The new camera, sponsored by Budweiser, would be known as the BudCam, and it transformed the quality of the coverage. Today, we're used to cameras that zip along a football field a few feet above the action, or capture the speed of a slapshot or a fastball, or how the track looks to a race car driver leaning into a curve. But such technology was cutting edge in 1987. The splash of the water, the intensity of the struggle, the slippery danger, and the exhilarating speed became palpably real to the viewer, showcasing ESPN's production values. With their customary passion for sports, the ESPN commentators explained the nuances of yachting to an audience largely unfamiliar with the competition in language that was not condescending but still compelling. Despite the odd late-night hours for live coverage of an event on the other side of the world, the ratings were enormous and the America's Cup became a television phenomenon. According to the *New York Times*, in a front page story, viewers were throwing parties at the homes of people with ESPN and finding late-night bars showing the broadcast in order to follow the race.

By serving the underserved, showing off the production quality, and enthusing like sports fanatics, ESPN created yet another franchise. On this occasion, the coverage did more than anticipated to put ESPN on the map as a mainstream television channel. Then, ESPN's credibility, popularity, production values, ever-increasing revenue, and the positive experience of the NFL Draft finally all came together. In 1987, ESPN achieved the Holy Grail of sports coverage when the NFL awarded a football package to a network that had been launched only eight years before.

The NFL is America's most dominant, popular, and lucrative sport by far, but at the time, commissioner Pete Rozelle was forced to reach beyond the big three networks for a television partner because a drop in ad rates made the incumbents balk at the NFL's proposed fee increases. To stimulate demand, Rozelle crafted a package of eight games that he offered to the cable industry. ESPN outbid a consortium of cable operators led by John Malone to secure those rights for a whopping $55 million per game.

An NFL game had never been broadcast on cable television before. *ESPN Sunday Night NFL"* became the channel's newest franchise and it launched with gusto. The first regular season game on August 16, 1987 saw the Chicago Bears at the Miami Dolphins, and secured the highest ratings ever for a cable channel. With that kind of programming, the sports world was compelled to pay attention. And given the exposure, ESPN took advantage, showing how differently it could produce sports television and enlivening the coverage with such new techniques as the Goalpost Cam, super slow motion replay, miked-up referees, and more field-level shots.

If the NFL package was an unusually bold gambit, it did not make ESPN timid. Gaining momentum with its success and growth during the 1980s, ESPN decided to take another calculated risk and seize the opportunity to become the dominant media outlet for sports. To do so, it needed coverage rights for the other professional leagues. Major League Baseball was the most critical missing piece. So, in 1989, ESPN paid $400 million for a four-year contract. It was clear to the number crunchers that there was no way the deal could make money, even with more advertising dollars and rate increases for cable providers. And in fact, while ESPN anticipated losing $60 million on the package, it ended up dropping twice that amount. Still, having professional baseball and football on the schedule was a heady accomplishment. By the mid-1990s, ESPN had arrived as a legitimate big-time network.

Create Your Own Outlet

Riding the rocket of its explosive growth, ESPN kept expanding and taking risks. The age-old question for media-based companies revolves around whether content or distribution is king. ESPN decided that the answer was both. Around the same time that it made its major investments into professional sports coverage, ESPN also expanded its distribution into new media offerings.

The first and most natural toe-dip beyond the ESPN cable channel was radio. The opportunity for radio programming showed up, practically uninvited and unannounced, one day in 1991 when ABC Radio executives visited ESPN and asked for 30-second spots that could be tucked into breaks during regular programming. The innocent invitation raised sensory antennae and the ESPN executive team met to discuss the suggestion. There was a sense among all those present that a larger opportunity could be at hand. John Walsh and Jim Allegro put voice to it, suggesting that maybe it was time for ESPN to start its own radio network.

That was self-evidently a good idea to Bornstein, so the hounds were unleashed. Sixty days later ESPN went live with 16 hours of programming per week. "It was a real feat," Jim Allegro recalled. Two new studios were ordered and arrived by truck. They were made of steel and heavy as hell. The first one was installed and the plan was to put the other on top of it, but then somebody realized that a second steel studio would be too heavy and would almost certainly cause the roof of the lower one to cave. So ESPN went back to the vendor and ordered another studio built out of wood. "We were running so fast," Allegro said. "We borrowed equipment, bought what we needed." Right up until the red light went on, pieces were still being put in place. At the last moment, someone ran down to the local Radio Shack and bought a wall clock that became the official timepiece.

The start, on January 4, 1992, was memorable. Keith Olbermann, who had just been hired as a *SportsCenter* anchor and was asked to be ESPN Radio's first announcer, went on the air. He led with a baseball scoop about feared free agent slugger Danny Tartabull signing with the New York Yankees. The newly hatched radio network never looked back, expanding to 24-hour programming within a few years. The entire endeavor was typical ESPN. It had been born of opportunity and launched fast, cheap, and barely under control. Yet, it met the standards of the quality of journalism coming out of *SportsCenter* while providing another outlet for ESPN's irreverence and humor. It served sports fans in a new and important way. And it tapped and developed inexpensive new talent who would become industry icons, including announcers Tony Kornheiser, a reporter with the *Washington Post* and now a host of Monday Night Football, Nanci "The Fabulous Sports Babe" Donnellan, and Mike Greenberg and Mike Golic of the *Mike and Mike in the Morning* show, not to mention Dan Patrick and Mike Tirico.

A second cable channel, called ESPN2 but known as the Deuce, required a much bigger investment and constituted a much bigger risk. If the idea of an all-sports channel had seemed ludicrous to critics a decade earlier, could ESPN double down and successfully launch a second all-sports channel? The lead-up was arduous, stressful, and energizing. ESPN went through its familiar urgent pacing in organizing and building a second studio, hiring the staff, seducing the talent, getting everything together faster and cheaper than a traditional network could dream of, all in time for the first broadcast on October 1, 1993. The epic party afterward was testament to the blood, sweat, and panic that had gone into getting there.

Bornstein believed ESPN2 would play a key role in keeping ESPN fresh, energized, and constantly at the forefront of sports fans' needs. The specific rationale for ESPN2 was that it would provide a distinctly different type of sports viewing for a distinctly different demographic. It was the early 1990s and extreme sports was the grassroots rage among testosterone-fueled young teenagers. The demographic for the major sports like NFL skewed higher end than that. So ESPN2 would feature alternative sports like snowboarding and motocross which appealed to 18–25 males. Everything about the channel reflected that—the bright colors of the studio, the casual clothes on the set, the extra-sarcastic tone in the voices, and, of course, the events themselves, more dangerous and unnerving than what ESPN was offering, steeped in the aesthetics of the hand-held camera and the amateur daredevil. But that notion never quite struck the sweet spot with viewers, cable companies, and advertisers. As a result, ESPN2 needed to evolve and grow until it became more comfortable in its own skin. Bornstein's gambit may have had its problems (a subject for Chapter 6), but the numbers don't lie.

From an initial 9 million subscribers, ESPN2 is now seen in over 90 million homes.

After ESPN2, the growth in new channels continued. ESPNews was launched in 1996, featuring 24 hours of sports news coverage. It served ESPN as kind of a continuously rolling CNN of sports, as well as a grooming area for new young talent, and a spillover for time-conflicted programs normally seen on either ESPN or ESPN2. Next, in 1997, ESPN acquired the independent channel Classic Sports Network and renamed it ESPN Classic. Again, critics might have once questioned such a move judgmentally—24 hours of sports on multiple channels, and now games in which the results were already known? But the idea of broadcasting classic sports invoked a keen understanding of the sports fanatic's brain. Big games are always up for discussion, even if they've happened decades before. Sports fanatics still mull over the details, the facts, the stories behind the events, and the historical implications, and they were more than happy to sit up late at night and get lost in a classic contest, even one they'd already viewed, and they were willing to pay their cable providers higher rates for the pleasure of doing so.

In 2003, under Bodenheimer's watch, ESPN ventured into the realm of new technology with its high definition channels broadcasting the same content as ESPN, ESPN2 and ESPNEWS. The evolution of high definition television was beset by the chicken and egg problem. The technological standards may have been in place, but before 2003 the future of that technology was totally in doubt. The networks and cable channels hesitated to invest in expensive high definition broadcasts until there were enough homes out there with TV sets capable of appreciating (and paying for) the extra quality. On the other side of the equation, most homeowners were reluctant to shell out for an expensive piece of technology when there was little programming available for enjoying its advantages. But the shift to high definition broadcasting made complete sense to ESPN from the standpoint of serving the fans. Indeed, Bodenheimer is adamant that credit for the idea goes to the employees of ESPN who knew that the only thing sports fans wanted more than sports on TV was sports with a crisper, clearer television picture.

(Electronics stores realize this, too, which is why they sell so many high definition big screen plasma TV sets in the lead-up to the Super Bowl.) ESPN understood that if it wanted to be the leader in sports television, it needed to continue to produce the best telecast possible.

As the first network to go HD, ESPN now produces more HD programs than any other channel, and the move has paid off. As Bodenheimer put it, "It does lead to increased viewing. People are making decisions about what to watch based on what's showing in high def." Once again, ESPN's willingness to see the product from the fan's point of view got it into a new market or a new game earlier than anyone else.

Stick with the Knitting

It would make sense that as it has become bigger, wealthier, and more established, ESPN may have lost the need to be creative and scrappy about its programming. The NFL and MLB rights deals would seem to be a case in point. But in fact, despite its resources and market command, ESPN continues to create its own game, crash parties, and expand cheaply and with almost reckless innovation into new areas with new sports, new franchises, and new programs. Bornstein talked frequently about the need to keep ESPN invigorated with reinvigorated broadcasting. That's part of the reason. But it's also true that heavy investments into professional sports and successful events have increased the vulnerability of ESPN to being hamstrung or held hostage. Indeed, those costly deals with the NFL, MLB, and in 2002 the return of the NBA, have led to some tough choices. ESPN was unable to hold onto NASCAR in 1999 and was forced to relinquish the men's senior PGA tour in 2001. The NASCAR loss, in particular, was a hard blow, since it was a wildly popular franchise that ESPN had invested a lot in to develop and promote. Recognizing that mistake, ESPN would eventually spend a lot to get it back.

The necessity may be different, but the patchwork approach to programming is just as important today as it was in ESPN's first few years.

By developing original programming and franchises in-house, ESPN can stay creative while keeping its costs and assets under control. The X-Games are a perfect example. Launched in 1994 as the first annual Extreme Games competition, the events are now held every summer and winter and feature outlandish extreme sports such as skateboarding, street luge racing, parachuting, and beach partying. The immense crowds, the credibility of the athletes, and the advertising dollars that pour in have shown that this franchise is very real and very successful. The X-Games have also given ESPN entrée into the younger male demographic that ESPN2 never quite captured.

The phenomenal popularity of poker is another franchise that ESPN locked onto early. Mark Shapiro was running all programming at ESPN when a young manager named Fred Christianson from alternative sports asked him out for a cup of coffee to pitch an idea. Christianson believed that ESPN's World Series of Poker was being given short shrift, and that more resources, more hours of coverage, and more promotion would help ESPN latch onto something that was growing fast. As Shapiro put it, "You have to breed your laboratory. You need an environment that rewards and encourages people to take chances and come to you with ideas. If that environment isn't nurtured and ideas are consistently shot down, people will stop bringing them to you." So, in spite of Shapiro's personal doubts, he decided to go for it. ESPN doubled the hours of programming, put poker onto its Sunday night schedule where it would get more exposure, produced the show with the kind of camera angles Christianson recommended, and did more promotion. "And the thing blasted," Shapiro relayed with amazement. "Poker was suddenly the third highest sport on our air."

Sticklers may have doubted that poker was a sport at all, but that's how ESPN builds new franchises—by serving the underserved fan. ESPN's 2001 acquisition of BASS, the "world's largest fishing organization," was another example of a patch ESPN picked up and added to the quilt. The bass fishing community may have seemed like an odd choice for an organization that produces Monday Night Football, but

BASS has 600,000 members, fishing is a growing global sport, and the annual BASSMASTER Tournament was a nice fit on ESPN2, harkening back to ESPN's early days of outdoor programming. Because ESPN owned the asset, any gains in growth and popularity derived from ESPN's work in promoting and developing the franchise will remain under control. Similarly, in June 2002 ESPN signed a six-year no-rights-fee deal with the WNBA in which expenses and revenue would be shared.

There are many more examples of creative patchwork programming that have kept ESPN innovative and growing, while not relying on its upper-tier success. *Dream Job*, a reality TV contest to become a sports anchor, *Around the Horn*, another debate format for discussing sports news, and original entertainment productions like *Tilt* and *Playmakers* have given ESPN plenty of new franchises to expand audiences while keeping costs down. I've never seen an organization so aggressive about new ideas. *SportsCenter* may be the single most successful show ever on cable television in terms of number of viewers, number of episodes, number of years running, and amount of ad dollars, but ESPN didn't rest on its laurels even with that franchise; it launched *Pardon the Interruption* instead. As a format, *PTI* was unlike anything else on TV. Two commentators—the vividly entertaining and cerebral sports journalists Tony Kornheiser and Michael Wilbon—heatedly argue and debate sports-related topics against the clock. And somehow, through the vitriol and energy, you get intelligent opinion with your excitement. Few thought it would be much of a hit, and some feared the new offering would hurt *SportsCenter* by splitting viewers, but *PTI* ended up out-rating *SportsCenter* while also actually lifting *SportsCenter*'s ratings as well as the ratings of other ESPN shows. Compare the format to staid PBS-style moderated sports discussions on other networks and you'll see how much more energy and interest is generated.

In its early years, ESPN's programming schedule was, by necessity, made of dozens and dozens of cast-off scraps. But when those threadbare or roughly torn pieces got woven together, they created an astonishingly comprehensive quilt. Back then, no one in the industry showed any concern as ESPN picked up a patch here, a patch there. It was only when the quilt was woven and the sports market was revealed to be lucrative that they tried to force their way back into the fray. But those that tried to emulate ESPN's tactics soon realized there were few cheap scraps left. ESPN's giant quilt covered just about everything.

And as I'm trying to suggest, by keeping that patchwork strategy in place, ESPN has promoted its ongoing growth. Big companies get complacent—it's in their nature. Once upon a time, IBM looked unassailable, the dominant company in the world's strongest growing industry. Then it let a college dropout named Bill Gates walk out the door with the rights to a few lines of computer code. Picture Gates thinking inside, "Microsoft is going to be bigger than IBM someday," and imagine an IBM exec thinking, "How cute." But that was the start of the age of Microsoft and the downscaling of IBM's vision. No company is immune—Bill Gates himself overlooked the importance of the Internet, the browser, and the search engine. Twenty years later a company called Google showed up as if a door to another universe had opened and a fully formed entity appeared.

ESPN has had its share of challenges. As its programming grew, large competitors like Fox Sports and Comcast and small competitors such as Outdoor Life Network, Speed Channel, and the Outdoor Channel (the last two of which were started by former ESPN CEO Roger Werner) arose to dedicate themselves to serving the territory ESPN had discovered. Franchises like NASCAR and the early rounds of March Madness were snatched away when they became valuable. ESPN's success in promoting anything it doesn't control inevitably comes back to haunt it. All those are good problems, but they are alleviated by ESPN's innate drive to develop stuff in-house and be cheap and creative in its programming. ESPN's ultimate product is its creativity and production quality, its attitude and irreverence, and its serve-the-fans mantra. As a result, it can develop any product or shift from any league and cover any event and still make it a winner.

CHAPTER FOUR KEY POINTS

"Serve the underserved"

In every market, there is a segment that is underserved, either by lack of service, product offerings, or quality. It is also important to remember that marketing research may not always expose a customer's real needs or wants, not because the research methods are flawed, but because customers don't always know what they want until they see it, have it, and experience it.

"If you want to be in the quilt business, start collecting and creating your patches now"

Too many companies enter markets to compete with established companies at their game, and on their scale. Start small and build. It wasn't DELL computers that almost brought down the mighty IBM, it was DELL, Compaq, HP, Apple, and Gateway that ate away at their market share collectively.

"For every business, there is a meta-business"

Who would have thought that news and commentary about sports would be such big business, not to mention celebrity news and commentary. What's next, a news show for all the news shows? Ever heard of *American Idol*? If you can't be a star, report on them, or create a show to discover stars. Derivatives didn't work out as well as Alan Greenspan thought they would for the U.S. economy, but derivatives and meta-business can work for upstarts or mature organizations. This applies even if you manufacture circuit boards—you get the metaphor.

"Content is king, but so is marketing. Oh, and distribution, too"

If you are a product or distribution company, you need to become a king marketer. Budweiser and Nike come to mind. If your business is about distribution, you need to think about a product or service—think of Amazon or Google. Whatever you are, continue to invest in the three legs of the tripod—content/product, marketing, and distribution.

"Stick to the knitting, if knitting is your thing"
Don't want to contradict the last learning point, but never forget your strength while exploring the other aspects that secure and expand your core competence.

Chapter 5

EXPAND
THE BRAND

Observers are still in awe of the way Jack Welch ran GE. What always impressed me about Welch was how easily and even gracefully he integrated all the many businesses of GE under the umbrella of one strong culture. From light bulbs to jet engines, from complex financial services to a major television network, GE has dominant business lines in incredibly diverse areas, and yet the way GE does business, the way it relates to customers, and the qualities of the GE people are amazingly consistent.

GE had a hundred years to become a conglomerate with a strong culture before Welch took the helm. When I thought about that, and then considered all the offerings and distribution outlets ESPN had developed in just 30 years, I was impressed by how gangly such a many-limbed octopus could have been and how gracefully ESPN seemed to glide through the water. In the thrust of so much change and development, how did ESPN manage to make the right decisions about products, people, and operations more often than not? During the early survival stage, there must have been moments when the right choice was a potential business killer and the expedient choice would have been wrong for the company long-term. At the height of its success, there must have been tempting opportunities to stray from the steady course and generate easy revenue or do something nervy to impress ownership. Yet, ESPN has shown an uncanny ability to avoid the wrong moves on its journey and stay true to its culture.

As I've mentioned already, the answer is so simple you can be excused for wondering if it isn't a statement of business book BS.

ESPN truly and deeply believes itself to be in the business of serving fans. Over the years ESPN has adopted several different strategic approaches to achieving that objective. In the early years, at least starting with Bornstein, ESPN set out to become the World-Wide Leader in Sports, or, as Bornstein put it in the ESPN values statement, "the premier sports channel." The objective was right, from ESPN's perspective, because achieving that kind of portfolio of programs and offerings would help ESPN serve fans better.

In Bodenheimer's era, the strategic mission changed somewhat to reflect both Bodenheimer's passion to preserve the corporate culture and ESPN's new circumstances. But the value of serving fans remained the same. By sticking to that philosophy, ESPN has followed the right course regardless of what else has been going on inside the company, in the marketplace, in the technological landscape, and even with new ownership groups. At every juncture, ESPN has only had to ask the question, "How is this going to serve our fans?" If the approach would enable ESPN to deliver more sports, more news, or more sports entertainment to those fans then it was a solid choice. That was the threshold for determining the rightness of a decision and it was the basis of the ESPN brand.

When in Doubt, Ask the Brand

Roger Werner was the first top executive at ESPN to talk consistently about the ESPN brand. Werner knew that creating a consistent and clear brand was one of the most critical tasks for a developing an organization in the media business and he took every opportunity to promote ESPN. In line with that, he started the ESPN marketing division to sell merchandise. It was a decision for the future, since there was little money in ESPN merchandise at the time, but that was Werner's forte as a leader: He was always anticipating the way the competitive landscape was going to look years down the road.

Bornstein faced a different challenge with the brand. Given all the acquisitions and growth in the 1990s, there was the possibility ESPN could lose its grip. For instance, when the ESPN brand began to get hot in the early 1990s, especially on college campuses, the temptations started to grow. You could slap the ESPN logo on skateboards, school notebooks, sneakers, or cereal boxes. But Bornstein was vigilant about avoiding opportunities that may have been lucrative or easy but didn't make sense from a brand perspective. As Bornstein puts it, "We were protective of the brand and there were a lot of things we didn't do. My point to my guys was that the day I see the shoeshine guy outside of Grand Central Station wearing an ESPN T-shirt is the day I know we've failed."

The brand was sacred, and the integrity of the brand was about sports and sports entertainment. That was a relatively clear concept when it came to programming and producing television shows. Whatever wasn't related to sports and sports entertainment didn't fit the brand and didn't belong on ESPN cable. For example, at one point, Bornstein launched a morning business news show to compete with other cable channels like CNN. It made sense from a demographic point of view. ESPN viewers were almost as interested in business and finance news as they were in sports news. But although the quality of the program and the journalism that supported it was top-notch, the show failed to catch on. The likely reason? It wasn't consistent with ESPN's sports brand. As it turned out, when it came to exploring product and marketing opportunities outside the familiar terrain of television, it was even more important to follow the brand.

Dick Glover was hired by Bornstein in November 1992 as the first employee of ESPN Enterprises, a group formed to grow ESPN not just as a media business with several channels but as a brand in many different arenas. Despite Roger Werner's forward thinking about merchandise, ESPN had very little to offer fans outside of sports television. Other than a home video business that was a complete mess and a few commemorative books published in coordination with Hearst Publishing, ESPN had never discovered an opportunity that made much sense. So Glover was charged with exploring new ideas outside the traditional realm and making sure they fit ESPN's overall strategy and brand.

One of the first possibilities Glover considered was the World Wide Web. This was very forward thinking of him, and a potentially risky area for a new executive to spend much time working on. Remember, at that time, e-mail was barely being used and there was no such thing as a browser like Netscape, Mozilla, or Internet Explorer that would allow people to access something called the Internet. Computer geeks were communicating and sharing information through what was known as electronic bulletin boards, however, and you could see the hint of future possibilities in that kind of computer-based networking. Glover, like other early adopters at the time, had a sense of the enormous potential of instant communication and news distribution, and he understood the degree to which this represented both an opportunity and a threat to the media business.

Those weren't easy arguments to make to a busy top executive, however, especially when no other media company was investing seriously in the technology. But in his discussions with Bornstein, Glover knew how to say the magic words. If ESPN was in the business of serving sports fans, then the Internet was just another means of doing so, and potentially a huge one at that. Bornstein gave the go-ahead to Glover to explore the possibilities of bringing ESPN content online. His only instruction was to do it as cheaply as possible, another mantra that hewed closely to the ESPN culture.

"Bornstein's idea," Glover said, "was to learn about this on someone else's dime." New Internet companies were eager to work with mainstream media enterprises in those early days. Glover had his pick of several, finally choosing a company called Prodigy (which was owned by Sears Roebuck and Company) over the more established CompuServe and another smaller start-up called AOL. ESPN had the brand and the content, and Prodigy had the technological expertise, so the two companies got started.

The work with Prodigy produced a web presence called ESPNNet. It gave ESPN some online functionality, enabling sports fans to access up-to-date sports statistics and scores. With the ever-evolving possibilities of information technology, however, there was no such thing as standing still. Soon, Glover led ESPN to join forces with Microsoft cofounder Paul Allen's firm, Starwave, in order to take the web site to the next level. But Starwave, cognizant of the fact that ESPN got all the glory out of its work with Prodigy, insisted that the joint venture be cobranded rather than have the exclusive ESPN name, suggesting SportsZone as a new moniker. Glover thought there was no value in that for ESPN, so the two sides went back and forth. The label, ESPNNet Sportszone was chosen as a compromise, prompting NBA Commissioner David Stern to call it the longest and most stupid name in history. Stern had a point, but Glover knew ESPN's Internet site would play well with fans.

In 1994, ESPN's web site had just been launched, but almost no one saw it as an important outlet for programming or a future area of growth. At the annual meeting of top executives and senior programmers, Glover sat quietly and listened to report after report detailing the many new projects in the works. It was amazing to everyone in the room how much growth the company was experiencing and how fast that growth was taking place. Near the end of the day, an executive asked Bornstein if he could name the one or two things that would be most important strategically for ESPN going forward. It's safe to say that every person in the room figured Bornstein would key in on the company's huge and very recent investment in ESPN2. But Bornstein never missed an opportunity to disturb and disrupt complacent thinking, and this kind of soft lob was too tempting to resist smashing over the net. Without hesitation he named the Internet and International as the critical priorities going forward. Glover remembered how the shock among the executives was palpable and all movement in the room stopped.

It was typical of Bornstein, consciously or not, to keep quiet with his views until he could have the most impact. Whatever else people had on their plates, they now knew that ESPN's web site and its international expansion were important to the boss and for the future growth of the company. So when Glover soon came knocking on their doors for content, expertise, and support, managers sat up and listened. In a way, the web site work helped to address another concern of Bornstein's: He was bothered by the existence of too many isolated silos within the organization. A new venture that required input from all over the company and that was a strategic priority of the demanding and hard-to-please CEO was an automatic silo buster.

The next year, at the same meeting, Dick Glover showcased the new web site. The seasoned television industry hands who filled the room were impressed at what could be done online. Glover compared projections for the growth of cable with the potential growth of the Internet in terms of the number of household computers that could be expected in the next 10 years. Based on those statistics, Glover insisted, there would come a point when more people would have access to ESPN. com than to ESPN's television channels. It was a sobering and disturbing statement, even as it bolstered Bornstein's view that the Web was critical going forward.

ESPN's Internet partner, Starwave, was soon bought by Infoseek, the Google-like search engine of its day, which then faltered and was bought by Disney. Disney had developed its own Internet business group and was aiming to be a significant player in the new technology. With Starwave, Disney developed the Go.Com system as a rival to such emerging Internet portal companies as Yahoo!. The idea was to create a gateway or hub for Internet users looking for content around entertainment, recreation, and sports—all spokes where Disney had expertise and leverage. At the time, ESPN was looking for a new technology partner to relaunch its Web presence with a keener focus on what the web site could and should do. The choice was between Universal Films and Disney's Internet group, both of which had compelling services to offer. Disney's vision made sense given ESPN's content strengths, however, so Glover went in that direction. He breathed a sigh of relief over that decision a year later when Disney acquired ABC Cap Cities, with ESPN as part of that deal.

The Go.com portal was part of ESPN's Internet address for years until Disney shut down its Internet media business following the collapse of the tech stocks. Regardless, ESPN's presence on the World Wide Web was a major achievement. Traffic was low at first because speed of access was exceptionally slow in those pre-broadband days and there were few active online users. But ESPN was one of the earliest news content sites on the Web, arriving before many of the mainstream news organizations. By establishing its Internet presence early and leading sports coverage distributed electronically, ESPN effectively pre-empted challenges from other sports-related content providers that might have otherwise found a low barrier to entry as a new competitor. Just think about the list of dot-com companies from the late 1990s and recall the Super Bowl advertisements from the likes of Pets.com. A sports news and entertainment web site should have been part of that mix of start-ups but wasn't, perhaps because ESPN already occupied the territory.

Today, despite competitors from the major networks, *Sports Illustrated* magazine, and the *SportingNews*, ESPN.com remains the most visited sports site on the Internet. The site has accumulated a string of accolades over the past 10 years as the top provider of sports information on the Web. What's more, ESPN was one of the few Internet ventures not to lose a great deal of money in development because it always relied on the services and know-how of partner companies. But in staking out its claim on cyberspace, ESPN did not have grand ambitions in mind. Instead, it merely looked at the Internet as another way of serving the sports fan, so building a presence there early (and cheaply) while keeping productive values high according to ESPN standards made complete strategic sense. "We were trying to bring the brand to a worldwide audience in ways we thought were important," Bornstein observed. "That's one of the reasons why ESPN is the leader of sports on the Internet. We were first, we were active early, and we kept working on it because that was what the brand needed."

ESPN Goes Abroad

The other area of strategic concern for Bornstein in that 1994 executive meeting had been International. Again, this made sense from a mission and brand perspective. If ESPN was aiming to live up to its claim as the "worldwide leader in sports" it certainly needed to have a dominant international presence. By 1996, ESPN had managed to develop some distribution internationally but traction was still weak. As a hired consultant, Geoff Mason wrote a report explaining what ESPN needed to do differently. Essentially, the firm lacked a good presentation about its offerings that it could use to convince potential international partners. Bornstein agreed and asked Mason to make the ESPN product more marketable for international distribution. Mason got the full backing of Howard Katz, who was head of programming at the time, and was thereby able to access as much ESPN content as he needed to satisfy potential joint venture partners outside the United States.

Bornstein was always averse to spending money unnecessarily, but he recognized the inherent value of global distribution. Whenever Mason called about a distribution opportunity that would cost some coin, Bornstein grumbled but supported the move. At that time, EuroSports was ESPN's predominant partner in Europe, but that entity was faltering. The Middle East and Africa were still afterthoughts. So most of the growth potential was in South America and Asia. Mason, Bornstein, and Katz put a lot of focus in those regions and the effort paid off. There were no major victories or sweeping accomplishments, but little by little, through a lot of spadework and attention, ESPN developed a global footprint, and is now seen in over 180 countries. Russell Wolfe, the current EVP of International, continues to build the global presence of ESPN and today, no other sports media company outside the United States can compare to ESPN in terms of programming and brand awareness.

ESPN Opens the Books

Back in Bristol, ESPN had two channels, the Internet, and radio, but one of the only media areas where ESPN still lacked presence was in print. Over the years, efforts had been made occasionally to leverage the relationship with 20 percent owner Hearst Publishing and do something related to print, but nothing came of it. Annual sports overviews were the best idea that turned up, but none of those projects had any significant value. Dick Glover was still immersed in the work of building ESPN's Web presence but he was also always on the lookout for other ancillary products that fit the brand. A light went on when *Sports Illustrated* established itself as an Internet competitor in combination with CNN. The move made sense. Both *Sports Illustrated*, the magazine, and CNN, the cable news channel, were owned by Time Warner; in the parlance of the day, it was thought that synergies could be achieved by combining the entities to create a giant news and sports information site online. The sudden threat got Glover thinking, and he wrote a memo with the provocative question, "Why should *Sports Illustrated* get a free run?" *Sports Illustrated* had ventured into ESPN's territory with a new point of attack. Shouldn't ESPN look at returning the favor? For every *Time* magazine, there was a *Newsweek*. For every IBM, there was an Apple. To be the worldwide leader in sports, ESPN needed to establish its own print magazine and compete with the vaunted *Sports Illustrated* on its own turf.

Bornstein loved the idea. The new Disney ownership had a strong publishing division that would need to be convinced, however. Glover figured the plan would die there, tangled in the bureaucracy of an enormous business. But the head of Disney publishing was a man named John Skipper, who happened to be a sports nut. Skipper was immediately fired up by the potential. In fact, if he could have designed his own dream job, it would have been to launch a sports magazine. Others in Disney thought a magazine was a stupid idea. In 1997, the rest of the world was abandoning print journalism for the Internet. Why would any sensible company want to go the other way? The final decision was up to Michael Eisner, Disney chairman and CEO. Knowing that Disney owned the Anaheim Angels baseball team and the Anaheim Mighty Ducks hockey team, Skipper developed a mock cover of *ESPN The Magazine* with Anaheim Angels' pitcher Jim Abbot on the cover. As luck would have it, Eisner was a big Jim Abbot fan. The presentation hit the right points of concern and the project was greenlit.

The first issue of the magazine was published a year later in March 1998. The launch was overseen by Skipper, who joined ESPN as a senior vice president, and John Walsh, the editor of *SportsCenter* and a former top editor at *Rolling Stone* magazine. *ESPN The Magazine* went for a younger demographic than *Sports Illustrated*. It focused on more outlandish athletes and stories, and exhibited that self-aware ESPN sense of humor. By any measure, awards, readership, advertising, and distribution, the magazine hit the mark. It also passed the internal test of allowing ESPN to take another step in becoming worldwide leader in sports.

Keeping Down the Number of Freight Cars

The successful launch of the magazine with Disney support was an example of how ESPN was able to leverage its new parent company's capabilities for great advantage. And indeed, the possibilities for doing so looked great on paper. Soon after the relationship began, senior managers from all over the Disney empire were brought to a corporate gathering and asked to give presentations about what their business units were doing. The ESPN executives who attended were impressed by the collection of capabilities on display and they could see that Disney was extremely well-managed. But although it was rarely openly acknowledged, some were quietly concerned about how well Disney would treat the ESPN brand. "We were fearful they didn't understand our brand," Glover said, "and the one thing we really did understand about our own business was our brand." There was the danger that, overtly or subtly, Disney might mishandle the ESPN brand, direct it in ways that weren't quite right, and start to weaken the connection with sports fans.

At the same time, there was curiosity about what else Disney could bring to the table. Disney's consumer products division was booming, for example. Every time Disney released a movie, it also earned hundreds of millions of dollars in revenue through the sale of merchandise. At a presentation about what Disney could do for ESPN, the consumer products group brought along a softball on which they'd stamped the number "$40,000,000." Tossing the ball over, they told ESPN that's how much money Disney's approach to consumer goods could generate for

ESPN annually. Bornstein, Glover, and the other ESPN executives were intrigued, if slightly skeptical.

The conflict within ESPN was always about leveraging the brand in ways that would add to the impact rather than subtract from it. "We'd think of ten opportunities every month," Glover said, "but then we'd say, 'Well, if we do that, it will help the brand in some ways and weaken it in others.' So we passed on a lot of stuff. We didn't want to hook too many freight cars onto the single ESPN engine." Yes, more products, more merchandise, more distribution channels, and other offerings would allow the ESPN brand to carry more freight, but would also slow the company down.

And yet, as the two companies got to know each other, a trust and rapport developed when it came to new ventures. Within Disney, there were other key executives like John Skipper who were passionate sports fans and admirers of ESPN, and they began to bring their ideas forward. Soon, with Disney's encouragement, ESPN was stepping well outside its traditional comfort zone and developing stores and themed restaurants. The ESPNShop and the ESPNZone were the results. Bornstein was initially a bigger backer of the restaurants than the stores, seeing a more direct fit, and the ESPNZone restaurants evolved into a kind of super-sports bar—a natural for ESPN—and helped the company set up a brand presence in such key urban centers as Times Square in New York City. An ESPNZone was the kind of place that a season ticket-holding executive with an interest in sports could bring clients for lunch; and it provided a perfect location for ESPN to do remote broadcasts in the midst of crowds of fans.

When You Get Big, Go Humble

All the growth and all the new offerings were turning ESPN into an empire. By the late 1990s, the organization was loaded with assets and secure behind its moat. It had an effective mosaic patchwork of programming that met the needs of passionate niches of sports fans, and it had the glorious crown jewels of mainstream sports with the broadcasting rights to the NFL and MLB. It had *SportsCenter* and ESPN.com. It had the ESPYs. It had amazing brand awareness, a lock on every important demographic, the top ratings in cable television, and national advertisers booked months in advance. It still had an irreverent attitude and a self-aware sense of humor; and it was still attracting those young, hungry, and passionate sports fanatics to come to Bristol and work like hell. What's more, because of its business model and the growth of the cable industry, ESPN generated more annual revenue than even the McKinsey report would have dared to predict. And now it was owned by a supportive and effective parent company that understood media, brand, and synergy. Truly, ESPN had become what it had long claimed to be, which was the worldwide leader in sports.

With size and success, however, there is the danger of complacency or arrogance. As Jim Collins states in his new book (*How the Mighty Fall: And Why Some Companies Never Give In*, 2009), the first stage of falling is "Hubris born of Success," when companies regard success as an entitlement, and lose sight of the underlying factors that created the success in the first place. Consider the trouble Wal-Mart or Microsoft got into when those companies became giants. Suddenly, the aggressive behavior that helped them secure the pinnacle of success came across differently, no longer admirable but threatening and bullying. ESPN needed to anticipate those kinds of problems and preempt them. It took new voices to warn of the traps that waited ahead and to help ESPN navigate a modified course.

Among those voices was Lee Ann Daly, a young, exceedingly smart, and aggressively articulate executive from the world of New York advertising who brought her emotions, her opinions, and her provocative ideas into every meeting, as though incapable of holding anything back. In the most positive sense, she was a disruptive force in the male-dominated executive ranks at ESPN, able to talk with the boys, and argue just as passionately for her position, but offering a counter view that was often entirely missing from their thinking.

Daly was hired into a senior position in the marketing division around the time of the Disney acquisition to help ESPN expand its business by matching the core competencies of Disney to the brand capability of ESPN. Her advertising experience, focused on branding outside traditional media, was a good fit, so she was thrown into the fray immediately. "We were trying to figure out, 'Okay, Disney has a really strong publishing capability, so what can we do with that? Disney has a really strong sight-based entertainment capability—what can we do with that?'" Very quickly, she found herself working on the ESPNZone franchise, *ESPN The Magazine*, and the relaunches of ESPN2, ESPN Radio, and ESPN.com. She also helped kickstart original entertainment programs such as the *Two Minute Drill* game show.

A lot was changing at ESPN in general. In 1998, Steve Bornstein left his position to head ABC, and George Bodenheimer succeeded him as president. Around the same time, Daly's boss, Judith Fearring, also left ESPN and Bodenheimer tapped Daly to be the new senior vice president of marketing. That's when the mission and brand of the company started to morph ever so gently.

Throughout Bornstein's era, the brand positioning statement of the company had always been expressed through the aggressive idea that ESPN was the worldwide leader in sports. Now, Daly talked to Bodenheimer persistently and persuasively about the need for a humbler mission that connected more directly and intimately with fans. "If your brand doesn't ring true with fans," Daly explained, "then you're messing with that relationship." The fans didn't care whether or not ESPN was the biggest name in sports or the most dominant content provider. The fans actually connected to ESPN's personality. It was the human aspect of that relationship that was important, not ESPN's footprint in the sports world or the extensiveness of its coverage.

To Bornstein that might have sounded like a politically correct attempt to make ESPN seem kinder and gentler. But Bodenheimer, with his understated and quiet personality, was naturally inclined toward Daly's idea of a more humble brand. He thought she was onto something, and he encouraged her to work through the ideas and test them out.

In coming up with new language for ESPN's mission and brand statement, Daly wasn't trying to reinvent the company or rewrite history. Instead, she was trying to connect the language of the brand to the ESPN values that already existed. Having worked closely with Bornstein years before in developing the original mission and values statement, I could have been excused for feeling defensive about efforts to change what had proven to be such a successful formula. But I loved what Lee Ann Daly, along with CAO Ed Durso and a few other executives, developed because it was a simple and perfect expression of what had always made ESPN successful. In Daly's articulation, the brand position statement changed. "We're not the world's biggest sports entertainment company," she said, "We're the world's biggest sports fan, and we exist solely to serve fans wherever they are."

Plenty of people at ESPN had described that personality over the years in exactly those terms. "We are just big sports fans," was a common refrain. ESPN was the guy you talked to at the water cooler about the playoffs. ESPN was the guy you wanted to sit next to at the bar when the big game was on. ESPN was the sports fan you actually liked, one with a sense of humor and a ton of helpful knowledge, not an obnoxious know-it-all. In other words, when it came to sports, ESPN was already humble and it didn't take itself too seriously. So, the new articulation was not a significant departure at all—and that's why it worked so well.

In official language the new/old ESPN mission became expressed as:

To serve sports fans wherever sports are watched,
listened to, discussed, debated, read about or played.

There was nothing radical about the words but their simplicity. It had been the rationale behind launching ESPN.com, for instance, and establishing the magazine and the ESPNZone restaurants. A Web presence made sense because that's where sports fans were gathering to learn more about their teams and their interests. Ditto for a sports-themed restaurant.

Once that articulation was accomplished, the marketing group got to work threading the new brand personality throughout the company. In terms of commercials, promotions, and shows everything was about connecting to fans in a more humble and self-effacing away while still being irreverent and passionate about sports. In reality, this was a challenge. ESPN was genetically programmed toward aggressive self-promotion across all platforms. If a big game was upcoming on ESPN2, every platform the company had, meaning every channel and news show, as well as the radio, web site or magazine, was relentless about letting viewers, readers, listeners, Internet users, or restaurant diners know the time and the place. With all those avenues, ESPN had the equivalent of hundreds of millions of dollars of advertising time available to it, and it spent that money carpet-bombing information. Daly was the first to question whether this was wise. "Do we want to use our ad time to shove information down people's throats or do we want to use it to make people like us more and spend more time with us?" According to Daly's new credo of a humble brand, the right answer was always the second one. On a business level, this also made sense because ad revenue was driven primarily by ratings and if viewers weren't invited in with genuine warmth they might not watch at all.

Still, business is business. A new balance had to be struck between navigating fans toward the information they needed and entertaining those fans in ways that made them "like us more and want to spend more time with us." As an example of how this balance was accomplished, at one point the marketing group started a campaign to inform people about the various times that *SportsCenter* was shown throughout the day. Instead of bombarding viewers with facts and details, the new campaign showed athletes and famous sports fans planning their actual daily lives around the *SportsCenter* schedule. So viewers and readers saw film director Spike Lee, a famous courtside New York Knicks fan, sitting in his library with all his movie and sports memorabilia on the wall, and his desk piled up with scripts, books, and computers. The campaign asked, "Which *SportsCenter* do you watch?" and listed the times and shows. It was a much more interesting and relationship building way of getting the essential information across.

"We needed to talk with fans, not at them," Daly explained. "We wanted to show them what's new and what's next, and take them behind the scenes and make them like us." Often, promotion at ESPN had been too inside, meaning ad spots were aimed not at sports fans but at sports fanatics, people who were in the know, people like the people working at ESPN. So when ESPN ran a commercial about Roger Clemens photocopying the letter "K" over and over, the average or casual sports fan didn't get it, while the avid baseball fan laughed because he or she knew that K's meant "strikeout," that Clemens was one of baseball's strikeout kings, and that he'd given each of his four boys a first name starting with K. The average person at Disney marketing, however, didn't know why that was funny, and it was over the heads of many viewers who would need to turn to their most knowledgeable (and possibly obnoxious) friend, the sports know-it-all, and ask. In its quest for a humbler brand, ESPN needed a persona that didn't talk down to those viewers who weren't in the know. So a new balance was struck. Whereas previously 80 percent of the ads had been directed to people who were keen insiders, by 2001 that mix was more like fifty-fifty.

"The reason for that was simple," Daly said. "We were trying to attract a broader audience." The desire for a broader audience was not just window dressing or busy work. Expanding the brand had become a crucial business need because both the competitive marketplace and the demographic was changing. ESPN may have been the worldwide leader in sports but ESPN's demographic (for the most part, the elusive young affluent male) was being lured from many different angles. On the one hand, a generation of sports fans who had grown up on ESPN were getting married, having babies, developing other interests, and finding their time filled with other activities. On the other hand, there was just so much more out there for them to consume. New cable channels like Discovery, the History Channel, and Bravo were making a strong run with original programming—travel and adventure shows, war documentaries, home improvement programs. The Internet was exploding and becoming a daily part of people's lives. Even "laddish" magazines like *Maxim* and *FHM* were trying to steal food off ESPN's plate. It became important with ESPN's positioning to expand its base by being slightly more inclusive while still satisfying the appetite of the crazed sports fan. It was a tricky balance and it spurred many anxious conversations and meetings because there was the fear that ESPN could go too far and alienate the supremely loyal customer.

In her advocacy for a humbler and more inclusive brand, Daly had George Bodenheimer's ear. With Bornstein, she'd been less easily heard, though she'd never been shy about making her point. For example, once when Daly developed a campaign to promote the X Games that featured Japanese television personalities and cartoon anime—a crazy jumble of noisy and weird stuff—she showed it to the top executives to get their reactions. Bornstein, never hesitant about offering critical feedback, declared that he hated everything about it. Daly answered, "Good. It's not for you." The demographic of the X Games was young males steeped in Japanese-style wackiness; they would *get* the ad and that was more important than Bornstein's tastes. Daly won her point because Bornstein was never resistant to a passionately articulated view. But few others in the company would have had the fortitude to tell Bornstein he was flat-out wrong.

Bodenheimer, however, listened closely to Daly's persuasive arguments. He knew she was an asset in building a brand and he acted on much of what she had to say, partly because what she had to say was consistent with what he had been thinking. That was where his leadership style differed so radically from Bornstein's. Like any CEO, he was not an expert in many of the fields that his executives were working in, but that was never a source of insecurity or concern. He didn't intrude or try to mark a project with his own fingerprints. Instead, he put people he trusted into positions of responsibility and let good work happen. The more experience I have behind the scenes in executive boardrooms, the more impressed I am by Bodenheimer's ease as a leader. Don't underestimate the guts it takes for a top executive to let go of the details and be persuaded by a counter-argument when the ultimate responsibility for the outcome of a strategy rests on his or her shoulders.

Leveraging

A brand is not just a message or an advertising campaign or an extension of the enterprise into restaurants or web sites. A brand is ultimately about product, which in the case of ESPN means programming. As ESPN's brand shifted in the late 1990s, it needed new programming to match the change that was taking place or it would risk mixing its messages badly. Just in time, another indispensable young executive talent arrived to take programming in new directions and to new heights.

Mark Shapiro understood the shift in brand better than anyone and physically lifted ESPN out of a rut and onto a new path. How did he do it? First, you have to understand that Shapiro is an entertainment industry phenom. If he were a political aide, he'd be the whiz kid who turned the unknown congressman into a presidential candidate. If he were an athlete, he'd be the kind of talent who took a perennially high-drafting team to a championship in a few short years.

When he graduated from college in 1993, Shapiro immediately jumped into sports television production, working for NBC Sports on the west coast. A year later, he got a call from a friend who let him know ESPN was looking to expand its presence out west. That was around the time of the ESPN2 launch, and one of the feature programs on the new channel was going to be called *Talk 2 with Jim Rome*, based out of Los Angeles. Shapiro got an interview, and was offered a position as a production assistant. It was practically entry-level, and a major step back—a lower rank, half the salary, no benefits, and only six months guaranteed employment. But still, he was tempted and discussed the merits of such a "big haircut" with his father. If the new show worked, he explained, and ESPN2 survived, there might be a lot more opportunity at ESPN than NBC Sports because of the way the network was growing. Shapiro figured it would take him 10 years to become a producer at NBC and maybe only 6 at ESPN. It was true that salaries and production budgets were lower, and cable was frowned upon as an inferior television product, but his gut told him the future was cable. His father agreed with the soundness of that reasoning and Shapiro called ESPN back to accept the offer.

Instead of six years, it only took Shapiro six months to become producer. He went from holding cables and operating cameras to running shows almost overnight. The ratings took off, and it was clear that Jim Rome was on his way to becoming a major broadcast talent.[1] Six months later, Shapiro was given a more established show in big ratings trouble and asked to turn it around. He managed that in short order, too, and the career ascent continued. Unlike the major networks where seniority was given a lot of weight, ESPN believed in rewarding performance with opportunity. Throughout his career at ESPN, Shapiro was held up publicly as an example of how far and how fast talent could take you at a network where performance and attitude was all that mattered.

In 1997, Shapiro was offered an opportunity at Bristol. The year 2000 was approaching and every media company was doing something to mark that momentous passage. Chronicling the century was a popular theme as TV channels, web sites, and magazines developed lists of the best movies, the best music, the best cars, you name it. ESPN, as the self-designated world-leader-in-sports, figured it should be the one to define the century in athletics. The vague idea was to look back at 100 years of sporting events and sports heroes, and cover all that in a multitude of ways. But Bristol needed someone to head that project up. Shapiro was only 26 years old, and nobody had him in mind for the top job, but Bornstein asked him to come in and interview for the number two position. Brazenly, Shapiro told his girlfriend (soon to be his wife) that he was going out there to get the big job, and if he didn't get it, he wasn't moving to Bristol.

As it happens, luck broke Shapiro's way. Three of the top candidates for the number one spot, all noted documentary filmmakers, had to drop out of consideration for various reasons. In his three-hour interview, Shapiro met Bornstein and Bill Creasy for the first time, as well as the heads of all the divisions that would be affected by the project. For Creasy, it was love at first sight. Meeting Shapiro reminded him of meeting the young Steve Bornstein back in Columbus, Ohio. Bornstein was impressed, too. The others on the interview panel were resistant to hiring Shapiro because he was so young and inexperienced, but Creasy and Bornstein had a strong feeling about him. Ten days later, they decided to offer Shapiro the job and throw him into the fire. The project was about to die for lack of leadership, so why not hand it over to the one person who was eager, available, and apparently capable of anything?

"I called it SportsCentury," Shapiro said. With a $25 million budget, the SportsCentury project would ultimately encompass 100 hours of programming on ESPN, ABC, ESPN2, and ESPN Classic while touching all of ESPN's other platforms, including significant pieces on the web site, four quarterly supplements in *ESPN The Magazine*, and an interactive exhibit that toured malls around the country. It won an Emmy and the first Peabody Award (the revered prize for excellence in radio and television broadcasting) ever achieved by ESPN.

Just as impressive as far as Bornstein and Bodenheimer were concerned was the fact that the SportsCentury project turned out to be profitable and it provided a how-to manual for leveraging ESPN's many platforms in an integrated way. What I mean is that SportsCentury had a component across the entire spectrum of ESPN's programming and this made it easier to market and sell the company's offerings. For an ESPN ad exec, for example, SportsCentury provided sales applications at multiple points, from the magazine to online to the radio to four different television channels. For someone in affiliate sales, SportsCentury bolstered the argument that ESPN's multiple channels made sense bundled together, even as they offered distinctive features. Perhaps most importantly, SportsCentury allowed ESPN to stake its claim as worldwide leader in sports across an entire century, including 79 years in which it had never existed. Talk about expanding a brand.

Bodenheimer was leading ESPN by then, and he was the one who made the SportsCentury project happen despite an organization's natural reluctance to allow anyone, let alone a newly hired 26-year-old producer, dip in and out across platforms. Shapiro got the credit for taking the ball and running with it, as they say in both sports and business. With that accomplishment to his credit, the opportunities at ESPN continued to open up. Since Shapiro had been immersed in the history of sports for 12 months, it only made sense to hand ESPN Classic over to Shapiro next. Classic had been faltering since its launch, gaining little traction with affiliate cable providers. Over the course of 18 months, Shapiro and his team turned affiliates and advertisers around on the value of ESPN Classic, more than doubling its reach to 55 million homes.

At that time, Lee Ann Daly was developing a more humble brand for ESPN, articulating a message through a series of campaigns that communicated to more general viewers. Shapiro, as a programming talent with some huge trophies under his arm, was one of the first to really see the potential of that move. "The strategy was starting to gain momentum," he noted. "We had the hard-core fans. But we needed to reach out to the casual sports fan, and we wanted more female viewers."

It's long been believed by entertainment and news executives that casual fans, and especially female viewers, are more drawn in by stories than by actual live events. That's why news coverage has reduced the amount of hard fact reporting, and replaced it increasingly with more narrative approaches by tying events to stories about the people affected by them and conducting lengthy personal interviews. In sports, that's why the coverage of such costly mega-events as the Olympics has come to include so many biography segments. Casual viewers are less interested in high jump attempts than they are in background stories of difficult journeys, dramatic turning points, and overcoming hardships.[2]

Fundamentally, ESPN had always been in the business of telling stories. Whether talking about upcoming games or background issues or reviewing highlights, ESPN anchors, reporters, and play-by-play announcers are good story tellers. But Bodenheimer knew there was an entire universe of great stories and documentaries related to sports that could broaden ESPN's appeal with new audiences and across different genres. ESPN had created an original programming unit to do so. For six months the new group faltered, but Shapiro had his eye on it, and believed the idea would be a winner with the right programming and leadership. So he asked to take the helm and Bodenheimer agreed, allowing Shapiro, at age 31, to include Original Entertainment with his responsibilities at ESPN Classic. Shapiro ran with it, and suddenly ESPN found itself in the business of producing original documentaries and scripted dramas.

Some viewed that as a radical shift for ESPN. Sports talk show hosts and hardcore fans derided the idea of ESPN making documentaries and fictional programs. ESPN was a sports broadcasting company, not a Hollywood studio. But critics overlooked the fact that ESPN had always considered itself to be in the business of entertainment as well as sports. The name itself stands for Entertainment and Sports Programming Network, after all. Former CEO Roger Werner, for one, considered the move to create original programming to be an echo of the early strategy of the enterprise, not a radical departure. For Shapiro, the balance was never in question. "Original programming was going to constitute 7 percent of the overall pie. We're not talking about MTV getting away from music videos. It was just a new blend, a nice shift in the balance."

It was 2002 and ESPN ratings had been falling for about two years. The reasons were complex. As Lee Ann Daly noted, some of that related to changing demographics, some to the explosion of new cable offerings and the diversions of the Internet and new magazines. But another contributing factor was that ESPN had become a victim of its own success. Securing rights to the NFL and Major League Baseball—an accomplishment by any measure—had used up a lot of revenue that might have gone to other sports programming. Meanwhile, franchises that ESPN had helped launch and popularize eventually became too expensive for ESPN to continue producing.

The first scripted program Shapiro's group produced was a drama about legendary college basketball coach Bobby Knight, called *Season on the Brink*, based on the terrific book by John Feinstein. In many ways, the production saga was a learning experience. There were plenty of problems, including issues with the director. But Shapiro was emphatic about getting the show on the air. ESPN drew heat for the amount of profanity in the broadcast, though anyone familiar with

Bobby Knight's conversation style knows that not including profanity would have stretched the bounds of the imagination. On that issue, however, ESPN made creative use of its multiple platforms. The movie was simulcast on ESPN2 with the swear words bleeped out. Critically, the movie was panned, but the ratings were a major success, achieving a combined rating better than a typical Yankees/Red Sox Sunday night MLB game and much, much cheaper to produce.

Without even looking at the ratings, however, Shapiro knew the original programming strategy was a success. On the Friday before the broadcast, *Season on the Brink* was the subject of a big article on the front page of the *USA Today* Life section. Now the ESPN brand was being talked about in circles where it had never managed to penetrate before. As Shapiro explained, "That's casual fans. That's female viewers. That's brand building. That was part of our goal, to expand the brand, to make sure that anyone who thinks of sports in any way—the fanatic or the casual fan, the recreational athlete or the retail consumer—thinks of ESPN first. We wanted to build the brand so that it's synonymous with sports, and that's what fueled original programming."

It was another feather in the cap for Shapiro, who would soon be offered a position no one except a president of ESPN had ever held before. Bodenheimer, with the moxy of a supremely confident top executive, gave Shapiro responsibility for all programming and production at the network. Like many great executives I have worked with over the years, Shapiro is a hungry student, which Bodenheimer was well aware of—he knew he was great, and would only get better. Shapiro was constantly leveraging the expertise of others, including Bill Creasy, one of Borsnstein's mentors, Don Hurta, who you will read about in Chapter 7, and myself. He is always in the process if refining his leadership. The promotion vaulted him over the heads of other executives with more seniority and responsibility. It was a testament to the cohesion of the executive team, and their commitment to the cause, that everyone recognized Shapiro's talent and supported the move. What's more, the promotion gave Bodenheimer his own Bornstein, and put balance at the top of the ticket.

Stepping into the Change

Organizations seethe with change. Leadership and employees turn over. Demographics shift. Technology evolves and sometimes makes radical leaps. In its first three decades, ESPN has experienced every kind of revolution and evolution that an organization can probably go through, including changes to major partners and ownership. The strategy of expanding the brand was one means by which ESPN has stayed vigorous and active about change, rather than reactive.

Bodenheimer, as well as a number of other key voices inside ESPN have pushed for more diversity at the organization for this very reason. Rosa Gatti, the long term PR executive, Ed Durso, Lee Ann Daly, and Mark Shapiro were among those who understood the need and advocated the change. If expanding the brand meant serving a broader audience of fans, it also meant making sure that all fans were being adequately represented by the programs, the points of view, the on-air talent, and the back-room management.

I'll admit something I probably shouldn't. Intuitively, I know that diversity is critical for long-term business success. However, if you look at the research, the data does not provide compelling proof that diversity truly is a competitive advantage for most organizations. As an old-school consultant, I have had my doubts about the importance of pushing diversity simply for diversity sake. Sometimes it seems a little too PC for my taste. I'm a believer in the meritocracy, which in its purest form recognizes, rewards, and promotes based on performance—not color, gender, sexual orientation, looks, ethnicity, weight, hair length, and so on. But I've heard articulate and convincing arguments by people like Gatti, Daly, and Shapiro that have opened my eyes and made me question my meritocratic views. As Shapiro put it, "Not only is diversity the morally or ethically right thing to do, but it's the right thing to do from a business perspective, too. You can't serve your viewers if you don't reflect your viewers. And it's not just skin color, it's diversity of thought, background, ethnicity, and perspective. If you're going to tell a story about the great Roberto Clemente, for example, you're not going to get it right if it's all white men in the room making the decisions. You can't capture the total impact of someone like that without knowing how he affected people from his region, background, and culture."

Shapiro is a big believer in making diversity an organizational priority. As a rule, he has insisted for a long time that his managers always hire the best candidate for a job, but that they make sure the pool of candidates has been expanded enough to include top people from diverse backgrounds. It's not enough for organizations to engage in the equivalent of the Dan Rooney (owner of the Pittsburgh Steelers) rule, whereby a single minority candidate has to be interviewed for every position. Managers have to stretch harder, find more and better applicants, and fill the ranks internally so that the succession pool is big and well stocked.

I think ESPN has come a long way on the practice of diversity, particularly when compared to other organizations. I know it has tried and I know it hasn't fulfilled everyone's expectations. But the reality is that sports, and Bristol, Connecticut, attracts certain applicants more than others. I don't know if everyone at ESPN feels the importance of the issue in their bones—we all come to work with our own blind spots and formative backgrounds. But I do think ESPN is generally ahead of the curve, and much of it is due to the fact that senior leadership, particularly Bodenheimer, understands the value at every level. Think about the female sports announcers, reporters, and anchors now working in the industry. I'm sure most women know there's still a long way to go, but the number and quality of the talent at ESPN and other sports networks is impressive.

Expanding the brand was a step ESPN had to take, and it's probably a critical step in the life cycle of any organization. You start with your well-known corner of the world, populated by your most passionate true believers. But eventually, if you're lucky and successful, you outgrow your old turf, and need to seek out more space. Hopefully, you do it in such a way that you don't hollow out your core.

In Bornstein's day, ESPN was filled with irreverent sports fans who were all about sports and little about themselves. But Bornstein knew that ESPN had to become a business to be successful, and so he focused his executives on what Jim Collins (in *Good to Great*) calls a "Big Hairy Audacious Goal"—becoming the worldwide leader in sports. ESPN needed a chip on its shoulder. It needed an insecure overachiever's desire for ultimate success. That was Bornstein's personality, too. By Bodenheimer's day, ESPN was the epitome of a successful business and needed to connect with that deeper sense of purpose as to why ESPN mattered. Essentially, he said, "We can't forget why we're here. We are a business. We've built this incredible institution, but we're doing this for the fans because we're just big sports fans ourselves. It's not about ESPN, it's about the sports, and it's about the fans." This is what drove the expansion of the brand. Business books are loaded with cases where companies have diluted, cannibalized, or even destroyed their brands because attempts at expansion were driven solely by short-term economic opportunism, rather than long-term customer service. Expanding the brand, making it humbler and more open, was a huge part of such a shift for ESPN. The move didn't negate the earlier evolution of the company or its success; it just helped the company look at the same world from a relational point of view. It reacquainted ESPN with the idea that what really mattered was the people, on both sides of the television camera.

CHAPTER FIVE KEY POINTS

"Let the mission drive the brand, not vice versa"
The mission of ESPN is to serve fans everywhere. When considering various brand extensions, they simply ask, "Will this help us serve our fans?" The clearer and more committed an organization is around its mission, the easier the decision making is around brand extension.

"Be more aggressive about protecting the brand than expanding the brand"
Established brands are sacred, and the integrity of the brand will impact your business for generations to come. Be clear and

strategic about what you will attach your brand to, but even more clear about what you will never attach to your brand, even if it appears lucrative at the time.

"When you get big, go humble"

With size and success, there is an inherent danger of complacency and/or arrogance. Believe it or not, it is easier to be the hunter than the hunted. Be humble at the top and develop a sense of appreciation in your culture. Never forget, if you are a dominant player in a given space, competitors will want to bring you down. But you are more likely to fail because you beat yourself.

"People behind the brand must reflect people in front of the brand"

Diversity has become a moral (or political) imperative to many great organizations today. At ESPN, diversity is a solid business and cultural imperative. Some may say that ESPN was a bit behind in this area, but I would argue that their belief drove their behavior. Many organizations simply behaved before they believed, which is why so many diversity initiatives have had such limited impact.

Chapter 6

PLAYING WELL WITH OTHERS

Sports is used as a metaphor for business so often, it sounds like a cliché. Sure, there are plenty of parallels. Organizations are like teams. Successful teams are composed of talented individuals and key role players, with the right chemistry thrown in and a good tactical motivator at the helm. An industry marketplace is like a league in which those teams compete. Now, go out there and win the game!

But, of course, both sports and business are a lot more complicated than that. In business today, for example, establishing good chemistry with the people you work with doesn't stop at the office lobby. Unlike a team on a playoff run, you don't have the luxury of an us versus the world mentality when it comes to partners, suppliers, and customers. You need to be skilled at developing relationships that bring value to all parties. In other words, if the partnership is strictly transactional in nature, in that it is simply a deal-based exchange, it will be unlikely that the relationship will be fully utilized. It is when relationships are transformational in nature, where the exchange is intended to create and realize long-term value for all, that all parties realize true synergy and mutual benefit.

If this critical capability to play well with others had been lacking at ESPN, the organization never would have made it. In some ways, that might seem counterintuitive to the ESPN culture. Fired up on the testosterone of competition and winning, seeing itself with plenty of justification as an underdog that received no respect from the rest of the industry, finding itself blocked at many turns by competitors and gatekeepers with hostile intent, ESPN could have been a bitter and secretive sort of company, focused only on its own needs. Instead, ESPN was forced by its circumstances and by the necessity of its Serve Fans mission to be in the business of partnering well. In fact, the attitude toward outside relationships has always been that if a program offering, deal, or financial arrangement doesn't work well for all parties involved, it won't work at all.

Playing Well with Owners

The truism of family life is that you can't pick your parents. (Parents, of course, know you can't pick your kids, either.) For CEOs and top executives, it's easy to believe that ownership is also something beyond your control. But the broad mix of ownership situations ESPN has found itself in, and the success it has gained through each circumstance, shows us that something can be done to leverage a relationship with practically any owner.

At the level of programming and production, ESPN acts and operates like an entity beholden to no master. But even before the red light went on in September 1979, ESPN has always been owned by one or more other companies. The first installment of that ownership cycle was born of desperation. A start-up with no principal backer is more like an orphan than an offspring and has only limited ability to choose its shelter from the storm. For ESPN, support came from the unlikely hands of Getty Oil and its principal representative in charge of non-core assets, Stuart Evey. The oil business was turbulent in the late 1970s, much like today, but the high price of oil meant producers like Getty were flush with cash and looking to diversify. ESPN never would have been a destination for that money if it weren't for Evey's passion for sports and interest in the potential of cable television. That's been a secret weapon of ESPN since its inception—the organization draws sports and media fanatics like lights attract moths, and key figures in ownership groups are no exception. The initial $10 million of Getty money was so desperately needed that founder Bill Rasmussen sealed his own fate when he signed the deal. He relinquished ownership of his precious venture so that it could survive, and soon saw himself escorted out the door as the organization moved on.

Evey, as I've said, was as hands-on an owner-representative as you could get in business. Like Dallas Cowboys owner Jerry Jones, he practically stalked the sidelines, cheering the team on, yelling at coaches, congratulating or consoling players even during the game. But as the controlling authority for the business, he had two inestimable virtues. First, he was skilled at managing the expectations and the support of the Getty executive team. Like a founder himself, he believed passionately in the mission even beyond all rational assessment. Despite the risks to his own career, he returned to the Getty well over and over again for additional funding when ESPN would have sunk otherwise. And he skillfully held off any doubts and questions that might have come from Getty headquarters, sparing the ESPN executives from the pressure of that additional burden. Although Evey was no gentle angel in personality, he knew the ESPN management team had enough to worry about and protected them like a mother bear protects her cubs.

Second, Evey understood the importance of putting good people in charge of your asset. In this, he established the conditions for future success, a service ESPN should appreciate forever. The top people Evey installed were special. Unlike executives at Silicon Valley start-ups these days, ESPN executives and managers weren't financially vested in the profitability of the company. And yet, they had the character and professional commitment to bust their bodies and brains for ESPN as if their own financial legacy was on the line. What's more, they hired key people who felt the same way, installing a generation of leadership that carried the ESPN culture forward.

The survival and success of ESPN shows that getting the right people involved in a start-up should be the first principle of good ownership. Personalities of owners and managers can vary as widely as the circumstances an organization faces. But ESPN demonstrated how much value an asset can achieve when good people are put in position to succeed. In turn, the ESPN leadership, from those early days until now, has always made it an unspoken principle to create a climate in which everyone is focused on the business of serving fans, not on the issues of owners or backers.

The difficulty of going to the well at Getty for such hefty investments wore on Evey and he was anxious to show some kind of return if the opportunity arose. He maintained his poker face, however, as the major networks started poking around ESPN in late 1979. By then, the realization of cable's potential was beginning to dawn on the conservative network heads. ESPN may have been sniffed at publicly by the television industry as a loser upstart, but the possibility of its survival and the potential value of the sports niche it championed was becoming apparent. Each of the big three networks had made investments into cable at that time with limited success. Perhaps they were hampered as much by their concern over offending local affiliates as they were by their own corporate sluggishness. ESPN as an established asset in the cable world began to look somewhat attractive, even if it was bleeding money.

Evey claims that he manufactured interest in ESPN by hinting to both NBC and ABC that each of the other networks was looking to take control from Getty. It was easy for a network to imagine that Getty might have lost its taste for the TV business. That didn't necessarily mean ESPN was a bad investment or an unworkable idea to a company that knew television well. ABC was the more creative and risk-oriented enterprise of the big three; and Roone Arledge, who had launched *Wide World of Sports* and brought the Olympics to the network, was curious. Apparently with Arledge's encouragement, ABC executives Herb Granath and Fred Pierce flew to Evey's office to try and make a deal. After a minimal back and forth, Evey sold 10 percent of ESPN's equity to ABC for $20 million, with an option to increase to 15 percent. ABC had deep pockets, and the purchase made sense as a way of expanding its sports offerings on cable without going through the struggle of launching another channel.

For Evey, the sale parried the growing concern at Getty that he was dabbling at ESPN as if it were his own hobby and wasting good capital on a poor investment. Suddenly, he'd established a price point for the channel that pegged its overall value at something attractive to Getty. Suddenly, ESPN was worth $2 million a point, doubling Getty's initial investment with only a 10 percent stake. In theory, Getty could recoup its total investment, earn a healthy profit, and still maintain control of ESPN by selling 49 percent of the business. In reality, the handshake with ABC may have been simple, but negotiations over rights and fees were complicated, and kept the money out of Getty's coffers for more than six months. But finally, ABC got its stake, Getty got its cash, and Evey got to breathe.

For ESPN, the deal was mostly positive with some potential downside. On the good side, an investment stake from a major network was an important sign of industry recognition and credibility. Since its inception, ESPN had been struggling in the hinterlands, earning nothing but disdain. Perhaps more important from a product point of view, having a television industry partner in the mix gave ESPN a better opportunity to access sports programming. Presumably all the cast-offs and scraps of sports coverage that ABC filmed but didn't use in its limited programming hours would be there for the taking by ESPN.

On the downside, there was concern about the meddling of an ownership group that actually knew the business, as well as the complexity of having a minority owner in partnership with a majority owner. What if the two ownership partners didn't get along? It seemed likely that Getty and ABC would commingle about as well as oil and water. According to Evey, Roone Arledge, in particular, had turned cold on the relationship by the time the celebratory party was held. Perhaps he felt it threatened or demeaned his sports franchise at ABC. But those issues were beyond the pay grade of the management at ESPN, so there was nothing to do but put their heads down and get back to work. In any event, the brutal schedule and the relentless demands of the enterprise required it.

As I mentioned, the trouble with ownership is that most of the time you can't pick your owners. This reality was emphasized to ESPN in 1984 when Getty Oil was purchased by Texaco. In an infamous contretemps, the takeover was extremely messy because Getty had established a deal in principle with Pennzoil to sell its assets before the Texaco deal was signed, in effect selling itself twice. Texaco had to leverage itself to the hilt to complete the $11 billion deal, one of the largest corporate transactions to that point in history. Accordingly, it was anxious to sell off all noncore assets immediately. A little television sports network in Bristol didn't rank in their strategic vision for the mammoth new venture.

ESPN's top executives saw an opportunity. The lack of any personal ownership stake had never stopped them from doing their jobs, but it did occasionally work its way up into the throat and stick there with regret. Roger Werner, in particular, was keenly aware of how much value the leadership team was creating, and how little they were earning in compensation. Werner and Bornstein visited one of their cable affiliates, Capital Cities, and talked to CEO Tom Murphy about supporting ESPN employees in buying ESPN from Texaco.

Capital Cities had a long history in cable, beginning in 1947 when it was called the Hudson Valley Broadcasting Company. It also had a long history as an aggressive purchaser of other media companies such as local affiliates around the country, radio stations, and even newspapers. To Werner and Bornstein, Capital Cities were great operators and would make terrific partners going forward. Tom Murphy also sat on the Texaco board, so it seemed possible he would know the right strings to pull to make such a purchase possible. Werner and Bornstein made their pitch, describing their view of the value of the asset, the future plans, and their belief in the quality of Capital Cities management. They'd buy ESPN themselves in a heartbeat, but they lacked the wherewithal to make the deal happen. Murphy listened, but seemed unimpressed. "It's a nice idea, but we have bigger things we're looking at," he told them. And Werner and Bornstein went back to Bristol without a deal.

They soon had other worries. Texaco was making no secret of its desire to unload ESPN. The most active interest came from Ted Turner, the cable mogul from Atlanta. Turner's vision was to combine ESPN with CNN and TBS—joining sports to movies and news—and create a superstation he could offer to cable operators for a dollar per subscriber. It was a brilliant plan. Grimes, Werner, and Bornstein flew to Atlanta to meet with Turner and discuss the numbers. Turner set what he believed to be a winning price on ESPN at over $280 million.

With its minority stake, ABC had the right to match and, to Turner's surprise, did just that. ABC had its reasons. Its own cable channel news station was failing and the success of CNN and the brash and loud Turner (the so-called mouth from the south) was probably an irritating reminder of that. They didn't want him stealing ESPN away from their control. Texaco unloaded ESPN at Turner's price to ABC. The deal earned almost $70 million of pure profit for what Getty had poured in over five years, not a bad return for Stuart Evey's investment.

Briefly, ESPN was fully owned by ABC. Unfortunately, ABC was already in trouble. Its share price was being hit hard on Wall Street and its overall operations were already encumbered by its size and the concern about its management team. Looking to lessen some of the pain, ABC decided to offload 20 percent of ESPN to Nabisco, the venerable biscuit and cookie maker, of all companies. ABC got $3 million a point for the equity stake, however, or $60 million, a 50 percent premium over the price set a year before, so it felt pretty good about the deal.

Now, instead of having a single parent, ESPN was quickly back in the hands of two businesses, one in and one outside the media industry. Within a few years, another upheaval took place. A change in FCC policies regarding media ownership opened the door for some new blood among the big networks. Tom Murphy hadn't been kidding when he said that Capital Cities had bigger and bolder moves in mind than a purchase of ESPN. In 1986, with the financial support of Warren Buffett, Capital Cities bought ABC, an organization that was far bigger and more prominent than itself. Then, just as that purchase had finished rattling the world of television, RJ Reynolds, the tobacco company from Winston-Salem, North Carolina, bought Nabisco. RJR Nabisco, the cookie and cigarette company, was itself a target a year later when the private equity firm KKR launched a hostile takeover bid in a leveraged buyout and picked up the business for an astounding $20 billion and an incredible amount of debt.

Once again, ESPN was the little asset that nobody wanted. Over the next few months, dozens of suitors made pitches for RJR Nabisco's 20 percent stake in ESPN. Bornstein practically begged Tom Murphy to snatch the shares up, but Murphy didn't believe in the business 100 percent. ESPN had just done an extremely expensive baseball deal, through which it was losing millions of dollars, and Murphy was skeptical that

ESPN's subscription revenue would ever outstrip the costs of the sports TV business. According to Bornstein, Murphy acknowledges that passing up full ownership of ESPN was one of the biggest financial mistakes of his storied career. In the end, the 20 percent stake was sold to Hearst Publishing for $170 million, almost three times what Nabisco paid for it.

In less than a decade, ESPN had gone through more ownership upheaval than seemed healthy. Going from Getty, to Getty and ABC, to Texaco and ABC, to ABC on its own, to ABC and Nabisco, to ABC and RJR Nabisco, to Capital Cities and RJR Nabisco, to Capital Cities and Hearst, meant a lot of shuffled seats around the board table. And yet, ESPN seemed untouched or unfazed by all that commotion, and was still proceeding on course toward fulfilling its long-term strategic objective of becoming the worldwide leader in sports, profitably. The reason was a combination of solid support and benign neglect. ESPN had been owned by a series of companies with bigger and more complex concerns. As long as ESPN management seemed competent and forward-directed—which they were in full—ownership executives could concentrate on other problems. On the financial front, remarkably, all the majority or minority ownership partners were always willing to reinvest dividends earned by ESPN.

In Capital Cities/ABC and Hearst, finally, ESPN had a solid rational ownership situation for the first time. In particular, Tom Murphy, the chairman of Capital Cities, and Dan Burke, his CEO successor, proved to be excellent overseers of the ESPN asset. In some ways, the legendary duo saw the world as ESPN did. Murphy had a great educational pedigree and could have worked anywhere, but chose to work for a small bankrupt UHF station in upstate New York because it gave him a chance to run something—a decision that seems in kind with the moves of a Bornstein or a Shapiro, who saw opportunity in cable decades later. In a hardscrabble operation, Murphy understood production and budget restraints, but he managed to succeed and grow the company many times over.

Murphy and Burke were not into extravagances, didn't approve of big salaries and bloated management teams, and favored sparse and efficient operations as much as possible. Indeed, ABC, which was not lean and mean, faced big cuts under their stewardship. But Murphy and

Burke were also not afraid to spend money when the risk was worth it. As bosses, they believed in hiring good people and letting them do their jobs unimpeded. They held managers accountable, but there was support. You could make big decisions as long as they were smart and well-reasoned. You could make big mistakes as long as they were honest mistakes. The cardinal sin in their world was dishonesty, and such betrayals brought immediate banishment.

With admiration, Warren Buffett called them "models of pleasant rationality"[1] and said they were like having "Ruth and Gehrig on your team."[2] He put his 18 percent shares in their hands as proxy. Bornstein, who was CEO during the Capital Cities/ABC reign, loved working for Murphy and Burke, and respected both men immensely. He didn't always agree with them, and he was frustrated from time to time with their resistance to putting big dollars into the business, but the independence of decision making and the entrepreneurial spirit they encouraged allowed ESPN to flourish during its most significant growth period throughout the early and mid-1990s. Murphy, in turn, was openly appreciative of ESPN. As he put it, "Capital Cities bought ABC because we thought we could run the television stations and make more money, which we did. But the thing that has actually been a huge break for us is the continual growth of ESPN. It has gone from losing $40 million to losing $20 million to breaking even to making $50 million to making $100 million. Now it's in the stratosphere."[3]

Murphy and Burke were always in business to make money for shareholders, and they were resistant to some of Bornstein's more expensive plans like buying up the regional sports affiliates across the country. The opportunity came in 1996 when Michael Eisner, in the middle of his turnaround of Disney, decided to get into the content distribution game and purchase a major network. Capital Cities/ABC looked like a good match, but Murphy and Burke knew Eisner could buy another network if he chose, and they did not relish such a competitor. After some tough negotiations, they struck a deal for $19 billion that was half cash, half stock, and Capital Cities (now called ABC again) entered the Disney fold.

Aside from the distribution of Disney programming on a major network, ESPN was the most valuable asset that Cap Cities owned, as far as Eisner was concerned. As far as the ABC and ESPN managers were concerned, Disney promised to be a very different kind of majority owner. There was continuity. Because Dan Burke retired, Tom Murphy returned as CEO of ABC and joined the Disney board. Other top talent at ABC were quickly brought into the top ranks at Disney. Indeed, Bornstein would be embraced by Eisner at first and made the head of ABC, and was for a time treated like a favorite son and potential successor at Disney. But there was also fear and anxiety. Murphy and Burke had been hands-off and supportive managers to a degree that is rare in American business. Michael Eisner, for all his creative acumen, was anything but a hands-off manager and could be extremely challenging with his management style. How would that change the mode of operation at ESPN?

Ultimately, any substantive fears were unfounded. Sure, individual personalities clashed and territory got redistributed, usually in ESPN's favor. Cap Cities had never interfered with ABC, but Disney quickly gave ESPN total control over ABC's sports franchise. But more than any issues of management or operations, Disney, which had the best brand in family entertainment and one of the most recognizable brands in the world, understood how valuable ESPN's brand was with the young male demographic. To Disney's credit, Disney let those two brand strengths coexist without interference. What's more, Disney gave ESPN immensely deep pockets, and the ability to buy or launch whatever it needed.

After so much change in its first 15 years, ESPN has had the same ownership group now for over 10 years, and it's working. Disney, as a media entity, is a giant, but a thriving one. ESPN has firmed up its preeminent status in sports under Disney's watch. Many tumultuous personalities have left the scene, and men who are "models of pleasant rationality," to recall Warren Buffett's words, now rule the day. In fact, George Bodenheimer's humble and self-effacing leadership style is a perfect match with Disney CEO, Bob Iger, who was groomed at ABC in the style of Tom Murphy and Dan Burke, and would have likely led their company if the merger with Disney had never happened. The Iger style and the ESPN experience served Disney well with the acquisition of Pixar in 2007. Negotiations restarted shortly after Iger became CEO, rescuing a relationship that looked to be headed for a very ugly divorce when Michael Eisner was in charge. Once again, a potential clash of cultures was avoided. As Iger explained, "There is an assumption in the corporate world that you need to integrate swiftly. My philosophy is exactly the opposite. You need to be respectful and patient."[4] Indeed, like ESPN taking over ABC's sports franchise, Disney has been secure enough to let Pixar leadership take over its precious animation studios.

In the end, the lessons of ownership seem simple. As much as possible, plow profits back into the business. Always be supportive of investments that improve the product and the market position of the company. And be content to let bright, capable managers work unimpeded in running the business. In return, ESPN has demonstrated how to leverage its ownership situation to its advantage. With Getty, that was about money. With ABC, it was about becoming a more credible sports programmer. And with Disney, it has been about maximizing the strength of the brand.

Playing Well with Business Partners

Almost more critical than its relationship with owners, ESPN has had to play well with its business partners. From day one, ESPN needed sports leagues and cable operators simultaneously. It needed content partners to satisfy its distribution partners but it also needed distribution partners for its content partners. Bornstein called it the one-two punch. The trick was convincing each side that the other was on board and making it all happen somehow at once.

College sports was the first step, and made sense as a relatively neglected area that underserved fans were clamoring for. In his proposal to the NCAA leadership group, Bill Rasmussen's proposal was all about meeting the NCAA's needs, not ESPN's. ESPN wanted to complement NCAA coverage, not threaten the relationships it had with the big networks. ESPN wanted to deepen and broaden NCAA coverage to include more sports and more schools over an entire year, not just when those sports were in network demand. When it came to fees, ESPN promised to tie the amount it paid to the NCAA to the growth in subscribers at ESPN. In other words, it was in the best interests of both parties to have a successful relationship. With that deal in place, Rasmussen was able to convince cable operators to carry the ESPN signal into homes. The relationship with cable operators was basically hat in hand. If ESPN was able to pay the affiliate fee and deliver content it would get the privilege of broadcasting its signal into the homes controlled by the cable operators.

It's widely acknowledged that ESPN survived because it secured NCAA football and basketball games. In particular, televising the early rounds of March Madness gave ESPN a cult following among passionate fanatics in offices and college dorms. But it's also true that ESPN coverage helped the NCAA immensely. Rights fees for the big sports have brought in hundreds of millions of dollars annually and helped fund many less popular sports and made excellence in those athletics possible. As Bornstein said, "We did a terrific job, there's no ifs, ands, or buts, but I think ESPN made a really positive contribution to the NCAA's popularity."

Rasmussen got ESPN into the broadcasting game through deals with the NCAA and the cable operators. Over the next couple of years, like a poor cousin, ESPN learned to live off the scraps of the major networks and the various leagues, aiming to please at every opportunity and prove its worth. Probably, this was the nature of the beast. Rasmussen's negotiations had not secured ESPN enough benefits, but ESPN had little to no negotiating leverage. Going forward, ESPN needed to benefit as much as its partners for an arrangement to make sense.

The most significant juncture in ESPN's history, and the turning point for the enterprise, was the decision to flip the cable affiliate revenue model and begin charging cable operators for the ESPN signal rather than pay cable operators for the same arrangement. I can hardly imagine how difficult this was to propose to cable operators, let alone convince them that it was in their best interests, but ESPN's reasoning was simple. ESPN was not going to survive if the cable operators didn't start funding its broadcast through rights fees. More importantly, the cable industry as a whole was not going to grow, let alone thrive, without those companies chipping in to pay for better content. Household subscribers were signing up for cable because it gave them better reception than the rabbit ears on top of the TV set. But they weren't going to buy an expanded package of offerings unless quality programming was being piped into their homes. They had options. They could stick with the free vanilla programming of the networks. If ESPN and other channels became must-have offerings, though, cable companies could raise their subscription rates and expand their number of households.

In these negotiations, ESPN relied on a multipronged approach. Werner and Bornstein made persistent and convincingly logical arguments about the necessity of the switch. Other top executives served as snarling attack dogs, fighting for the right numbers. But George Bodenheimer, working on affiliate sales from Denver, also showed early signs of his value as a top executive by developing key alliances behind the scenes and building trust among the parties. ESPN could never have brought the cable operators along without those allies. In the end, reason, relationships, and the pressure of hard economic times combined to make the arguments convincing. The cable industry was in upheaval, as many hundreds of companies were quickly shrinking to a few dozen. The survivors needed life preservers and ESPN was offering one. In the end, ESPN achieved its objective of flipping the model. But it was only able to progressively raise its fees over the years because it lived up to its side of the bargain, providing broadcasting content that household cable subscribers felt they needed. At the same time, the surviving cable companies grew rich on the quality of the programming that ESPN and other cable channels were able to deliver because they were finally earning sufficient revenue.

During its early years, ESPN built up its credibility by producing consistent, creative programming and making money for its partners. That credibility paid off when ESPN was given the opportunity to bid on a package of NFL games. Those rights were going to cost serious dollars, and ESPN was in competition for them with a consortium of cable operators. At the same time, ESPN could never have swallowed its potential deal with the NFL without the support of cable operators. An interesting and difficult balance of interests was required.

Bornstein and Bodenheimer came up with a creative plan to buy the package of NFL games, then divide up the costs of the rights fees and pass them on to the cable companies in the form of increased surcharges. Those cable operators would then be able to raise the rates they charged their household subscribers because they had a compelling product to offer. Meanwhile, ESPN would produce the games and sell the national advertising, while cable operators could sell the local advertising. The logic of the plan was beautiful. For ESPN and the cable operators, the arrangement was a classic win–win. ESPN became the first cable channel to show the NFL and was able to swallow the costs by sharing them with the cable operators and make money by building their national advertising accounts. Meanwhile, the cable operators got the NFL for pennies, sold the ad time on local stations, and thrilled their customers. It was the greatest programming to ever hit cable, and football fans loved it.

Once established, the formula for successful partnership with the cable operators became simple and clear. As long as ESPN was continuing to provide must-see programming, cable companies needed to help support ESPN's costs with increased rights fees. In return, cable companies were able to build their asset base and grow their subscribers. The league partners benefited, too, as ESPN became more successful. Major sports like the NFL, MLB, and the NBA got a new outlet in ESPN to compete with the four major networks and drive their rights fees to unparalleled heights. And ESPN produced excellent programming that helped grow the fan base. What's more, between *SportsCenter*, all the various ESPN channels, and the magazine and web site, ESPN had the platforms to promote its programming more aggressively and effectively than a major network.

The circumstances vary, but ESPN also takes a partnership approach with sports franchises that are outside the major sports leagues. With

Arena Football and the WNBA, ESPN has become outright business partners, sharing costs and revenues together. That kind of creative partnering gave those sports a national outlet they wouldn't otherwise have had, and in some cases made their very existence possible. For ESPN, including such sports on the programming schedule helps meet the needs of underserved fans while imprinting its brand over all sports, not just the ones that the major networks cover.

The Battering Ram and the Velvet Glove

ESPN learned a lot from its ownership situations over the years. It learned that mergers and acquisitions work best when two partners value each other's culture, content (products and market), and capabilities. Companies that combine without considering all three realms rarely succeed. Good cultural fit isn't enough without the strategic assets to make the endeavor worthwhile. There is a clear consensus in management research that a merger that looks good on paper doesn't last or meet its potential if the corporate cultures are at odds.

Getty was an ownership partner that could never have lasted long-term because of the tremendous difference in culture. The way Getty made decisions, thought about assets, and looked at market share wouldn't work if applied in the television industry, but Getty had other virtues in terms of how it handled its asset. Capital Cities and Disney were ideal ownership situations because all three realms made sense. As in love, relationships work best and last longest when each party avoids trying to change the other. ESPN benefited from ownership partners that did not impose an alien way of doing business on it. Even Disney, so careful of its brand and so knowledgeable about entertainment, retail, and marketing, was respectful and supportive rather than interfering with ESPN management. Instead, it allowed ESPN to leverage the Disney resources and knowhow that made sense for ESPN's own vision.

ESPN's wins and losses as an owner have followed the same pattern. In the case of its acquisition of Classic Sports, for example, the product was a good fit but the culture was a miss. Even though ESPN Classic is a successful part of the ESPN platform, few of the Classic employees were still with ESPN by the end of the first year. On the other hand, the acquisition of BASS worked well in every aspect. As a niche, sports fishing was a good offering for ESPN, and the BASS leadership and employees have stayed engaged and committed to what ESPN and BASS are trying to do together. Lessons have been learned.

Rupert Murdoch called sports a "battering ram for pay television." In announcing his plans to develop a global pay television network through British Sky Television in 1996, Murdoch explained, "Sport absolutely overpowers film and everything else in the entertainment genre." Murdoch's DirecTV satellite dish system in the United States was also built on providing a package of sports games that sports fanatics couldn't live without, namely the NFL Sunday Ticket.

ESPN has the same battering ram but uses it in different ways. Content and distribution are a game that requires partnerships, but ESPN has always taken the view that such relationships should be win-win. Even with league commissioners and cable owners who hold very different perspectives, ESPN has done a great job of reminding their partners that they all share the same goal—bringing quality sports to the fan. The secret to making sure everyone sees the objective in the same way is to figure out the deal clearly up front and live according to the agreement that was struck. To be sure, at this stage in the game, several negotiations with various partners of ESPN have had their share of strained emotions. Inevitably, each party will think they are being fair, while the other will feel slighted in some way. Unfortunately, most decisions and deals are not black and white, and the subjectivity becomes magnified with emotion. But as my dad said many times, "You'll always succeed in business if you honestly seek to never screw anybody, all the while never allowing yourself to be screwed."

It's been relatively easy for ESPN to see through the thicket of the confusion that naturally grows in business. ESPN looks for every avenue and every option to serve fans better. If that means ESPN should support a competitor, build a partnership, or buy a franchise, then the way forward is clear. This is the power of having such a compelling mission that is embraced by all. Like most successful enterprises, ESPN knows that strategic growth is organic, but driven by a careful matching of internal capabilities and the leveraging of partnerships.

CHAPTER SIX KEY POINTS

"Seek transformational, not transactional, partnerships"
ESPN always had the attitude that if an outside relationship doesn't work well for all parties involved, it won't work at all. It's easy to just do deals, but to do deals that lead to other deals, and ultimately, partnerships, is the high-yield objective. Go into a deal with the hope of developing a lifelong partnership.

"Clarify the goals, roles, and procedures (GRPs) up front"
Most partnerships fail because not enough time, effort, and thought went into clarifying the goals, roles, and procedures up front. Be clear on what each party expects to gain from the relationship, hammer out who will be responsible and accountable for the various aspects of the arrangement, and proactively think how you can best work together—the process and procedures of the relationship.

"Like relationships, partnerships demand work"
In my career, I have witnessed too many partnerships, mergers, and acquisitions fail because so little care and attention was given to the nurturing and development of the relationship. Companies will expend tremendous time, thought, analysis, effort, and capital to create a partnership, then assume that once the deal is done, it's done. In reality, it's just beginning.

Chapter 7

BLOW THE WHISTLE, SPOT THE BALL

When I worked with Steve Bornstein on ESPN's original mission and values statement, I knew we were putting together a document that would have an impact. Despite his skepticism—that harsh questioning before diving in—he took the task very seriously. He considered the character of the organization deeply and thoroughly and then he carefully constructed a blueprint for future success based on the most important qualities and strengths. One of the few key areas Bornstein highlighted was risk taking, the subject of this chapter.

Risk taking had been an element of ESPN's mode since day one. Of course, ESPN was a start-up and an argument could be made that risk is an integral part of any venture launched under uncertain circumstances. But there are plenty of start-ups that are risk-averse. They feel they're not ready yet to take a chance, and must secure more funding or market share, a better balance sheet or credibility before they take big chances. If that were the case at ESPN, this book would be about a small cable channel covering local sports in Connecticut. ESPN's founders and early leaders were never afraid of seizing an opportunity when that also meant seizing enormous risk. From the first major decisions, when Bill Rasmussen elected to go with satellite broadcasting and went national and 24-hour instead of local and limited, opportunities were embraced because they fit with the larger vision. Other leaders like Bill Grimes and Roger Werner embodied that philosophy in their own way, and made it live in the culture of the organization.

When Bornstein articulated that sense of risk in the mission and values statement, here is what he wrote:

> From the start **aggressive thinking** and **risk taking** have been at the heart of our success. We must constantly practice and encourage these qualities to secure our future. We must feel free to honestly disagree with one another while knowing when to treat mistakes as learning opportunities. In our competitive environment, creative risk taking can net us huge rewards.

That was the recipe—the formula ESPN followed. But if we're going to appreciate how well ESPN adhered to that philosophy, it's best not to assess the successes of ESPN, since those are well-known and documented here and elsewhere, but the failures. You can look back at any company's achievements and point to the bold thinking and supportive environment that supposedly contributed to the wins. But what happens when the ball is dropped or the screwup occurs? By definition, risk taking and aggressive thinking cannot always lead to successful outcomes. So how did ESPN handle losing?

Adjust and Make it Work

The early spirit of innovation and risk-taking was only partly due to desperation. There was also a looseness to the place, in spite of the long odds and the difficulties getting money and programming content. Rules and policies were scarce or nonexistent. Even at the strategic level, there was a view that charging toward opportunity was more important than considering all the potential pitfalls. For the young, hungry, and relatively inexperienced people working in production, a sense of "what the hell, no one is watching us anyway" brought a lightness and innovation to the ESPN programs. Different camera angles. New ways of showing the events. Irreverent humor in the broadcasts. The older hands balanced this by being incredibly disciplined around timing, schedules, budgets, and top production values. That yin and yang set in as the organization's way of operating: fun inter-twining with pride. There was no model for how to do things best, but there was always a standard of excellence to maintain and an ambition to achieve.

Roger Werner credits his predecessor Bill Grimes with establishing that tone. The heated, chemically unstable, and inherently desperate days with Rasmussen, Evey, and Simmons were always high pressured and high stakes. It was make good or go home. Grimes was more optimistic, pleasant, and sunny to be around. He brought a sense of fun to the enterprise, and took the pressure off the rank-and-file to whatever extent possible. Most importantly, Grimes instilled a spirit of open-mindedness and creativity, a feeling that you should never be afraid to take chances.

If something didn't work out, that failure was never the subject of an inquisition. The attitude was, "Let's just admit defeat and go on to Plan B." ESPN didn't have the time for lengthy postmortems and it didn't need the emotional baggage. What it needed was speed and forward momentum. Even significant decisions were made without a lot of deliberation and hand-wringing. Moving quickly was more important. The leadership and the management believed it was better to make a midcourse correction than to remain in place and go nowhere in a hurry.

"It was not a fear-driven climate where people were afraid to make mistakes," Werner noted. "It was an opportunity-driven climate where people were encouraged to think creatively, make decisions, and get moving." Grimes may have been more easygoing and above the fray than the analytical Werner, but the style of decision making and risk taking was shared by both men. When Werner assumed the top post, his biggest leadership decision was overturning the affiliate fee payment model that had been industry standard for so long that it might have been written on clay tablets and handed down by Moses. In large areas and small, Werner insisted that what could work better must take precedence over what had always been done. If there was a more creative, efficient, or productive way to do something, then try it. If it didn't work out, try something else.

Bornstein, in turn, continued that trend, working deliberately to foster an organization in which opportunity was the major incentive.

He could be harsh and skeptical in his questioning of an idea or a proposal—so much so that gentle souls withered under the glare—but that kind of rigor was applied to strengthen rather than tear down. If you withstood the assault, he backed you fully, and he never made the failures personal.

When Bornstein looks back on the biggest mistakes of his tenure, he doesn't point to missteps but missed opportunities. The opportunity Bornstein regrets most came when ESPN had the chance to buy stakes in regional sports networks around the country. "I had this dream," Bornstein said, "that would have precluded anybody else from ever taking us on. I always thought that if someone could acquire all the various regional sports outlets, they could cobble together a very effective competitor to ESPN." Cap Cities were supportive owners. They bolstered, through their own cultural practices, ESPN's attitude of encouraging innovation. But Cap Cities did not understand programming like ESPN did and they did not like to spend money when it did not align with their larger plans. So Bornstein could not get them to sign on to the plan.

Rupert Murdoch, who still saw sports as a "battering ram" for television and entertainment, had no such hesitation. FSN, or Fox Sports Net (otherwise known as the Fox Sports Regional Network), was formed basically on the acquisition plan that Bornstein warned Cap Cities about. Murdoch's News Corporation bought up regional sports networks around the country. Then they acquired the play-by-play rights to the big teams and events in each area, and went head-to-head with ESPN by broadcasting the most popular programs nationally.

Not getting the green light for his acquisition proposal was less a personal blow to Bornstein than a frustration of strategy. The promised land of total sports domination had been tantalizingly in reach before being pulled out of his grasp. Bornstein understood the reality behind the Cap Cities decision, just as his predecessors had understood the limits of their ownership groups. As Werner put it: "Every time we had a new owner who didn't understand what we were doing, we had the expected pressures, particularly the off-base questions and challenges to the cost side of the business." But ESPN never gave itself an excuse for failure, however justified. It adjusted to each setback and moved on.

So ESPN acknowledged FSN as a new competitor and got aggressive in areas it could control. On the advertising sales side, it showed advertisers how ESPN's national advertising opportunities were superior in value to its new competitor's regional footprint. On the programming side, ESPN continued broadcasting all its sports nationally, while also expanding to new programs, new franchises, and new channels. In the end, FSN blinked first and lost its focus. Although Murdoch's network is a serious competitor to ESPN and gives sports fans an alternative, the rise has not threatened ESPN's market leadership, and FSN, in my opinion, has failed to realize all the potential benefits of its regional strategy. That doesn't mean to say that ESPN wouldn't love to have the chance to go back in time and snatch up those regional networks before News Corporation got them. But nobody let the missed opportunity become an excuse or a diversion. Instead, it served as a rallying cry.

As with the regional sports gambit, Bornstein also failed to buy the Golf Channel for similar reasons when the opportunity presented itself. He'd always thought that a dedicated golf channel would make a great vertical integration with ESPN's other channels but couldn't get the go-ahead. An opportunity to secure a major ownership stake in car racing was lost for different reasons. Bornstein had the chance to buy into the Daytona 500 but hesitated. "The deal was done and I didn't pull the trigger and I lost it. It would have been significant for the health and wealth of ESPN." Recognizing what had been missed by failing to act, ESPN, in future years, would be quick to make ownership investments into other leagues and franchises like the WNBA.

Take a Chance, and Make it Happen

The steroidal growth of ESPN during Bornstein's tenure was built on bold decisions to acquire and develop new channels. Even the wins, however, were spotted with complications. Depending on who you talk to, for instance, ESPN2 was either the most successful launch in cable television history or a venture that was misconceived and misbranded. ESPN2 was supposed to be the radical sister of ESPN. It was meant to be wild, extreme, and younger, broadcasting sports that weren't mainstream, or sometimes even considered sports at all in conventional terms. So how should its success be measured? On the one hand, ESPN2 expanded faster to more homes than any other cable channel, including ESPN, ever had. Of course, that meant more revenue, a bigger footprint, more outlets for advertisers, and so on. On the other hand, much of that growth was clearly due to the leverage ESPN had with cable companies to bundle offerings. Absent such pull, there was no stampeding rush to pick up the channel.

Adjust and make it work. Bornstein applied his particular programming genius to the problem. More or less downplaying the extreme sports focus of ESPN2, he decided to broadcast events that sports fanatics absolutely could not live without. The key opportunity came when ESPN2 scheduled Duke versus North Carolina in NCAA basketball. Number one versus number two was too much for a sports fan to resist. The calls to cable operators came in. "What do you mean I don't have ESPN2?" The freakout was palpable.

The shift in programming toward the mainstream was enough to give ESPN2 some cache. By the time ESPN renegotiated with cable operators, a deal was struck whereby ESPN2 was included in more home packages. The growth of the channel accelerated from there. But in terms of brand and position, ESPN2 remained the weaker stepchild. It should have been marketed and positioned as an outlet for more ESPN, an extension of the mother channel the way BBC2 is for BBC, giving sports fans additional opportunities for what they already wanted. The channel also lacked leadership. Without an executive solely in charge of ESPN2, the channel was always an afterthought before Mark Shapiro took that role.

ESPN Classic had its own problems but ESPN resolved them more quickly because of the lessons learned with ESPN2. When Classic

Sports was acquired by ESPN during the last of the Bornstein years, it seemed a natural fit. More of the sports games that sports fanatics wanted, spiced with nostalgia. But Classic, as I mentioned in the previous chapter, was a poor fit from a cultural standpoint and its leadership immediately left. What's more, despite a hefty $175 million price tag, ESPN soon learned that broadcasting archival programming was rife with complicated rights issues. In essence, the network had paid for some programming it wasn't actually able to buy.

If ESPN Classic was going to be successful, Bodenheimer believed the channel would need its own leadership. That was a shift in managerial approach, since previously either Bornstein or Bodenheimer had overseen everything personally, and no one from a lesser rank had been assigned to head a particular channel. But ESPN2 showed the benefits of hands-on, aggressive, and creative control. Fresh off his success with SportsCentury, Mark Shapiro was a bold but logical choice for Bodenheimer to make. However, for the other executives and managers at the company, whether in programming, affiliate sales, or advertising, it was a startling change in direction. Suddenly, people who had reported only to the head of the company were reporting to the head of a single channel, and a 28-year-old boss at that.

Bodenheimer applied his relationship building skills and his humble leadership style to smooth any ruffled feathers. "We need a face and a spokesman for Classic," he said, "and Shapiro will work with you guys closely." Overall, the move to delegate authority for the channel to a single captain worked well. Shapiro drove everyone on all cylinders for the next 18 months while the channel grew from 20 million to 55 million homes.

To keep growing and stay on top, the leadership believed that ESPN needed to continually innovate and even reinvent a portion of itself on a regular basis. Whether it was a different way of producing the game, a new segment on *SportsCenter*, or an entirely new channel, it was more important to stumble and pick itself up then it was to stand still and never fall.

Remain Friends and Have a Short Memory

Conflict was common at ESPN. At the leadership rank, arguments were often heated and profanity-filled. People who worked at ESPN and then worked somewhere else have remarked at the difference. At most American corporations, fighting is taboo and executives rarely scream at each other, though they may not function well as a team. At ESPN, the team was highly functional in spite of the arguments, because the conflict was not personal, it was passion. It was about arguing your point of view forcefully, openly, and with incredible candor. Bornstein was good at picking fights. He challenged points of view and forced sharp analysis out of the proposals and ideas people brought forward. Even Bodenheimer, who is more personable and somewhat conflict averse, encourages conflict around him. To this day, he pushes his executive team to embrace what he refers to as a "culture of candor." He wants to hear opposing views and operates as though the best way to work out a good approach is to have two passionate advocates going at it in front of the boss. ESPN has always been led by people who fight to get the right answer. In my experience, that's much better than a group that avoids necessary conversations and touchy subjects because they might lead to hurt feelings.

Not everyone could handle that. But people who thrived at ESPN understood that the intensity of the argument ended at the office door. In the hallway, the parking lot, or at the restaurant, the live wires were about friendship and shared experiences and good times. Those who couldn't shake off the conflict didn't last. They took their hurt feelings and moved on.

With business partners such as leagues, cable operators, and ownership, the same principle applied. ESPN was passionate about doing what it thought was right, but it never allowed the arguments to kill the relationship.

ESPN launched its original entertainment programming figuring that its expertise in sports and storytelling would be a huge asset in developing narrative documentaries and scripted entertainment. Some partners were less than supportive of the unconventional move, particularly when those documentaries and entertainments infringed on their brand or territory. *Playmakers*, for example, was the first drama series produced by ESPN. As a show about a fictional professional football team where drug abuse, steroid use, gang violence, spousal abuse, promiscuity, and homosexuality were portrayed as daily aspects of athletes' lives, *Playmakers* offended the NFL, famous for its buttoned-down image as the "No Fun League."

Shapiro, as head of programming and production (which included EOE, ESPN Original Entertainment) championed the show and pushed it through in spite of the NFL's protests. He got away with it because neither Bodenheimer or Disney CEO Michael Eisner seemed to realize how big and controversial *Playmakers* could become. Once the show aired, the NFL's anger with ESPN redoubled and that further amplified the critical and viewership attention. The NFL's reaction, many at ESPN felt, was unjustified. Still, with the intense hurt and anger, how could ESPN continue to antagonize its biggest league partner? In the end, it couldn't, and so ESPN canceled *Playmakers*, despite its critical acclaim and cult status, after only a single season, knowing it was better to get along than to break a trusting relationship.

Fans may have been disappointed, but they would have been more disappointed if the relationship between the NFL and ESPN had grown hostile. Shapiro argued against the decision and fought the good fight, but at the end of that meeting, despite the disagreements, "we walked out as one." He had a passionate and personal attachment to a creative project, but there were no regrets or lingering bitterness once the cancellation decision had been made. "I don't regret," Shapiro noted, "and I don't live in the past. I have a real knack for being able to let things like that roll off me like water."

Shapiro's ability to forget the intensity of emotion, focus on the important things, and move on is typical of successful ESPN executives. A parallel can be drawn with top athletes. They say a great pitcher, quarterback, golfer, or goalie is always blessed with a short memory. A bad throw, shot, or goal is quickly shaken off. Then the mind returns to the moment and the body readies for the next bit of action. Great leaders are similar. They may be thoughtful and inquisitive and passionate, but they don't spend a lot of time looking in the rearview mirror. They save their reminiscing for later. They forget about the pain, frustration, or regret of failure, and focus instead on what they can control—the circumstances of the present and the opportunities going forward.

The No Blame Zone

Theoretically, as the aggressive head of original programming, Shapiro could have been made the fall guy for the "failure" of *Playmakers*. In reality, *Playmakers* was too well received and Shapiro too valuable and productive an executive for any corporation to blame. In any event, Bodenheimer, like Bornstein before him, doesn't play that game. In Bodenheimer's eyes, it wasn't a mistake to launch *Playmakers*, it just didn't work out the way it needed to, and so a midcourse correction was made. In the meantime, Shapiro was given the continued green light for more original programming, some of it just as controversial as the *Playmakers* series. You can imagine the dampening effect if Bodenheimer had said, "Original entertainment is too risky. We don't want to offend. Let's stick to the knitting and do what we do best." The brake on creativity, innovation, chance-taking, and boldness would have been a severe drag on the organization's forward momentum and ongoing evolution.

This kind of attitude has been consistent through many years and circumstances. When Dick Glover was developing ESPN's early Internet site, Bornstein's instructions were to do it on some other company's dime. So Glover looked for technological partners, as I mentioned earlier. The top providers at the time were Prodigy, Compuserve, and an upstart called AOL. Prodigy offered Glover a one-year deal for technical support that also included a $10 million payment to ESPN for advertising. AOL had recently gone public and wanted to forgo any cash payments and offered stock warrants instead, giving ESPN the option to buy shares at a set price. Glover brought both offers to Bornstein for deliberation.

Bornstein listened to Glover's assessment of the offers and the companies as though he was completely ignorant of the Internet business. Glover said that AOL was the more aggressive company, but Prodigy was the industry leader, with around 1.1 million subscribers compared to AOL's 400,000. Given the extended market share and the $10 million in cash, it made sense, on balance, to work with Prodigy. Bornstein pressed him further. It turned out that he actually knew plenty about AOL and Prodigy. In fact, he was an early AOL member with an e-mail address that would be impossible to get today, SteveB@AOL.com, sitting right next to AOL owner Steve Case's address, SteveC@AOL.com. Once again, Glover was surprised at how thoroughly Bornstein understood the issues in advance, and how deliberately he pushed his executives to make their case. As Glover put it, "Bornstein knew more than you knew, but he never let you know that." In the end, Bornstein was satisfied with Glover's arguments and agreed with the strategy. ESPN went forward with the Prodigy offer.

After AOL bought Time Warner, Glover and Bornstein shared a few drinks and calculated how many hundreds of millions of dollars AOL's warrants would have been worth if ESPN had made that deal. They could only laugh. There was no blame involved. The Prodigy relationship had accomplished clear goals: ESPN got advertising money in the bank, and learned a lot about developing a Web presence at a time when other media organizations were floundering or ignorant. Instead, regrets landed on an entirely different front. Glover and Bornstein realized that they'd chosen the wrong partner. AOL was better than Prodigy, even though it was smaller and had less money. In the Internet world, it was the scrappy overachiever and ESPN should have recognized a kindred spirit. What's more, a better partner might have meant a better product. "The reason we ended up making the wrong decision was not about money," Glover said, "but because we got away from thinking about the customer and the fan. That was one of the tenets constantly preached into our brains: Think about it from the fan's perspective." The unexpected payoff when AOL's warrants turned to gold was just symbolic of the other missed opportunity, the chance to serve fans better.

If you did a postmortem of ESPN's failed mobile phone strategy, you might come up with a similar assessment. ESPN launched its Mobile ESPN phone with a great commercial at the Super Bowl in 2006 when the Pittsburgh Steelers played the Seattle Seahawks at Ford Field. The spot showed a young male office worker walking down a busy city street, scanning his cell phone while dreamy music played and athletes of all kinds dodged, shot, raced, or jumped around him. Then the caption arose: "Welcome to sports heaven." And a moment later, the voiceover said, "Introducing Mobile ESPN. Sports fans, your phone has arrived."

What wasn't to like? Like the first broadcast in 1979, ESPN was offering sports fans another service that enabled them to access sports and sports news whenever, wherever they wanted. Of course, some questioned whether ESPN should be in the mobile phone business at all. But ESPN had also gone into the Internet business, the restaurant business, the publishing business, and the retail business without stumbling, so why should mobile phones be any different?

As ESPN would discover, the mobile phone business was more complicated to organize, operate, and finance than anything they'd been involved in before. Technical capabilities aside, there were a couple of things about the Mobile ESPN service that didn't seem to fit with the way ESPN operated. Most alarmingly, the launch of Mobile ESPN meant that ESPN customers would be receiving a bill from ESPN for the very first time. That seemed in strong contrast to the relationship ESPN had always had with fans. On top of that, the price point was much higher than ESPN would have liked, there was no family plan included in the pricing options, and the customer service needed to be outsourced.

Ultimately, there was a feeling among some insiders that the idea was conceived, given the green light, and launched to create another $50 million a year business, not necessarily to better serve fans. So when it stumbled and faltered, many were not surprised. Serve fans was the critical tenet Glover spoke of, and ESPN ignored or forgot that rule to its detriment. For $150 million in investment ESPN had netted a mere 30,000 customers, nowhere near the number it projected. Almost a year after the 2006 Superbowl, ESPN announced that the Mobile ESPN phone would be shut down. In a midcourse correction, the content part of the service would be migrated to established carriers and offered to fans that way. The intellectual property and content that was developed may prove to be worth the investment in the long run; what ESPN realized, like IBM before them, was that they are far better off as a service and content provider, and should leave the hardware business to others.

So how did ESPN handle this public and pricey failure? In his internal memo, Bodenheimer wrote: "Growth and innovation often involve taking risks and ESPN has not shied away from aggressively seeking to improve our business at any point in our history. Mobile ESPN was one such undertaking with many challenges and in the best tradition of ESPN the Mobile team built the finest wireless service for sports fans." Bodenheimer then went on to explain the reasons he felt the plan hadn't met expectations. Then he ended, "I would like to thank all of them [ESPN staff] for a remarkable job in conceiving and launching this product. We are very proud of all you have accomplished."

Nobody was fired. No heads rolled. No one was accused, in hindsight, of bringing a bad idea forward. That message reminded me of a few stories I'd heard about other business failures where risk and innovation were involved. At 3M, for example, an executive wanted to use the Post-it Notes glue technology in binders for school children. At all levels of analysis, the product looked good. Parents were spending a lot on bulky binders, and three-hole punches were messy and cumbersome. Post-it glue was surely an elegant solution meeting an unknown customer need. The research supported the idea. The presentation to the top executive team was a success. The project got the go-ahead, and many millions were spent getting behind the new product. In the market, however, it failed utterly. So what did 3M do to the manager with the bright idea? It rewarded his innovation by sending him and his family to the Virgin Islands for a week. In contrast, I know of many examples firsthand where an executive was fired because a new product or service failed to meet performance expectations.

If a company is serious about risk taking and aggressive innovation, it needs to support and reward those behaviors. If it only rewards risk that leads to positive outcomes, and punishes risk that leads to negative outcomes, the message will be clear. Don't take a chance. Don't put your best ideas forward. Stay low. And watch out.

ESPN, like the best innovative companies, has never been about heaping blame when bad outcomes occur. It accepts bad outcomes as the inherent risk of risk taking. Companies that grow organically innovate continually. Occasionally, they need to be reminded that innovation must be in service of the customer. That's what failure is for.

The Don Hurta Rule

If one corollary of risk is the need to reward risk-taking behaviors, the other is the need for urgency.

In my experience, companies that lack an innovation capability are often guilty of doing too much due diligence. As McKinsey consultants are fond of saying, they tend to "boil the ocean" and won't make a risky move until they've proven that everything is absolutely going to work. The problem with such "analysis paralysis" is that the threshold for taking a chance becomes established at such a high level that change never happens. The conditions are never exactly right. As effective business leaders know, there's no such thing as perfect competition and there's no such thing as total certainty. One client of mine used to say that "[he] succeeded not because he was so damn smart, [he] just did his homework, and unfortunately experienced and exercised all possible failure options."

My close friend Don Hurta called this imperative "the need to make a $#@&ing decision." Don was an independent consultant who specialized in Risk and Game Theory, who I tried to hire for years. He loved working with me and my firm, but loved the risk and game of being on his own too much to formally join a firm. The good news is that we loved working together, and found ample opportunities to do so. The first client I introduced Don to was Ingersol Dresser. Later I brought him into Goldman Sachs and Avaya, and in every situation, I could see how people were struck by him. He was a tough, clean-cut ex-Marine with no BS about him. He was also a PhD in mathematics and an extremely clear thinker. Maybe it was his military background, or maybe it was that combination of brutal clarity and sharp intelligence, but Don was the kind of person you wanted to follow into battle. As a consultant, I'm more concerned with interpersonal relationships, emotional intelligence, and leadership development. Don was all about strategy, hard data, and calculated decision making. We made a nice balance.

By the time I brought Don to ESPN in 1998, the company was becoming big and successful. There's a need in that stage in the life cycle of any aggressive company to avoid becoming complacent and stay hungry and urgent. The first time Don met with the executives and managers he challenged everyone's thinking around risk. Don had a simple graphic, a drawing of a pointer with a sliding dial that indicates how risky or conservative a person, a decision, or a situation might be.

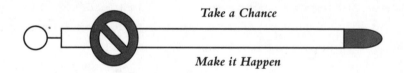

Take a Chance

Make it Happen

Don was always pushing people to move further up the scale to a level they weren't necessarily comfortable with.

Don's point was that people are usually more risk-averse than they realize. They think they're a 7 on a 10-point scale when they're actually a 2 or a 3, thus the "no" symbol on the lower end of the scale. This was difficult information for some high-powered executives to accept. So Don would use a few examples. I remember when he asked everyone in the room how much insurance they had. Then he proved with statistics that we were all overinsured. Of course, that's how insurance companies make money—they take in more in fees than they pay out—but it was an interesting demonstration, and it got into people's heads and began to challenge their understanding of risk.

Don didn't care how much insurance the executives in the room had, of course, but he did care how much risk they were taking in their respective roles within the organization. In his view, ESPN needed to keep its risk meter at a 5 or a 6 on his scale. Too high on the risk scale and those executives were being irresponsible—everyone understands that. But too low on the risk scale and those executives were also being irresponsible. That was a trickier concept to grasp. But, as Don explained, if you're not taking risks, you're not innovating, and if you're not innovating, you're not growing, and if you're not growing, you're being irresponsible to your shareholders.

If you boil the ocean, if you get bogged down by analysis paralysis, by the time you finally act, the opportunity will have been lost or the competition will have beaten you to the punch. The antidote was to "just make a $@#&ing decision." In fact, that's what ESPN had consistently done in the early days. While other companies were taking their time, arguing through the ramifications, boiling the ocean, hesitating, ESPN was making decisions and acting. Its tolerance for risk was not irresponsible. It never destroyed a partnership, blew a production, or overstated its ability to meet an obligation—but it never hesitated to jump on an opportunity. When satellite communications signals became available, ESPN snatched them up, mere weeks before the bigger competition caught on. When it was apparent that a cable company couldn't make any money under the traditional revenue model, ESPN didn't wait for consensus or for some other channel to establish a new precedent, it led the revolution. When ABC came to ESPN and asked about filling radio spots, ESPN launched its own radio network in record time. When the America's Cup was a success and people demanded more coverage, ESPN didn't wait for the following year to fulfill that demand, it immediately changed its programming. When the NFL put up a package of games for bidding, ESPN didn't worry about breaking the bank, it leaped on the opportunity. Over and over, ESPN was first to a new opportunity because its tolerance for risk was a 5, not a 2, and it left other companies behind as a result.

Don's message was timely because ESPN was getting bigger and it needed to be reminded about how it had generated its own success. Interestingly, my involvement with ESPN started to narrow as Don became part of the team. I had been there for the mission and values work, the leadership development and feedback, the emphasis on team building and human capital. But Don became the hard-edged voice of reason with the Patton-like speeches that ESPN needed to hear. If ESPN had always been able to find the right leader at the right time, then Don was the right advisor at the right time. I could have been the jealous boyfriend, but I was plenty busy on my own, and Don was so grateful for the introduction. Something in him connected strongly with the leaders at ESPN and the way they thought and saw the world. "I love these guys," he told me. Young leaders like Mark Shapiro feasted on his words. He wasn't telling them anything they didn't know at some level. But he was affirming their core beliefs and making them stronger and more confident in their leadership.

I learned later that Don never charged ESPN for any of the work he did. To him, it was too much fun. Don wasn't averse to making money. He had a thriving and lucrative consulting practice with top clients around the world. But ESPN was different. He accepted tickets to big games or the ESPYs for him and his family. But he wouldn't send in a bill. It was such a concern to Bodenheimer that he called and asked me if I could talk Don into giving them an invoice. Don refused to ask for a nickel. I last saw Don at the ESPYs in Los Angeles with his daughter, so proud, so happy, and as he had always done, he hugged me and thanked me for introducing him to his beloved ESPN.

Then Don got sick and passed away more suddenly then any of us expected. It was a hard blow. But at his funeral, the ranks of ESPN executives were many and strong. Several months later, I got a box in the mail from his son who now works at the NFL, and opened it. Inside there were hundreds of those Take a Chance pointers Don passed out at his presentations. I picked one up and could hear his voice in my head as clear as day.

"Just make a $@#&ing decision."

CHAPTER SEVEN KEY POINTS

"Take a chance, make it happen"

Any big decision that involves some element of risk demands thorough analysis and due diligence. However, speed of decision making must also be factored into the process. At some point, you need to pull the trigger, make the decision, and make adjustments along the way. Truth is, you will need to make adjustments anyway, so why not get started a few days before your competition. If you've got a good idea someone else out there has it too.

"Reward risk-taking behavior, not just outcomes"

If you value (smart) risk taking, then you must reward the process and the behavior, not just the successful outcome. Organizations that only reward the outcomes will find themselves doing so less and less frequently over time. Risking too little is just as dangerous to an enterprise as is risking too much.

"When (not if) you make a mistake, stop, learn, and move on"

Remember that some great decisions were made with faulty decision-making models, and some poor decision were made with great decision-making models. Bottom line: Mistakes will happen if you are an organization that values risk taking. Therefore, when a mistake happens, blow the whistle quickly, watch the instant replay, learn from the process to enhance your decision making going forward, and move on.

"Stay friends and have a short memory"

Business friends and partners are valuable assets to any enterprise. Inevitably, one party is going to frustrate the other. If you are in a company that values risk taking and aggressive thinking, like ESPN, then be prepared to make mistakes, make adjustments, ask for forgiveness, and be willing to "forgive those who have made mistakes against you."

Chapter 8

ARE YOU
HAVING FUN?

One of the questions Don Hurta liked to ask the folks at ESPN was this: "Why do you exist as a company?" Given ESPN's serve fans mantra, the answers to his question were quick. Most people replied with something like: "To provide the world's best sports programming." But Don curtly shot down all the variations on that theme and asked ESPN executives to think harder. As business types, they reached for the next level in their hierarchy of needs and answered: "To make money." But Don said that wasn't good enough either.

"Your purpose," he told them, "is to make as much money as you possibly can, for as long as you can."

Now, I know I can be sentimental, but that seemed a little cold for an enterprise with the spirit, humor, creativity, and boldness of ESPN. Still, I'd heard the same kind of talk from ESPN leaders like Bornstein and Werner. As I considered the challenges ESPN faces now, I kept thinking about Don's statement of purpose. Bornstein put it slightly differently but just as bluntly. "In the old days of broadcast television," he mused, "back in the 1950s and 1960s, anybody's idiot cousin could run a television station and make money. But were they earning 20 percent profit margin or 75 percent? So that's a challenge for ESPN in the future. They're going to make money, but are they making the most money?"

After 30 years of existence, ESPN finds itself in a rare spot. In the sports media world, it is the Roman Empire. For many years there were other competitors. Some were more dominant like the cultured Greeks. Others were pesky territorial challengers like the Samnites or Etruscans.

And then there were threatening invaders like Hannibal's elephant army from Carthage. Now there is only Rome, and all roads lead to Bristol. But can the ESPN empire avoid its own decline and fall?

Right now, it seems as though the life cycle of American corporations has become compressed. Rome wasn't built in a day, but ESPN was built in a mere generation. Couldn't its decline and fall come just as quickly? In recent years, we've witnessed the downfall or shrinking of many once-vigorous institutions. Financial houses like Lehman Brothers and Bear Stearns come immediately to mind and there are many others in the auto industry, computer manufacturing, retail, and accounting. Some companies fail to see the new competitive landscape until it is almost too late. Some fall victim to what Jim Collins cited as the second stage of decline, which is the "Undisciplined Pursuit of More." Some stumble in their transition to a new generation of leadership. Others discover that their paradigm-busting innovations in service or distribution have been imitated so thoroughly that what made them market leaders at one time no longer distinguishes them today—in other words, that "deviation from the start" is no longer a deviation. In fact, hungrier risk-taking upstarts are already leaving them behind.

As I have noted earlier, my colleague and friend Marshall Goldsmith wrote the wonderful book, *What Got You Here, Won't Get You There*, which focuses on the little discussed paradox of leadership. In the book, he talked convincingly about the pitfalls of success. According to Marshall, success is its own trap. Size and power separates you from the rest of the world and blinkers you from reality. Everyone around you and everything you see reinforces what you already believe to be true. You assume that what made you successful in the past will continue to make you successful in the future. To generate more success, you need to recognize a complex new reality, one that encompasses your current status and the obligations that entails, while still managing to adapt to the needs of the future.

It ain't easy, and it's what keeps diligent CEOs up at night worrying when everyone else has turned off their BlackBerrys. Veteran leaders quickly bring up such concerns. From his vantage point, as a former head of ESPN and the founding CEO of two other start-up networks, Roger Werner put it this way: "When a company really achieves maturity, you face multiple challenges. You need to sustain an environment that's opportunity oriented, where people are still encouraged to try new things, even when the cost of failure has gotten higher and higher. It's also harder in a mature environment to squeeze another dollar of profit out of existing business models. So you have to be very adept at managing the cost side of the business while finding every opportunity for additional top line revenue growth."

As Werner explained, maintenance and management are critical skills now at ESPN, but you still need to keep growing. You also have to worry about the kind of people you draw to or retain at a mature organization versus a start-up. Institutions, after all, tend to appeal to more conventional or conservative types, while start-ups attract people who are more tolerant of risk and change. Can you keep the values and mission of the organization fresh even when the CEO has made the same speech a thousand times? Can you stay in tune with your customers and adapt to their evolving needs, especially when those needs shift suddenly? Can you take advantage of your momentum and dominance without becoming complacent or arrogant?

The challenges seem so complicated that it makes you appreciate the simplicity of Don Hurta's message. "Your purpose is to make as much money as you possibly can for as long as you can." While that sounds purely mercantile at one level, the beauty of Don's proposal is that it keeps an organization focused on what's important. Don wasn't advocating making as much money as you possibly can in the short term. In fact, he was saying that if you focus only on immediate gains, even huge ones, you might sink your fortunes in the future. Instead, if you're trying to make as much as possible for as long as possible, you need to worry about lots of other things, too.

ESPN can only make the most money for an extended time if it does everything right. It needs to continue to serve fans, create new games, expand the brand, continue to build its pipeline of leaders, work with partners, and take risks. It can't grow complacent. It can't get too

arrogant. It can't overlook the competition or the changing technological landscape.

But how exactly does an organization manage all that? When
I thought of boiling all that complexity down into something more
simple I heard a second voice in my head, and this time it was George
Bodenheimer's.

Bodenheimer understands that ESPN has become so big and
powerful that it is an institution, and that an institution faces its own
unique challenges. In developing a response to those challenges he
doesn't wearily recite the same bullet points over and over. Instead,
for Bodenheimer, the challenge comes down to one critical question: "Are you having fun?" He's not talking about squirt-gun fights
in the hallway or jokes at the water cooler, he's talking about satisfaction, enjoyment and energy, or what management gurus now refer to
as "employee engagement." Bondenheimer is an optimistic realist. He
knows that employees are not always going to be having fun, but he knows
that it is human nature to focus on the not so fun stuff in life, and forget about the opportunities, joys, and blessings that lie before us all; to
Bodenheimer, it's a matter of perspective.

Years ago, I developed a model that I use when executives are
struggling with their careers. It's a simple three C model (see Figure 8.1),
that illustrates the three factors of perspective. Before we make a decision about work, relationships, where we live, and so on, it is important
to have a clear perspective about all the variables involved in the decision. In thinking through the variables, I would have my clients separate
the various aspects of their job into three segments; The first segment
is "Celebrate"; In nearly everything we are engaged in as humans
(jobs, relationships, neighborhoods, where we live, what we drive, etc.),
there are aspects that we truly enjoy, and in essence celebrate because
of the joy, satisfaction, and fun that they create. The second segment
is "Change." In everything we do, there are aspects that we would all
love to change. These are things that are not ideal, but given that they
are in our sphere of control, we can make a concerted effort to
change them in a way that increases the celebration factor. The third

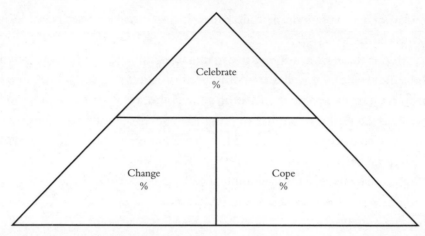

Figure 8.1   The Three C Factors of Perspective

segment is "Cope." Unfortunately, there are aspects in our lives that are neither fun nor changeable. These are variables that are not very enjoyable and lie outside of our sphere of control; therefore, we can only cope with them as best as we see fit.

I share this model not because this is a chapter on perspective, but "having fun" in one's job is driven by one's perspective. Great leaders, I have learned, have a way of reminding their employees of the real joys and opportunities of their work. One such way is to ensure that the organization does its fair share of celebrating victories and accomplishments. If having fun is an outcome, then it's important for leaders to celebrate the inputs to reinforce the behaviors that are required to achieve that which is cause for celebration. It is also important for leaders to empower their employees to take initiative and change that which is squelching the fun and satisfaction factors, while being very clear to only spend time and effort on those aspects that can truly be changed. Once I developed this model, I realized that this is what Bodenheimer does intuitively. His celebration factor always seems to be above 65 percent, and he is always concentrated on the 20 percent of change that is needed to keep ESPN on top. Finally, I never heard him bitch and moan about the 15 percent that he has to cope with day to day, and in maintaining this balance, his leadership by example is extraordinary.

Bodenheimer knows that if you're having fun at least 60 percent of the time or so, that means you're winning market share, working creatively, enjoying the camaraderie of your colleagues, satisfying fans, and growing the business. Similar to Cyndi Lauper, Bodenheimer maintains the conviction that at the end of the day, employees and fans "just want to have fun."

"Are you having fun?"

It's a question we need to ask ESPN.

The Perils of Market Leadership

In the early days, the fun was easy. You joked around to take the pressure off. There were no rules and policies. You were young. You worked hard and played hard. You were constantly scrambling to convince partners, convince leagues, convince viewers and athletes that you were worth taking seriously. You told yourself you didn't care because no one was watching. Of course, you cared like hell, and were driven by the mission and the immense opportunity. The world may have been barely aware of your existence but it was waiting for you to conquer it.

One of the most common accusations ESPN faces today is that it has grown arrogant. The accusations come from a variety of sources. Cable operators that once worked vigorously to restrict or impinge on ESPN's growth now find themselves with little leverage when ESPN raises rates. More than any other cable channel, ESPN has the content, the brand, and the advertising sales to back up its demands. But the cable operators are the ones stuck applying the rate increases to the customer in terms of higher subscription fees. That can't help but generate resentment.

Another accusation is that ESPN is so big it can distort the coverage of sports. As Bob Costas put it, "Money has always had an impact on the way sports and television do business, and today with networks paying billions to leagues like the NFL, how much do the dollars determine the way sports is covered?" In other words, from a journalistic standpoint, will ESPN cover its league partners as vigorously and thoroughly as it should? Or will it soft pedal through touchy issues? After all, ESPN pulled *Playmakers* to soften the wrath of the NFL—what's to keep it from sitting on a negative story, too? On the other side of the coin, does ESPN cover leagues or sports thoroughly when they are not in business together? Some conspiratorial fans and critics have their suspicions.

And then there are those in charge of advertising dollars and accounts who complain about ESPN's ad rates. In the spring of 2008, for example, a PowerPoint presentation criticizing ESPN was eagerly circulated among industry insiders. It was called, "The Emperor's New Clothes: How ESPN's Multi-Platform Strategy Hasn't Improved Ratings." The argument is that ratings for ESPN shows and events are not that high, that cable fees and ad rates keep going up regardless, and that leagues in business with ESPN do better than those that are off the reservation. Ultimately, according to those critics, a multi-platform strategy is less effective at reaching the numbers ESPN claims. On the other hand, ESPN is also accused of over-promotion across its platforms. With the magazine, multiple channels, web site, radio, and the restaurants, ESPN can hammer an announcement or marketing campaign more or less relentlessly. People who watch ESPN for a living—other journalists, rabid fans, athletes, and coaches—frequently bristle at the repetition.

I haven't written this chapter to make excuses for ESPN, but to assess the business challenges of its current position. In that sense, it's interesting to consider these criticisms. So let's tackle each one, starting with the accusation of arrogance.

Arrogance can be the armor of the powerful, and when you're big, you get arrows shot at you from many angles. Is arrogance a problem at ESPN? It can't be easy to remain humble when you are the clear market leader. Whereas ESPN once went to the cable operators or the leagues with hat in hand to beg for a few scraps to weave into that larger patchwork, now those executives travel to Bristol to seek out meetings and work out deals. No one worries much about the arrogance of the underdog—it's only an issue when combined with power and leverage.

I have no doubt that ESPN executives understand the strength of their position. They have the ability to squeeze hard during negotiations. Fans, cable operators, and ad agencies benefit when ESPN gets a good deal from the leagues. Leagues get richer when ESPN gets more revenue from cable operators and advertisers. It's not a zero sum game, and it's impossible to make all parties happy about everything. But business is about providing service that meets customer needs while generating as much revenue as possible. Or, as Don Hurta said, ESPN is in business to make as much money as it can for as long as it can. Arrogance can hurt that prospect if an organization's business relationships or brand are damaged, so that's where the worries arise.

Interestingly, although ESPN is not and never has been the most humble organization, it has always been about the sports fans first, and itself second. What's more, although ESPN has had executives in the past who were thought to be arrogant, its current CEO is a truly humble man. Recall Bodenheimer's admonishment of Mark Shapiro for pressing too hard on a league executive. As a teacher and a leader, Bodenheimer is not against using ESPN's leverage to make a better deal, especially when it serves fans. But he's also a strong counterweight to the rough-and-tumble testosterone of business. He has the long view when it comes to relationships and the brand. Plenty of top level companies get into trouble because of arrogance. An organization that dominates an industry can benefit a lot from a humble, but purposeful leader like Bodenheimer.

The accusation of conflicting interests in coverage is another area where ESPN may be a victim of its own success. It's a tricky thing, for example, for a business entity to be reporter of, producer of, and partner with the content. But within ESPN, there's a line between church and state, between editorial and business, just like there is in any quality news organization, major network, city newspaper, or magazine. The business pressures on content producers in every media organization are tremendous. But I don't think they're any different at ESPN then they are at CBS or the *Washington Post*. ESPN gets equal heat from both sides—the leagues and the media critics—for the way it covers stories or events, which seems to indicate it's maintaining a decent balance, not making any one side too happy.

When it comes to the accusations that ESPN's ratings are not high enough to justify its advertising rates, well, that's an interesting business question. Rumors suggest that the "Emperor's New Clothes" report originated from a competitor, putting those criticisms in a different light. Perhaps that was just a fun way for a competitor to take a shot at an industry leader. But the criticism struck at the heart of a media organization's modern reality. With hundreds of options, people flip compulsively from channel to channel. With repeats of events and shows, and devices like Tivo and DVR, people watch those shows when they want to, not when they're offered. When an entity like ESPN has many different outlets—those multiple channels, the web site, and the magazine—how do you measure how much exposure the customer is getting? What's more, from a marketing standpoint, how do you resist using all those outlets as promotion tools? More than any other media organization today, ESPN is the ultimate multi-platform service. In the late 1990s, experts predicted the rise of such businesses, but although the advantages are self-evident in ESPN's healthy revenue, can the measuring sticks of yesterday do an accurate job assessing the impact? ESPN is concerned about the aggregate numbers of fans it reaches, and that's consistent with its mission: *Serving fans wherever sports are watched, listened to, read about, or discussed.*

Is it a fool's errand to worry too much about criticism, or do you need those voices to be watchful about your own predicament? Success puts a target on your back. As in politics, if you don't have the stomach for the street fighting, you're better off getting out of the game.

The Perils of Keeping and Losing Talent

Another problem with success is the difficulty of keeping talent. As a new organization, ESPN was successful in large part because of the tenaciousness, creativity, and intelligence of its first employees. In its junior years, it sucked talent to Bristol and away from New York and Los Angeles. There are many stories of people who were willing to sacrifice the money and the prestige of an established network for the opportunity and excitement of a rapidly rising one.

As a growing organization, ESPN retained many of those people. That's a good thing. Organizations need to keep more people than they lose. The stability in culture, work processes, and sense of teamwork pay dividends. But organizations also need fresh energy, ideas, and approaches, not to mention diversity, to keep evolving and meeting new challenges. That became increasingly difficult at ESPN. What's more, ESPN has always been the kind of environment that rewards merit and risk taking over seniority. But how do you keep that philosophy alive in an organization as it becomes an institution loaded with 20-year veterans?

One way is to establish poster children. When Mark Shapiro came to Bristol he was frequently lauded as an example of what aggressive thinking, risk taking, and creativity could accomplish and how it would be rewarded. It didn't matter that Shapiro was only 32; his talent got him the job as executive vice president of programming, leaping over the heads of his former bosses. It was an incredibly sound move. ESPN's ratings had been in somewhat of a slump for the previous eight quarters, and Shapiro turned that around immediately. He also reinvigorated ESPN's productions with new ideas, new talent, and new approaches. But at the age of 35, in a career that was incomparable, he left ESPN and joined Washington Redskins owner Daniel Snyder, as the CEO of Red Zone, a firm that soon bought the amusement park chain Six Flags. So how did ESPN lose one of its most celebrated employees?

One problem that many successful organizations face is the lack of room at the top, and the accumulation of talented and highly prized lieutenants that can be poached by other firms. Every previous CEO at ESPN had moved on to something ostensibly larger or more lucrative after a number of intense years at the helm. Bodenheimer was different. He'd been at ESPN his entire career; a move to California with ABC or Disney had its challenges, given his young kids, parents in the area, and so on, and he still had much he wanted to accomplish in Bristol.

Shapiro, at number two, knew he wasn't going to become number one any time soon. Furthermore, unlike many ambitious executives, Shapiro loves Bodenheimer, and did not want to see him leave the post where he has had enormous impact and success.

ESPN is fortunate to have the outlet with ABC and Disney. That was an excellent path for Bornstein, which allowed Bodenheimer to rise at ESPN. Likewise, when Bill Grimes was president of ESPN and Roger Werner had been in the number two spot for a few years, he made the shift to ABC in order to find room to grow, before returning to ESPN after Grimes left to run Univision. Perhaps a similar path would work for Shapiro? Disney interviewed Shapiro for the number two job at ABC Entertainment. Depending on who you ask, Shapiro either didn't want or wasn't offered the job. If he wasn't offered it, Disney must have been banking on the idea that Shapiro loved sports too much to leave ESPN so quickly. In fact, Shapiro loved entertainment and Hollywood as much as sports, and Dan Snyder's enterprise satisfied those needs plus Shapiro's own entrepreneurial urges.

When I asked Shapiro about his own motivations for leaving, it was that entrepreneurial freedom he talked about. As number two at ESPN, Shapiro had been in place during a particularly invigorating period during which ESPN obtained the rights to Monday Night Football, extended the contract with MLB, and got back NASCAR. However, Shapiro recognized the new challenge of success. "We'd spent so much getting those three properties that there wasn't going to be as much left over to experiment with. And I'm not that. I'm not a maintenance guy. I looked at the future and I looked at the past. I'd had a real opportunity at ESPN and been there for an incredible growth curve, and got rewarded in a terrific way. But I saw that the immediate future wasn't going to be about the growth that I'd been lucky enough to participate in. ESPN is going to grow—don't get me wrong. But they're going to grow in bits and pieces as opposed to the quantum leaps." So Shapiro, the kind of employee who fit ESPN like a glove in a growth phase, wasn't the kind to stick around for the consolidation, especially when there was little room at the top.

It's never easy losing top employees, though it's also a fact of life. However, the leadership at ESPN has a lot of bench strength and stability, indicating that talented executives remain committed to the organization and energized by the challenges. The consistency through the decades has been remarkable for an organization that has experienced so many ownership changes and has never relied on the steady hand of a founding CEO. ESPN has brought in few top executives from outside organizations. It promotes from within or across its partnership with Disney as much as possible.

ESPN is also not bedeviled by the problem of a founding CEO lurking in wait. The growth of Dell, Starbucks, and even Schwab, was driven by strong and creative founders who then supposedly passed the big chair to a successor. But when those organizations subsequently stumbled, the founders stepped back in, relieving investors, employees, and customers in the short term but creating uncertainty about the long term. The quest for the next, younger clone of the founder naturally results. ESPN has gone from leader to leader without faltering. Each of those leaders was steeped in ESPN's ways for years before they became the top executive. Fortunately for ESPN, this trend may continue, but it will be a challenge in the long term.

The Perils of Unexpected Competition

It's a truism of modern business that you don't always know where your toughest competitors are coming from. Motorola was on top of the world before a rubber boot and pulp paper company in Finland called Nokia got into the mobile phone business. Similarly, while mobile phone providers like Nokia, Motorola, BlackBerry, and Samsung competed against each other, Apple jumped into the market and outgrew everyone. Particularly in information technology–related industries, innovation can quickly break paradigms that seem like they should last forever; and customers are just as quick to change their loyalties.

By launching itself as a 24–hour cable channel broadcast on satellite, ESPN upset the gravy train of the big three networks. For decades they'd divided the sports spoils among them. Then ESPN changed the rules of television broadcasting and viewing. With its patchwork strategy and its prominent brand, ESPN staked a powerful hold on that new marketplace, one that has yet to be successfully challenged. Turner tried and didn't see it through. Fox Sports Network tried, and has certainly become a major player in sports television, but hasn't threatened ESPN's health. The most recent competitor, Comcast, has also taken on ESPN but has made far less headway than Fox. Some leaders like Bornstein and other key industry figures we spoke to believe that ESPN's position is unassailable. The moat has been dug. The battle is over. The victory is final.

So where will the revolutionary challenges come from? ESPN anticipated the threat of the Internet, got in early and skillfully, and made expanding its brand into cyberspace look easy. Likewise, ESPN was at the forefront of High Definition broadcasts and hasn't allowed anyone else to stake a claim with better quality productions. The most recent trend is for leagues themselves, or for dominant sports franchises like the Yankees, to get into the broadcasting business. They own the content, so why shouldn't they pipe it directly to fans and circumvent the middlemen like ESPN, Versus, or FSN? But those networks have struggled to rise above their images as corporate mouthpieces, just as they've struggled to develop programming that is compelling enough to bolster their games. If the mighty NFL is still fighting like hell for distribution with its network, headed by Steve Bornstein no less, than how can a lesser league, even as vaunted as MLB, pull it off? It's difficult to see the day when we go to a hundred different channels for our sports events instead of just a few.

And yet, it seems inevitable that as digital technology expands and improves, viewership will splinter. ESPN was probably ahead of its time with Mobile ESPN, just as Apple was with its hand-held Newton. People will be watching their sports news and games on small gadgets wherever, whenever they like. Control of content and editing of what is consumed is migrating from producers' hands to consumers. The Wiki-fication of television is on the way. We might also go bigger and broader in our spectacles. High definition broadcasts are nice, but three-dimensional broadcasts will be the new state-of-the-art. Soon, you might be able to watch the Superbowl in a movie theater, and the picture will be so realistic you feel like you're on the field. You might be able to watch the U.S. Open on a virtual reality screen in your family room.

Will ESPN remain at the forefront of that much technological change, willing to invest, take risks, be first? The likelihood is good if it sticks to its serve fans mission. After all, sports itself, and the fascination with it, seems to be timeless. From the first Olympics to the Roman Coliseum, sumo wrestling, jousting, to whatever it is we're doing a hundred years from now. There will always be sports.

For the Fun of It

With so much to worry about, so many threats and critics, so much change, so much that goes into broadcasting even the simplest game, is it any wonder that Bodenheimer keeps asking the employees of ESPN, "Are you having fun?"

ESPN has been a remarkable story. Consider its origins as the dream of a sports fanatic. Consider its revolutionary changes in the way sports were broadcast and the cable business was run. Think of how it established a leadership core steeped in a strong culture. How it looked for scraps and cast-offs, then turned those programs into a wonderful tapestry. How it reinvented the ways in which sports were produced and changed television. How it kept the purse strings tight as a matter of operational discipline but loosened them wide when the opportunities were worth it. How it established and expanded its brand. How it not only survived a tumultuous ownership history but excelled through its ability to leverage partnerships. How it handled failure and mistakes without regret, embracing risk, change, and growth. By doing all that, ESPN has made the most money for the longest time, fulfilling its raison d'être according to the measuring (or more accurately, pointer) stick Don Hurta applied. But I maintain that ESPN is still more than all that.

There's a spirit to the place and a sense of something special. It's still there, and it brings a note of pride and a hint of strong emotion to the voices of the tough old salts I talked to as I wrote this book. Perhaps Dick Vitale, the ESPN announcer whose voice embodies NCAA basketball, put it best when he was enshrined in the Basketball Hall of Fame. "I've been stealing money talking about a game, getting paid." The love of sport, the appreciation of camaraderie, the satisfaction of creativity, energy, and success—that's what Bodenheimer wants to preserve in the atmosphere at ESPN, and I must say, he is truly off the charts when it comes to EQ (Emotional Quotient) or as it is referred to in business parlance, Emotional Intelligence. As I stated in earlier chapters, he is as capable as any executive I've met.

The CEOs before him, especially Bornstein and Werner, dealt with very different challenges. There was a need for analytical sharpness and strategic acumen, pure, unadulterated IQ. And the fun was easy. It came with the building up. Now, there's a concern that the organization stay young at heart and enthusiastic—that's the energy it taps for meeting new challenges.

Bodenheimer embodies the principle of management by walking around. He's always in circulation, meeting senior leaders, managers, and employees. When he's not physically connecting, he's jotting notes, sending messages, checking in. I've gotten my share. They make you feel special. They invigorate your sense of loyalty and make you want to contribute more. I've read that Joe Torre, one of the greatest managers in baseball, does the same thing. It's called checking the pulse. You need to understand what's happening among the people you work with. It's good for business, and it helps to percolate ideas to the top, but it's also about enjoying the game. Ultimately, we relate sports to business so readily for those reasons. Work is not always fun or fulfilling. There are times when Bodenheimer himself will admit that he's a 6 on a scale of 10. But on balance, are you having fun? Is the work you're doing bringing enjoyment to others?

At ESPN, more often than most organizations I've known, the answer is usually yes.

CHAPTER EIGHT KEY POINTS

"Make as much money as you possibly can, for as long as you can"
The profit motive rules business for very healthy reasons. The current economic crisis taught many that you can make a lot of money in the short term, but if it is generated by a business model that fails to take into consideration long—term sustainability, all parties will end up losing.

"Take fun seriously"
As a leader, make fun a business imperative. Fun is different for everyone, so empower people to identify, create, and exercise that which brings them joy in their work. Since the central good of any talent management program is to attract, retain, develop, and excite employees, realize that fun impacts all elements, and must therefore be taken very seriously.

"Commit to leadership development, but realize you will lose some of your investments"
All great institutions that are known for leadership development (GE, McKinsey & Company, Goldman Sachs, P&G, etc.) inevitably know that they will lose star performers to others. Great leaders want to lead, and unfortunately, the farther one goes in an organization, the fewer the opportunities are for top leadership positions.

"Success not only attracts competition, it intensifies it"
A by-product of success is the attraction of fierce competition. Look at the impact that Tiger Woods has had on the level of talent in the PGA. This point may seem obvious, but this is why you can never rest with your success.

Notes

Chapter 1: Turning Fanatics into Fans

1. A quote that some attribute to Palmer's esteemed golfing colleague, Gary Player, but one that certainly fits golf, business, and life in general.
2. John Curand, "Taking Aim at Bristol," *Sports Business Journal*, March 17, 2008.
3. Don Ohlmeyer, when speaking on HBO's *Costas Now*, April 29, 2008.
4. John Curand, "Taking Aim at Bristol," *Sports Business Journal*, March 17, 2008.

Chapter 2: Think Like an Incumbent, Act Like a Challenger

1. Lisa Featherstone, "Wage Against the Machine," June 27, 2008. http://www.slate.com/id/2194332/pagenum/all/#page_start.

Chapter 3: The Right Leader at the Right Time

1. Jon Meacham, "God, Politics, and the Joyful Warrior," *Newsweek*, June 23, 2008.

Chapter 4: Create Your Own Game

1. Craig Reiss, "John Walsh: The King of Cable Sports," *Cable World*, August 19, 2002.

Chapter 5: Expand the Brand

1. In 2007, I heard Rome raving about Shapiro on his radio program, marveling about the rapid advance of a young kid behind the camera with a brash sense of command who ended up being everyone's boss.

2. Don Ohlmeyer, when he was speaking on HBO's *Costas Now* about changes he made to ABC's *Monday Night Football*, described the attitude in the crassest terms as, "Fuck the fans." In other words, fanatic sports viewers would tune in no matter what, but casual viewers needed special distractions and enticements. ESPN never viewed it that way, but the anecdote articulates something about the difficulty of balancing hard core and casual viewers when trying to achieve big ratings.

Chapter 6: Playing Well with Others

1. Stratford P. Sherman, Research Associate David Kirkpatrick. Capital Cities' Capital Coup, *Fortune*, April 15, 1985. http://money.cnn.com/magazines/fortune/fortune_archive/1985/04/15/65799/index.htm.

2. An interview with Tom Murphy. August 4, 1995. http://www.charlierose.com/shows/1995/08/04/1/an-interview-with-tom-murphy.

3. http://www.hbs.edu/entrepreneurs/pdf/tommurphy.pdf.

4. Brooks Barnes, "Disney and Pixar: The Power of the Prenup," *New York Times*, June 1, 2008.

References

Becker, Ernest. 1973. *The denial of death*. New York: Free Press.

Bossidy, Larry, and Ram Charan. 2002. *Execution: The discipline of getting things done*. New York: Crown Business.

Buckingham, Marcus, and Donald O. Clifton. 2001. *Now, discover your strengths*. New York: Free Press.

Collins, Jim. 2001. *Good to great*. New York: Harper Collins.

Collins, Jim, and Jerry Porras. 1997. *Built to last*. New York: Harper Collins.

Collins, Jim. 2009. *How the mighty fall*. New York: Harper Collins.

Deal, Terrence, and Allen Kennedy. 1982. *Corporate cultures: The rites and rituals of corporate life*. Reading, MA: Addison-Wesley.

Feinstein, John. 1989. *Season on the brink*. New York: Simon & Schuster.

Godin, Seth. 2007. *The dip*. New York: Penguin.

Goldsmith, Marshall. 2007. *What got you here, won't get you there*. New York: Hyperion.

Hirshberg, Charles. 2004. *ESPN 25*. New York: Hyperion.

Katzenbach John R, and Doug K. Smith. 1993. *The wisdom of teams*. Boston: Harvard Business School Press.

Kerr, Steve. 1975, December. "On the folly of rewarding A, while hoping for B." *Academy of Management Journal*: 769–783.

REFERENCES

Kim, W. Chan, and Renee. Mauborgne. 2005. *Blue ocean strategy*. Boston: Harvard Business School Press.

Lewis, Michael. 2003. *Moneyball*. New York: Norton.

Meacham, John. 2008, June 23. "God, politics, and the making of a joyful warrior." *Newsweek*: 31–33.

Ourand, John. 2008, March 17. "Taking aim at Bristol." *Sports Business Journal*.

Rasmussen, Bill. 1983. *The birth of ESPN:* New York, QV Publishing.

Reiss, Craig. 2002, August 19. "John Walsh: The king of cable sports." *Cable World*.

Smith, Anthony F. 2007. *The taboos of leadership*. San Francisco: Jossey-Bass.

About the Authors

Dr. Anthony F. Smith is cofounder and managing director of Leadership Research Institute, based in Rancho Santa Fe, recognized as one of the leading management consulting firms in the world, specializing in leadership development and assessment. He has been an active consultant for over 25 years in the areas of organizational change and assessment, team building, executive coaching and development, and leadership training and design. Besides ESPN, he has served clients in a variety of fields, including, American Express, the National Football League, the Coca-Cola Company, The National Geographic Society, Seimans AG, The Walt Disney Company, Deutsche Bank, Spencer Stuart, Hewlett-Packard, KKR, Goldman Sachs, and McKinsey and Company.

Anthony has served on the teaching and research faculties of several universities, including the University of California and the Tuck School of Business at Dartmouth, and received a visiting professorship at the EAP European Graduate School of Management at Oxford, U.K. He holds a B.A. and M.A. in the Behavioral Sciences and earned his Doctorate from the School of Leadership Science and Education at the

University of San Diego. Following his Doctorate, he was appointed as a Post-Doctoral Fellow of social anthropology at the University of California, where he studied leadership and cultural change. His research, writings, and reviews on leadership have appeared in several publications, including the *European Journal of Management*, the *Journal of Leadership Studies*, *BusinessWeek*, *The Economist*, *The Investors Business Daily*, and the best-selling books *The Leader of the Future* and *The Organization of the Future*. He is also the author of the critically acclaimed business book *The Taboos of Leadership*, published by Jossey Bass. He serves on several boards, including the V Foundation for Cancer Research. Anthony lives in Rancho Santa Fe, California. He can be reached at www.espnthecompany.com or www.dranthonyfsmith.com.

Keith Hollihan is a writer who has collaborated with Smith and many other top business and leadership experts on books and articles covering the gamut of issues that leaders face today. He is also coeditor of *The Art and Practice of Leadership Coaching: 50 Top Executive Coaches Reveal Their Secrets, Enlightened Power: How Women Are Transforming the Path to Leadership*, and *coauthor* of the best seller *Everybody Wins: The Story and Lessons Behind RE/MAX*, all of which are published by Jossey-Bass, an imprint of Wiley. Keith lives in Minneapolis, Minnesota.

Index

Index

Index